THE WORLDS OF JAPANESE POPULAR CULTURE

Gender, Shifting Boundaries and Global Cultures

This lively discussion of Japanese popular culture brings an anthropological perspective to a broad range of topics, including sumo, manga, women's magazines, morning television, karaoke, horse-racing and soccer. Through these topics – many of which have never previously been addressed by scholars – the contributors also explore several deeper themes: the construction of gender in Japan; the impact of globalization and modern consumerism; and the rapidly shifting boundaries of Japanese culture and identity. The book offers a view of Japan as a postmodern consumer society. The international team of scholars includes experts on literature, sport, film and linguistics, offering a broad spectrum of analysis. This exciting and innovative study will be of interest to anyone curious about Japanese culture, as well as readers in sociology and cultural anthropology.

Dolores Martinez is a lecturer in anthropology with reference to Japan at the School of Oriental and African Studies, University of London. She co-edited *Ceremony and Ritual in Japan* with Jan van Bremen. Her articles on religion, tourism, women, ethnicity and Japanese tourism have appeared in numerous edited volumes.

CONTEMPORARY JAPANESE SOCIETY

Editor:
Yoshio Sugimoto, La Trobe University

Advisory Editors:
Harumi Befu, Kyoto Bunkyo University
Roger Goodman, Oxford University
Michio Muramatsu, Kyoto University
Wolfgang Seifert, Universität Heidelberg
Chizuko Ueno, University of Tokyo

This series will provide a comprehensive portrayal of contemporary Japan through analysis of key aspects of Japanese society and culture, ranging from work and gender politics to science and technology. The series endeavours to link the relative strengths of Japanese and English-speaking scholars through collaborative authorship. Each title will be a balanced investigation of the area under consideration, including a synthesis of competing views.

The series will appeal to a wide range of readers from undergraduate beginners in Japanese studies to professional scholars. It will enable readers to grasp the diversity of Japanese society as well as the variety of theories and approaches available to study it.

Yoshio Sugimoto *An Introduction to Japanese Society*
  0 521 41692 2 hardback 0 521 42704 5 paperback
D. P. Matinez (ed.) *The Worlds of Japanese Popular Culture*
  0 521 63128 9 hardback 0 521 63729 5 paperback
Kaori Okano and Motonori Tsuchiya *Education in Contemporary Japan*
  0 521 62252 2 hardback 0 521 62686 2 paperback

THE WORLDS OF JAPANESE POPULAR CULTURE

Gender, Shifting Boundaries and Global Cultures

EDITED BY

D. P. MARTINEZ

CAMBRIDGE
UNIVERSITY PRESS

PUBLISHED BY THE PRESS SYNDICATE OF THE UNIVERSITY OF CAMBRIDGE
The Pitt Building, Trumpington Street, Cambridge, United Kingdom

CAMBRIDGE UNIVERSITY PRESS
The Edinburgh Building, Cambridge CB2 2RU, UK
40 West 20th Street, New York, NY 10011–4211, USA
10 Stamford Road, Oakleigh, VIC 3166, Australia
Ruiz de Alarcón 13, 28014 Madrid, Spain
Dock House, The Waterfront, Cape Town 8001, South Africa

http://www.cambridge.org

First published 1998
Reprinted 1999, 2001

Typeface Baskerville (*Adobe*) 10/12 pt.   *System* QuarkXPress®   [BC]

A catalogue record for this book is available from the British Library

Library of Congress Cataloguing in Publication data
The worlds of Japanese popular culture: gender, shifting boundaries
and global cultures/edited by D. P. Martinez.
p.   cm. – (Contemporary Japanese society)
Includes bibliographical references and index.
ISBN 0-521-63128-9 (alk. paper) – ISBN 0-521-63729-5 (pbk. alk. paper).
1. Popular culture – Japan. 2. Japan – Civilization – 1945–
I. Martinez, D. P. (Dolores P.) 1957– . II. Series.
DS822.5.W67 1998
306'0952–dc21   98–7086

ISBN 0 521 63128 9 hardback
ISBN 0 521 63729 5 paperback

Transferred to digital printing 2003

Contents

List of Contributors   ix
Acknowledgements   xi

Part I Introduction

Gender, Shifting Boundaries and Global Cultures   1
D. P. MARTINEZ

1 Sumo in the Popular Culture of Contemporary Japan   19
YAMAGUCHI MASAO

Part II The Male Domain

2 Transformational Magic: Some Japanese super-heroes
and monsters   33
TOM GILL

3 *Akira*, Postmodernism and Resistance   56
ISOLDE STANDISH

4 Japan's Empty Orchestras: Echoes of Japanese culture
in the performance of karaoke   75
BILL KELLY

Part III The Female Domain

5 Vampires, Psychic Girls, Flying Women and Sailor Scouts:
Four faces of the young female in Japanese popular culture   91
SUSAN NAPIER

6 Japanese Women's Magazines: The language of aspiration   110
   KEIKO TANAKA

7 *Nonchan's Dream*: NHK morning serialized television
   novels   133
   PAUL A. S. HARVEY

Part IV Shifting Boundaries

8 Media Stories of Bliss and Mixed Blessings   155
   HALLDÓR STEFÁNSSON

9 The Cult of Oguricap: Or, how women changed the
   social value of Japanese horse-racing   167
   NAGASHIMA NOBUHIRO

10 Soccer *shinhatsubai*: What are Japanese consumers
   making of the J. League?   181
   JONATHAN WATTS

Index   203

Contributors

TOM GILL is a research assistant at Kyoto Bunkyô University. He has worked in Japan as a teacher, journalist and translator. His PhD fieldwork was conducted in a day-labouring district of Yokohama.

PAUL A. S. HARVEY is an Assistant Professor in the Faculty of Language and Culture at Osaka University. His most recent publication was a chapter in *Women, Media and Consumption in Japan*, edited by Lise Skov and Brian Moeran.

WILLIAM H. KELLY has recently completed a PhD on karaoke in Japan, in the Institute of Social and Cultural Anthropology, University of Oxford. He has also done comparative research on karaoke performance in the United Kingdom.

D. P. MARTINEZ is a Lecturer in Anthropology at the School of Oriental and African Studies, London. She edited *Ceremony and Ritual in Japan* with Jan van Bremen, and is currently working on a book about divers (*ama*) in Japan. She has published articles on subjects including Japanese women, ethnicity and television.

NAGASHIMA NOBUHIRO is Professor of Social Anthropology in the Compartment of Social Anthropology, Hitotsubashi University, Tokyo. He has worked in East Africa as well as Japan and has a particular interest in cross-cultural comparison of gambling, horse-racing and wine-drinking. His publications include *Keiba no jinruigaku* (the anthropology of horse-racing).

SUSAN NAPIER is Associate Professor of Japanese Literature and Culture at the University of Texas at Austin. She is the author of *Escape from the Wasteland: Romanticism and realism in the works of Mishima Yukio and*

Oe Kenzaburo, and *The Fantastic in the Modern Japanese Literature: The subversion of modernity.* She is currently working on a book on Japanese animation.

ISOLDE STANDISH is Head of the Japanese Department at King Alfred's College in Winchester. Her research reflects her background in the areas of film, media and politics, and in Japanese and Korean. Her PhD was entitled *Myth and Masculinity in Japanese Cinema.*

HALLDÓR STEFÁNSSON is Professor of Anthropology at Osaka Gakuin University in Japan. He has published several articles on ancestor worship and death rituals in Japan, South Korea and Taiwan. His recent work is concerned with gift-giving and gender in Japanese society.

KEIKO TANAKA is a Lecturer in Japanese at the Oriental Institute, University of Oxford. She is the author of *Advertising Language: A pragmatic approach to advertisements in Britain and Japan.*

JONATHAN WATTS is the Tokyo correspondent for the *Guardian* and a staff writer for the *Daily Yomiuri.* His association with Japanese soccer dates back to 1991, when he joined the Yatake Sunday league team in Kobe.

YAMAGUCHI MASAO teaches at Shizuoka Kenritsu University, and was formerly Professor at the Tokyo University of Foreign Studies. His numerous publications cover many aspects of Japanese culture as well as commentary on global society.

Acknowledgements

An edited book is always more the result of the hard work and patience of contributors than of any single one person. In the case of this text, I am more than usually indebted to all the contributors who, in the years since we first discussed this book, have re-written and updated their chapters more than once. Special thanks must also go to Keiko Tanaka who double-checked the Japanese and Tom Gill who did last-minute checking on Japanese sources.

The preparation of the book was greatly helped by the hard work of Jacqueline Ryle and Tony Watling who typed in much of the text; and by a grant from the School of Oriental and African Studies Research and Publications Committee. Thanks must also go to Kodansha Publishing for their permission to quote the text in footnote 16 on pp. 70–1. This book would not have been possible without the comments of my husband David Gellner, whose practical and moral support have been essential to all my work. My own chapter has also benefited from the input of an Oxford ISCA seminar in 1996. I am also indebted to Joy Hendry and Arthur Stockwin, who suggested that I edit the book in the first place, as well as to Stella Harding, who helped me sort out the details of Superman's life. Roger Goodman has been supportive of the project from the start and has answered innumerable queries about getting the book published. Finally, I am grateful to Professor Sugimoto and to Phillipa McGuinness at Cambridge University Press, whose enthusiasm for the work made it possible to keep at it!

PART I

Introduction

Gender, Shifting Boundaries and Global Cultures

D. P. MARTINEZ

Japanese popular culture is so rich and varied that no single book could do justice to it, and this volume is only one recent attempt to describe the "worlds" to be found under the deceptively simple heading of "popular culture". The chapters in this book present a variety of topics, ranging from traditional sumo to the more recently successful introduction of football. The book's contributors include Japanese as well as British, Icelandic and North American writers, all of whom offer a diversity of views of what Japanese popular culture is and how it is best approached and understood. The unity of the book lies in its predominantly anthropological approach – of the ten contributors five are anthropologists; the others include a linguist, two experts on literature, a journalist and a film theorist – and in its implicit assumption that Japan is the unit of analysis. But, we might ask, as Yoshio Sugimoto did in the first book of this series (1997): which Japan? Male manager-dominated middle-class Japan? The Japan of the Kantô region, dominated by Tokyo, or the Japan of the Kansai region where Osaka and Kyoto are the important cities? Is it urban Japan or rural Japan, the Japan of small nuclear families or of the single young woman? Is there one Japanese society? The essays in this book argue against the view of a single Japanese culture. Yet we cannot ignore the common assumption that Japan the nation and Japanese society are one single thing: in fact that *is* the assumption upon which most nation-states are constructed (Gellner 1983). While the reality of contemporary Japan is far more complex than any single model could well describe (cf. Mouer and Sugimoto 1990; Weiner 1997), it would be simplistic to ignore the connection between the nation-state, with its ideology of a shared "Japaneseness", and popular culture.

1

If asked, most Westerners probably could outline what this image of Japan is: a homogeneous society, where hierarchy and formality continue to be important. A country where men still are dominant and all work for large companies as modern "samurai" businessmen. Japanese women are held to be gentle, submissive and beautiful, and yet also appear in the foreign media as pushy mothers obsessed with their children's education. Japanese children, by extension, must be miserable automatons who do nothing but study all day and half the night. Japanese society is portrayed as one where esthetics and harmony are highly valued, and yet feudal violence lives on in the guise of the *yakuza* (gangsters). In short, images of this modern state still depict it as a place of contradictions, difficult to understand for any outsider naive enough to try. Matters are not helped by the fact that the Japanese themselves hold these images up as valid representations of their own society.

Anthropologists should be foremost in debunking some of these images of modern Japan, but they must do so in the face of a national culture which stresses similarity over difference. In this Japan can be compared to many other modern nation-states. As Anderson (1991) notes in his important analysis of modern nationalism, one of the factors crucial to the development of the nation-state was the invention of the printing press and, as a result, the appearance of the first mass media: newspapers and novels. Both media assumed that readers shared a common language, a set of common experiences understood by all, a basic level of literacy common to a large portion of the population, and a capitalist economic system which would market the mass-produced newspapers and books. Homi Bhabha picks up this theme in his introduction to *Nation and Narration* (1990), expanding on the idea that the modern "imagined community" which is the nation requires its own forms of narration.

I have argued elsewhere that we might best understand these forms of narration, which are embodied in various types of the mass media, as myth (1992): myth not as false history, but rather as a series of continually re-worked narrations which reflect and reinforce the values of constantly changing societies. As Samuel and Thompson (1990) argue, these are the myths we live by: not neo-Marxist dominant ideologies, but something closer to a view of culture which shapes and is shaped by society. Approaching popular culture as *the* culture of the nation-state implies a unity of vision. Arguing that popular culture is part of the domain of the mythic acknowledges that the mass media have both a political, or ideological, dimension and a deeper, more symbolic and psychological aspect which allow the messages they convey to mean diverse things to different people at different times and to be shaped, re-worked and re-formulated over time.[1] Thus we can have a popular culture of the Japanese nation which also reflects the diversity of

Japanese society at a given moment and which can also accommodate changes throughout time. Moreover, as a form of myth, popular culture is able to travel and be transformed, attaining the level of global culture as well.

As the chapters for this book were written, it soon became clear that aside from the mythic dimension there were three central themes which all the contributors touched on: gender, the question of global culture, and the shifting of boundaries within Japan. Yet, because of the complexity and diversity of Japanese society, these three categories should not be seen to be limiting; in fact they are linked in so many ways that any discussion of these themes raises new issues, questions and interpretations at every turn. Before discussing these themes, however, it is necessary to define a few terms and to say something about the anthropological premises of this book.

Popular culture and anthropology

To the average person living in an English-speaking society, "culture" is a term with a variety of meanings, one of which is so common as to be unquestioned: culture is about the intellect, about high art, about distinctions between classes, about superior knowledge.[2] In contrast, *popular* culture is the culture of the masses; it is not about art or the intellect and is frequently held to be of no merit whatsoever. Debates surface in Britain every year as to whether the study of popular culture or the funding of forms of popular entertainment are somehow debasing our society. In this debate we see enacted all sorts of issues of class or distinction[3] which to an anthropologist are fascinating, but not necessarily central to what an anthropology of popular culture should be *about*. That is a different problem altogether and one premised on another definition of "culture".

In anthropology as well, the term "culture" reveals itself to contain a variety of meanings: it can refer to the materials produced by a given society (its art, as well as tools, baskets, buildings, etc.); or alternatively to the symbolic or signifying systems of a society. For a structuralist or postmodernist anthropologist there is perhaps no conflict in these two main anthropological meanings of the term: the materials produced by a society are also capable of having symbolic value, and thus the anthropologist's job is to explore the relationships between material culture and symbolic culture. It is the interaction between these apparently separate aspects of society that must constitute the focus of an anthropological study of popular culture.

By defining the anthropology of popular culture as the study of the interaction between the *apparently* separate realms of the material and the symbolic, I am, in fact, saying nothing that an anthropologist would see as unusual. Whether studying the relationship between the wrapping of gifts and polite language in Japan (Hendry 1993); the meaning of body-painting and mythology in the Amazon (Lévi-Strauss 1968–77); or the presentation of bracelets, necklaces and the meaning of prestige in the Trobriand Islands (Mauss 1970 [1925]), anthropologists have always explored this interaction. What is unusual, perhaps, is that I am including popular culture in the same realm. For here we encounter an interesting problem: since the study of anthropology has long been associated with small-scale or pre-capitalist societies, many anthropologists remain suspicious of studies done in larger or more complex societies and popular culture is most often associated with the latter not the former. In fact, whenever we find traces of global popular culture in out-of-the-way places – rock music in Ladakh, India, for example – anthropologists are just as likely to label this as evidence that the original culture has somehow been spoilt.

Accepting the need to understand modern nation-state formations, and, beyond that, the globalization of modern culture, has led some anthropologists to come to consider popular culture in terms of consumption (Miller 1987). For Daniel Miller it is not necessarily how and what people produce that constitutes postmodern culture, but how people consume the products of capitalism, and what products, that constitutes culture. In doing this, anthropology would appear to be following the path trodden by sociologists and writers in media studies: but what anthropology has to offer is somewhat different from these well-established disciplines.[4] Writers in cultural studies often take it for granted that the writer and reader share a common culture. In contrast, the anthropologist works in a more difficult terrain: making connections between various, if not all, aspects of a foreign culture in which she has studied and lived. In a world increasingly aware of shared technologies and in which images, music and products are also shared, this leaves the anthropologist working in the domain not only of similarities, but of continued differences. This is the domain where culture resists globalization: assimilating, appropriating and producing its own version of, for example, how to market and play football.

It is here that anthropologists have their new arena of study: in the connections made between areas as diverse as, say, cartoons and religion. It is the links or relationships between the "invented" traditions of the nation (Hobsbawm and Ranger 1983) – its mass-produced culture, and the deeper connections to older culture, such as folklore – that constitute an exciting realm in the anthropology of modern societies. Nowhere is this more evident than in the anthropology of the popular culture of that most complex of modern (or postmodern) societies: Japan.

Thus I wanted the contributors to the book not to be afraid to make connections between the world of the material and the symbolic, for it is precisely within this relationship that we find the domain of popular culture. This domain is never static; it is always changing, shifting and is often called upon to mean different things to different people. Whenever writers felt unsure of the connections they had made, I had only one bit of advice to give: ask a Japanese child, or young man, or young woman, what *they* think. So while each author makes different assumptions about what constitutes popular culture, the closest this book comes to fixing the terrain is in Chapter 10, with Jonathan Watts' use of Miller's (1987) theory of modern consumption.

Part of the reason for allowing this sort of conceptual fuzziness to remain can be explained by trying to define popular culture in the Japanese context. Kato Hidetoshi, one of the leading sociologists of Japan, makes an important point in the 1989 *Handbook of Japanese Popular Culture*. Translating "popular culture" into Japanese is not easy: he prefers "mass culture" or "*taishû bunka*". Immediately we are confronted with an important problem: are Western notions of culture, particularly the division between high and low or elite and mass culture, actually universally valid? Japan is an interesting example, for practices which we might label elite or high culture, have, under the guise of what is Japanese, become more and more the domain of the huge middle class. Japanese women are studying tea ceremony, classical dancing and classical instruments in large numbers and women are also the main supporters of imported Western high culture, such as the theater, classical music, ballet and opera. When several million people participate in "elite" practices, how can we not label them as popular, or part of mass culture? In this volume, with its emphasis on forms of culture which a Western reader could easily identify as "popular", we attempt to broaden the understanding of this issue for Japan by including analyses on sumo (Yamaguchi, Chapter 1), on the event of the royal engagement (Stefánsson, Chapter 8), and in the manner in which several of the chapters attempt to link the postmodern with older traditions (see especially the chapters by Gill, Standish and Napier).

Many of the contributors to this book implicitly argue against the notion raised by Powers, again in the *Handbook of Japanese Popular Culture* (1989), that popular culture belongs to the realm of international culture. The idea is that in the USA this culture is homogenized until it loses its international quality, while in other countries, such as Japan, it retains its "foreign" label as part of its prestige or interest value. This might suit anthropologists who would like to dismiss popular culture as not worthy of study, arguing, for example, that it is not really of the society being studied or that it belongs to the domain of representations of representations, the hyperreal but not the real (Baudrillard 1983). This argument is not, in fact, taken up by Japanese scholars who have long been concerned with questions about the effects of the mass media on society, in a manner mirroring work done in the West. All the media in Japan are seen to have home-grown roots, whether or not the technology or some of the formats, or both, came from the outside. Thus, samurai dramas and kabuki theater, medieval novels and modern fantasy fiction, Buddhist cartoons and the *manga* (comics, cartoons) industry are so much a part of each other that it makes no sense to call the mass culture of Japan "international" in its character. Parts of it are international and export well, others can only be understood in a Japanese context. Moreover, it is ironic that the most international of "cultures" is actually elite culture, including the arts, opera and ballet: these are all aspects of culture which might easily be labeled global in that they command large international markets.

Finally, and it is most important to re-iterate the point, popular culture (and not just in Japan) is not only *mass* culture, the culture of the imagined community: it is culture consumed, and consumed in various ways, by different people. Another reason, then, that I have not asked the contributors to fall back on a particular theory intended to "explain" popular culture was that I wanted them to take the concept as a given and to explore its various uses and meanings.

The domains of male and female

Of all the themes to be found in this book, gender comes to the fore: every chapter refers to the male and female in Japanese society in one way or another. In fact, when I had to decide how to organize the book the most obvious section divisions were precisely those of gender, followed by sub-divisions of age groups. Part II covers the male domain, beginning with Tom Gill's chapter on children's programs (mostly aimed at boys); this is followed by Isolde Standish's analysis of the blue-collar male adolescent love of *bôsôzoku* (reckless driving) spectacle; the section ends with Bill Kelly's exploration of the white-collar male-dominated world of karaoke. Part III, "The Female Domain", is structured in a similar way: Susan Napier closely examines the depictions of the pre-adolescent and adolescent girl in the world of *manga* (both comics and animation); Keiko Tanaka looks at how young women are targeted as powerful consumers by magazines; and Paul Harvey examines the links between housewives, nation-building and morning dramas on Japanese television.

Yet, these divisions are in some ways too simplistic and readers should be wary of drawing conclusions from the way in which I have chosen to arrange the chapters. For example, little Japanese girls watch many of the same violent programs which are targeted at boys; and I have seen Japanese girls just as fascinated by walking, roaring Godzilla toys as they are with their dolls. The film *Akira* may well have grown out of the blue-collar *bôsôzoku* sub-culture, but it was popular in a wide segment of the Japanese population; just as karaoke, so much a part of a white-collar man's life after work, is popular now amongst women as well as young men. *Manga* about pre-pubescent girls are read by a wide variety of people and are often created by men,[5] just as important women's magazines may have their policies decided by their male owners (Tanaka, Chapter 6 in this volume). And all Japanese, from the 1950s onwards, have been exposed to the high ideals and aspirations depicted in morning dramas by the simple act of sitting with their mothers as they watched television.

Given this warning, what generalizations may be made about gender as represented in Japanese mass culture and what can be said about the relationship between age, gender and consumption? As almost every recent work on women in Japan has argued,[6] there remain sharp divisions between the male and female domains in Japan and yet they are also held to be complementary and necessary for the construction of the social. It is generally held that women are associated with the inside, the private domain (*uchi*) and men with the outside, public domain (*soto*). Yet, as Susan Napier and Halldór Stefánsson in this volume note, the female was, and still is, often associated with the outside (*soto*), with outsiders and thus with dangerous powers; para-doxically, of course, these outsiders were necessary and had to be incorporated as "insiders", that is, as wives and mothers.

In contrast, the construction of maleness in Japan is rarely con-sidered, but it can be said that, given its strong patrilineal emphasis, the men of a household are associated with the inside (*uchi*), although their work is often done in the public, outside domains. In essence women are aliens in the male domain and yet *must* enter this domain if society is to be reproduced. Thus, Japanese women are both a source of danger to the norm and the very means of perpetuating that norm. It then becomes possible to depict Japanese women as both symbolically dangerous (as does Napier), as well as the very source of all that is Japanese (as does Harvey), and thus able to mediate between the two poles (as Stefánsson argues): what is important to understand is that these are women at different points in their life-cycles. While as young unmarried workers they are depicted as vampires, goddesses and girl-children with wild powers, women are also targeted as powerful consumers: the wielders of large economic resources which are free to be spent on luxury and leisure items, such as trips abroad or fashion items (Tanaka), or consumer goods associated with new fads, such as soccer (Watts). Within the same society, the standard model of the middle-class and middle-aged Japanese housewife is of a woman at the center of the household, the one who makes all decisions: the good wife and wise mother, the bearer of all that is Japanese, who is also a powerful consumer and economic decision-maker.

Men, on the other hand, are rarely considered as part of the study of gender in Japan, although as Cornwall and Lindisfarne argue (1993) we cannot understand the construction of what is female in any society without seeing how it is constructed against and through what is male, and vice versa. Such constructions of gender are often complex and dynamic, so that although it is structurally neat to argue that Japanese women are associated with the outside and danger and men with the inside and stability, reality is far more difficult to pin down. And representations of reality reflect this difficulty. So men in Japan are also associated with traditional Japaneseness (Yamaguchi and Nagashima), the stable center which resists change; and, yet, they are also capable of being dangerous outsiders (Gill and Standish). The difference, perhaps, between the male and female case in Japan has to do with class and status: women might be said *always* to be dangerous "Others" even when they are "domesticated" as wives and mothers; in contrast it is only men on the margins – motorcyclists, gangsters, gamblers, etc. – who fall into this category. It could be said that women cannot free themselves of their ascribed status association with danger; men, on the other hand, by moving into the middle-class white-collar world of the company man, can change class and therefore leave the status group of marginal, dangerous outsiders.[7] Elsewhere I have argued that even this simple model is complicated by considering age: a young woman is more dangerous than a middle-aged married woman, as is a young man, and so on (Martinez 1995).

Furthermore, both Chapter 1 by Yamaguchi Masao and the final section of the book, "Shifting Boundaries", might well be read as examples of how some of the boundaries in Japan have shifted, or are in a never-ending process of shifting. Sumo, an ancient Japanese tradition suffused with religious symbolism, and linked to the world of the theater through kabuki as well as to the imperial family, is, as Yamaguchi reveals, as much a part of Japanese postmodern popular culture as are the imported sports of horse-racing and soccer. Moreover, as Stefánsson argues, sumo might be seen as a "masculine" aspect of Japanese modern culture, not yet ready to be polluted by contact with the outside world, while the more "feminine" imperial family is leading the way in making Japan a more "international" nation. The adoption of horse-racing and soccer (both introduced in the nineteenth century by the British) might also be seen as part of Japan's internationalization but, as Nagashima notes, it has taken women a long time to become part of the racing scene in Japan; and Watts outlines a century-long struggle to make soccer popular, which has finally succeeded by marketing the game as a product that could appeal to young Japanese women as well as men. The boundaries between male and female, inside and outside, what is dangerous and what is stable, are constantly being negotiated and it is in the arena of culture which is labeled popular that we can see some of this negotiation taking place. Paul Harvey's examination of women's morning dramas and their history explores well some of the facets of this symbolic "give and take".

The global and the local

It follows from what has been said that much of the book may also be read as different analyses on the themes of globalization and modern consumerism, for the success of each aspect of popular culture described is not uniquely a Japanese phenomenon. It might help to think of popular culture in general and of Japan in particular in terms of Marshall McLuhan's modern oral tradition (1966). Like the great oral epics of old, much of popular culture is in a form accessible to people everywhere and anywhere but, oh, how it changes in translation! Lee van Cleef was just as popular in Japan as Clint Eastwood, the hero of the westerns in which van Cleef was so often the villain. Godzilla in his early incarnations was favorite Saturday afternoon children's viewing in the USA, but as Gojira in Japan he has had a much longer – though not so varied – life. Japanese rock stars do not travel well, while British and American ones obviously do. Japanese films which are not greatly appreciated in Japan have become cinema classics in the West, while great Japanese favorites never make it to the West. As Kelly notes, the idea of karaoke has traveled, without any of the music so popular in Japan coming with it. Soccer now might be labeled the world's only truly global sport (if only those North Americans did not skew the picture) and horse-racing cannot be far behind. In the realm of children's culture, Thomas the Tank Engine has been a big hit throughout modern societies, while Postman Pat cannot be exported to Japan because his four fingers appear to be symbolic of Japanese *yakuza* (gangsters). And, in a case of never-ending borrowing, the *Jū Rengâ*, which became the *Power Rangers* in the US (with new Western actors intercut into the fighting scenes) have been re-imported to Japan with the Western actors dubbed into Japanese!

The examples could be endless, but the point is the same: we can dismiss popular culture as being somehow empty of meaning and not worthy of study and miss much of what is going on in all societies. Or it could be argued that the meaning of such representations is so culturally specific that it is impossible to understand the popular culture of other societies save in a Marxist relationship of ideology being imposed on the brainwashed consumers of the various media. Or it could be acknowledged that the relationship, as the above examples show, is much more complex – different consumers get different things from the mass media and are targeted as specific groups by manufacturers and advertisers (Moeran 1996). The question we might ask once more is how is it that an anthropology of popular culture continues to use a discourse now often derided by postmodern anthropological theory (cf. Moeran 1990; Mouer and Sugimoto 1990): that is, how dare we continue to write about Japan as a unity? How can we decide what is Japanese and what is alien? This question is central to an issue raised here earlier: the construction of the culture of the modern nation-state.

Thus, although the recent trend in modern anthropological studies of Japan is to try to move away from analyses of models of what *is* Japanese towards some more meaningful depictions of what it feels like to *try to be* Japanese (cf. Kondo 1990; Rosenberger 1992; Sugiyama-Lebra 1984), it must be understood that studies in the latter mode depend on the models so often derided in the former. The crucial point is that the rhetoric of the Japanese state remains one of a homogeneous national identity. In this Japan is similar to many modern nation-states in that it has had to construct a model of a unitary identity shared by all citizens (cf. Hobsbawm and Ranger 1983; Yoshino 1992). Identity no longer depends on religious models (although it may be based on such older models, just as Confucian ideals remain important in modern Japan), or on loyalty to one particular ruler/leader, but on the wider construct of the imagined citizenship of the imagined national community. This nationalism depends on the mass production of mass culture and, while the logic of capitalism (late or otherwise) demands diversification, the underlying logic of one identity (the Japanese) as different from that of their neighbors (let us say, Korea and China) remains crucial to the construction of the nation-state.

This construction is not, as has been noted so brilliantly by Carol Gluck (1985), easily arrived at. It is not, as Hobsbawm has argued, best understood as part of an analysis done only from "above", but needs also to be "analysed from below, that is in terms of the assumptions, hopes, needs, longings and interests of ordinary people" (1992: 10).[8] We need to consider both the elite and common, the urban and rural (cf. Robertson 1991), and the normal and uncanny (cf. Ivy 1995). Most of all, it is not static (cf. Tobin 1992): the foreign is quite capable of being imported and "remade in Japan" and this is not only true of Japan, but of any modern nation-state.

Most importantly, popular culture can be a tool for creating a sense of unified identity, but it can also reflect regional differences (Harvey, Chapter 7 in this volume), differences between nations (cf. Martinez 1997); as well as being subject to the demands of "the public". Any *Star Trek* fan or cultural studies theorist can relate how public demand and interaction with the mass media can change and influence the media (cf. Jenkins and Tulloch 1995; Tulloch 1995). This parallels, in an important way, the relationship between the citizen and the state, so much so that understanding the mass media has become an integral part of the analysis of modern politics (Dickey 1993; Pharr and Krauss 1996).

Given the argument that popular culture is an important aspect of modern nationalism, how then are we to account for the culture that travels – that becomes mass not only at home, but also abroad? I have already argued that this is due to the mythic aspect of mass culture, its ability to be about many things at once; but it is also due to the ability of "consumers" to consume differently icons which we might naively believe to be culturally specific (Gillespie 1995). One example from Japan is the way in which new or imported forms of mass culture often acquire a *dô*, or specific "way". The Japanese emphasis on correct forms and styles makes the process of "domestication" (Tobin 1992) an efficient one, and works well as part of capitalist marketing, as Tanaka argues in this volume.

The relationship between the global and local is far from being easy to pin down or analyze. Despite postmodern theorists who emphasize the way in which the economic has bled into the cultural (Harvey 1989; Jameson 1991) in order to produce the homogenized, de-contextualized, mish-mash of postmodern culture, the fact remains that products of all sorts are, as Tobin argues, "domesticated" (1992): individual, ethnic, regional and national concerns seem to dominate. Thus *Akira* is read differently by different spectators; horse-racing and horses have a meaning different for the Japanese than for the British; and sumo is appreciated for different reasons in different places. Ien Ang, a media specialist, has often noted that the audience is almost impossible to find, pin down and generalize about (1991), and if we do so, we must do it armed with empirical data. It is here that anthropology has a valid contribution to make to the study of popular culture.

Reflecting society

While in the past anthropologists have tended to avoid the study of Japanese popular culture,[9] other specialists have not. There exists a serious literature of film analysis and criticism, as well as a large body of literary analysis. One of the more recent studies of Japanese popular culture still in print is Ian Buruma's *A Japanese Mirror* (1984), which argues that popular culture represents all the repressed violent and sexual desires of the Japanese. Provocative and occasionally highly perceptive in its overview of one aspect of Japanese popular culture, Buruma's work leaves us asking if Japanese culture is really so utterly male-dominated.

Similarly, Brian Moeran's (1989) analysis of historical/samurai dramas raises important questions about how popular culture may mirror, or even attempt to resolve, moral and ethical issues for modern Japanese people; but such an approach only tells part of the story. An NHK[10] producer once confirmed my own theory about the popularity of historical dramas by telling me that the dramas filled the need of creating a shared history for the modern nation. Analyses of science fiction along structuralist lines (Matthew 1989), or baseball in terms of Zen (Whiting 1990), or comics (*manga*) in terms of coping with Japan's defeat in the war (Schodt 1983) are only partial explanations for what goes on in Japanese popular culture.

What might be said to be the missing ingredient in these analyses? From an anthropological point of view what is missing are the voices of both producers and consumers of popular culture. Some efforts have been made in this volume to redress this: Harvey talked to writers of home dramas; Tanaka uses the history of magazines to reveal some of the aspirations of the producers and talked to young female magazine readers; Watts and Gill rely on the use of published material on marketing soccer and children's television respectively; and Nagashima interviewed writers of horse-racing *manga*. Conversely, Gill also relied on the network of children with whom his five-year-old son played; Kelly discussed karaoke with many informants; Nagashima was there, listening to the reactions of seasoned betters when women invaded the paddocks; and Watts did a small, controlled study based on interviews with Japanese, as well as actually being there when soccer began to succeed in Japan. All the contributors, through their knowledge of Japanese and large familiarity with Japan might be said to have achieved the anthropological goal of participant observation: through living, working and studying in Japan they may well have come close to articulating a Japanese point of view.

Comment should be made, perhaps, on the apparent differences between the various approaches taken by the foreign scholars and by the "native" anthropologists – do the latter reflect Japanese society better or differently than the former? First it should be noted that three of the "foreign" scholars are resident in Japan (Gill, Harvey and Stefánsson) and one of the "natives" has long lived in the UK (Tanaka), somewhat skewing any neat typology we might try to create. If we include the

Japanese Japanese anthropologists, Yamaguchi and Nagashima, along with the resident-in-Japan scholars, the broad generalization could be made that these five experts approached the task of making wider connections much more readily than some of the others in this volume. Stefánsson concurs with Yamaguchi on the link between sumo and the imperial family, while Harvey is not afraid to think and ask about the nationalist implications of women's television dramas. Gill makes broad links in terms of color, Taoist symbolism (as does Yamaguchi), Japanese words and the world of children's programs. Nagashima is ready to consider the psychological implications of the cult that grew up around a race horse and makes assertions in a way that many a non-Japanese would hesitate to make. However, Napier, a well-known expert on Japanese literature, draws on her knowledge of both the language and of visual media to make broad connections amongst folklore, traditional forms of the Japanese novel and the broader theoretical literature on feminism, psychology and vampires.

Again, I hesitate to argue for clearcut differences between native and foreign attempts at understanding Japanese popular culture in this volume. If I must point to one large discrepancy between the local and the foreign researchers it is, perhaps, in the natives' ability to view their popular culture with an ironic detachment: who else would dare to link kabuki, sumo and the imperial family while exploring sumo's connections with Korea, rural Japanese traditions, Taoism, Shintoism and esoteric Buddhism? Yamaguchi does this with a subtlety that many a reader might miss: by linking sumo with kabuki and the imperial family, and its fortunes with the political rise and fall of the imperial line he implies that this very Japanese "tradition" might well fall into the category of a modern invented tradition of the sort that all nation-states have. Elements can be linked to the past, but the pulling-together of the tradition into its current form can only be understood in light of the formation of the modern nation. So too with Nagashima's look at the intrusion of women into the closed, tough, masculine world of gamblers; in his attempt to understand what motivated these women he must also consider the emotional commitment men have to gambling. In the end we are given a picture of both sexes acting out some form of fantasy: each imbuing the same figures with different meanings. Further, by including himself as both participant and observer, Nagashima raises a broad question about the nature of "traditional" anthropology: do researchers ever get to enjoy themselves? We do, but we only write about it if someone asks us to consider, for example, popular culture.

What conclusions might be reached from this diverse set of studies? I have already discussed the importance of gender, the presence of local and global issues, but ultimately what these chapters all seem to be describing is a society in which change is rapidly occurring. The arena of popular culture which each chapter presents might well be said to be an arena of *negotiation* in which tradition, the present, the future, a Japanese identity, gendered identity and class/status identities are all reflected, reinforced, fragmented, re-created or created anew. In short, popular culture is the best possible means through which to examine the process that is often called "national culture".

Thus my initial warning about taking the gendered and age divisions of the book's structure too seriously: it is precisely these categories that are being questioned. As Stefánsson argues, women who can be associated with the household, and thus the inside (*uchi*), are being seen as mediators with the outside world in the quest for internationalization. As Napier points out, despite their association with tradition and the home, women have been long marginalized, so it might seem only logical that these marginals who are both insiders and outsiders be given the task of making Japan more international. In looking at the two chapters together we get the impression of the past and present being re-worked, the images of women being re-made (Imamura 1996) and the future thus being ensured. This point is made all the more powerfully by Harvey, whose work on home drama (Chapter 7) makes clear that one aspect of these future-oriented dramas is that of nation-building. So Japan must become more international and women are crucial in this goal, but they must also retain a foot in the past, in ancient traditions, acting out the roles of mothers and wives as well as innovators. It is perhaps no accident of history, then, that the new Crown Princess seems to fill all these roles perfectly, nor that several chapters of the book refer to her as a pivotal figure in modern Japanese culture.[11]

Japanese men in this case seem to get left behind. Yet the representations of men in this book are many: as Kelly describes them, they are the modern white-collar employees, playing out the structures of corporate hierarchy in karaoke; for Standish they are class outsiders, dreaming that traditional Japanese values will see them through in a post-nuclear world; through Nagashima we glimpse a sector of the male world where even modest employees could rub shoulders with gangsters and pretend to know danger, a continuation perhaps of ideas nurtured through watching *Ultraman* and *Ryû-Renjâ* in childhood. Static and passive, trapped in tradition as these images of men might seem, we are shown their attempt at belonging both to the hometown and the wider world through Watts' analysis of the growing interest in soccer – which may be marketed at young women, but is played and supported by young men.

And all the while advertising agencies, PR companies, television surveys try to keep up, to target the right consumers, to sell a new product, to reflect the changing world. The relationship between the shifting ideologies represented and the notion of a dominant ideology being articulated becomes complex: was it the strong yen which led to young Japanese women traveling and did magazines detect this and respond with articles on travel; or did the magazines see the potential and, with advertisers, push the idea of travel overseas? Tanaka does not venture to answer this question, but it was probably a bit of both.

Thus we are left where we began, with a variety of media (magazines, television, films, sports and comics) that teach us something about Japan as a nation where the group is still important and memories of the war are reproduced in science fiction portrayals of the future. The analyses of these media also reflect a varied, diverse and dynamic society; a society in which, as Kelly notes, homogeneity is the apparent dominating value and yet heterogeneity is also important. Readers will, I hope, become interested in Japan; think about new aspects of Japanese society; question some of the assumptions made about the proper domain of anthropologists; or of theories in relation to popular culture; and, I may even hope, will never think about popular culture in the same way again.

Notes

1 This notion of symbols which change their "content", as it were, over time has been developed in the Japanese context by the anthropologist Ohnuki-Tierney (1987; 1990; 1994).
2 See Williams (1983) for a brief overview of the evolution of this idea.
3 The book *Distinction*, by the French anthropologist Pierre Bourdieu (1984), is an interesting and all-too-rare attempt to look at how certain status groups in French society distinguish themselves from each other. This study documents, through surveys, how knowledge of and the consumption of different types of books, music, art, and even food and dress, are used to mark status and class distinctions.
4 Yet, while positing that an anthropology of popular culture is different from a sociology of popular culture, there are also important similarities: in recent years, for example, both disciplines have relied on Marxist and neo-Marxist analyses.
5 On these themes especially, see Schodt's seminal work on the subject, *Manga! Manga! The World of Japanese Comics* (1983), and his more recent textbook *Dreamland Japan: Writings on modern Manga* (1996).
6 See the introduction to *Women, Media and Consumption in Japan* (Skov and Moeran 1995) and various essays in Imamura's *Re-imaging Japanese Women* (1996) for some recent examples of this.

7 Clearly then, I agree in part with Nakane's description of Japanese society (1971) as one in which status is achieved, not ascribed, but – and this needs greater emphasis than Nakane gives it – this applies only to a small section of the male population.
8 Some sociologists of popular culture have pushed this idea further with the argument that culture is formed not just by "producers" but in an interaction with consumers (see especially: Lull 1988; Morley 1986; Silverstone 1981).
9 Early exceptions to this include Ruth Benedict's pioneering study of Japan, *The Chrysanthemum and the Sword* published in 1946, for which she read novels and studied films (all in translation); and David Plath's *The After Hours* (1964), an edited study of various aspects of leisure in Japan.
10 Nihon Hôsô Kaisha, Japanese Broadcasting Company, the nationwide broadcaster, the BBC of Japan.
11 In this students of Japan would appear to be more attuned to the national *Zeitgeist* than were those of Britain who were taken by surprise by reactions to the death of Diana, Princess of Wales.

References

Ang, I. 1991 *Desperately Seeking the Audience.* London: Routledge.

Anderson, B. 1991 *Imagined Communities, reflections on the origin and spread of nationalism.* London: Verso.

Baudrillard, Jean 1983 *Simulations,* trans. Paul Foss, Paul Patton and Philip Beitchman. New York: Semiotext(e).

Benedict, Ruth 1946 *The Chrysanthemum and the Sword.* Boston: Houghton Mifflin.

Bhabha, H. (ed.) 1990 *Nation and Narration.* London: Routledge.

Bourdieu, Pierre 1984 *Distinction: a Social Critique of the Judgment of Taste,* trans., R. Nice. London: Routledge and Kegan Paul.

Buruma, Ian 1984 *A Japanese Mirror: Heroes and villains in Japanese culture.* London: Jonathan Cape.

Cornwall, A. and Lindisfarne, N. 1993 *Dislocating Masculinity.* London: Routledge.

Dickey, Sara 1993 *Cinema and the Urban Poor in South India.* Cambridge: Cambridge University Press.

Gellner, E. 1983 *Nations and Nationalism.* Oxford: Blackwell.

Gillespie, Marie 1995 *Television, Ethnicity and Cultural Change.* London: Routledge.

Gluck, Carol 1985 *Japan's Modern Myths: Ideology in the Late Meiji Period.* Princeton: Princeton University Press.

Harvey, David 1989 *The condition of postmodernity: an Enquiry into the Origins of Cultural Change.* Oxford: Basil Blackwell.

Hendry, Joy 1993 *Wrapping Culture: Politeness, Presentation, and Power in Japan and Other Societies.* Oxford: Clarendon Press.

Hobsbawm, E. J. 1992 *Nations and Nationalism since 1780, programme, myth, reality.* Cambridge: Cambridge University Press.

Hobsbawm, E. J. and T. Ranger (eds) 1983 *The Invention of Tradition.* Cambridge: Cambridge University Press.

Imamura, Anne E. (ed.) 1996 *Re-imaging Japanese Women*. Berkeley: University of California Press.

Ivy, Marilyn 1995 *Discourses of the Vanishing: Modernity, Phantasm, Japan*. Chicago: University of Chicago Press.

Jameson, F. 1991 *Postmodernism or the Cultural Logic of Late Capitalism*. London: Verso.

Jenkins, H. and John Tulloch 1995 "Beyond the Star Trek phenomenon: reconceptualizing the science fiction audience" in their edited *Science Fiction Audiences*. London: Routledge.

Kato Hidetoshi 1989 in *Handbook of Japanese Popular Culture* edited by R. Powers and H. Kato. Westport, Conn.: Greenwood Press.

Kondo, Dorinne K. 1990 *Crafting Selves: Power, gender and identity in a Japanese workplace*. Chicago: University of Chicago Press.

Lévi-Strauss, C. 1968–77 *Structural Anthropology*, trans. Claire Jacobson and Brooke Grundfest. London: Athlone.

Lull, James 1988 *World Families Watching TV*. London: Sage.

Martinez, D. P. 1992 "NHK comes to Kuzaki: Ideology, Mythology and Documentary Film-making" in *Ideology and Practice in Modern Japan* edited by R. Goodman and K. Refsing. London: Routledge.

——1995 "Women and Ritual" in *Ceremony and Ritual in Japan* edited by Jan van Bremen and D. P. Martinez. London: Routledge.

——1997 "Burlesquing Knowledge" in *Rethinking Visual Anthropology* edited by M. Banks and H. Morphy. New Haven and London: Yale University Press.

Matthew, R. 1989 *Japanese Science Fiction: a view of a changing society*. London: Routledge.

Mauss, Marcel 1970 [1925] *The Gift*. Glencoe: Free Press.

McLuhan, Marshall 1966 *Understanding Media: the extensions of man*. New York: New American Library.

Miller, Daniel 1987 *Material Culture and Mass Consumption*. Oxford: Blackwell Publishers.

Moeran, Brian 1989 "Confucian Confusion" in his *Language and Popular Culture in Japan*. Manchester: Manchester University Press.

——1990 "Introduction" in *Unwrapping Japan* edited by Eyal Ben-Ari et al. Manchester: Manchester University Press.

——1996 *A Japanese Advertising Agency, An Anthropology of Media and Markets*. Richmond, Surrey: Curzon.

Morley, D. 1986 *Family Television, Cultural Power and Domestic Leisure*. London: Comedia.

Mouer, R. and Sugimoto Yoshio 1990 *Images of Japanese Society, a Study in the Social Construction of Reality*. London: Kegan Paul International.

Nakane, Chie 1971 *Japanese Society*. Harmondsworth: Penguin.

Ohnuki-Tierney, Emiko 1987 *The Monkey as Mirror: Symbolic Transformations in Japanese History and Ritual*. Princeton: University of Princeton Press.

——(ed.) 1990 *Culture through Time, Anthropological Approaches*. Stanford, California: Stanford University Press.

——1994 *Rice as Self*. Cambridge: Cambridge University Press.

Pharr, S. J. and E. S. Krauss (eds) 1996 *Media and Politics in Japan*. Honolulu: University of Hawaii Press.

Plath, David (ed.) 1964 *The After Hours*. Berkeley: University of California Press.

Powers, R. 1989 "Introduction" in *Handbook of Japanese Popular Culture* edited by R. Powers and H. Kato. Westport, Conn.: Greenwood Press.

Robertson, Jennifer 1991 *Native and Newcomer: Making and Remaking a Japanese City*. Berkeley: University of California Press.

Rosenberger, Nancy (ed.) 1992 *Japanese Sense of Self*. Cambridge: Cambridge University Press.

Samuel, R. and Paul Thompson (eds) 1990 *The Myths We Live By*. London: Routledge.

Schodt, Frederik L. 1983 *Manga! Manga! The World of Japanese Comics*. Tokyo: Kodansha International.

——1996 *Dreamland Japan: Writings on Modern* Manga. Berkeley, California: Stone Bridge Press.

Silverstone, Roger 1981 *The Message of Television, Myth and Narrative in Contemporary Culture*. London: Heinemann.

Skov, Lise and B. Moeran (eds) 1995 *Women, Media and Consumption in Japan*. Richmond, Surrey: Curzon.

Sugimoto, Yoshio 1997 *An Introduction to Japanese Society*. Cambridge: Cambridge University Press.

Sugiyama-Lebra, Takie 1984 *Japanese Women: constraint and fulfillment*. Honolulu: University of Hawaii Press.

Tobin, Joseph J. 1992 "Introduction: Domesticating the West" in his edited *Re-made in Japan*.

——(ed.) 1992 *Re-made in Japan, Everyday Life and Consumer Taste in a Changing Society*. New Haven and London: Yale University Press.

Tulloch, John 1995 "The Changing Audiences of Science Fiction" in *Science Fiction Audiences* edited by H. Jenkins and J. Tulloch. London: Routledge.

Weiner, M. (ed.) 1997 *Japan's Minorities: the illusion of homogeneity*. London: Routledge.

Whiting, Robert 1990 *You Gotta Have* Wa. New York: Vintage.

Williams, Raymond 1983 *Keywords: A vocabulary of culture and society*. London: Fontana.

Yoshino Kosaku 1992 *Cultural Nationalism in Contemporary Japan, a Sociological Enquiry*. London: Routledge.

CHAPTER 1

Sumo in the Popular Culture of Contemporary Japan

YAMAGUCHI MASAO

Introduction: Sumo and Japanese culture

Until recently sumo in Japan was considered to be a pre-modern sport, a product of feudalism; moreover, it was thought to be resistant to modernization since it would not change features such as its traditional hairstyles, or the wearing of kimono, etc. However, sumo has survived all this criticism and is currently enjoying a renaissance in Japan, as well as tremendous popularity in many other countries including the UK,[1] Spain, France and the United States. It should be noted that the way the sport is appreciated seems to differ from country to country; that is, it is consumed differently in different places.[2] In Spain sumo is enjoyed more as a fighting sport, while in the UK it is also its ceremonial and stylized aspects which attract people. In Japan, as this chapter will argue, the reasons for the sport's renewed success are more complicated and lie in its association with both theater and the emperor as well as in its retention of various elements which are related to "traditional" Japanese religion.

Paradoxically, it also seems that sumo's current popularity in Japan can be explained by the fact that the sport reflects both the urban culture of the Edo period (1603–1867) as well as being seen to spring from a deep stratum of rural culture. As will be explained below, sumo includes various elements of agricultural ceremonials and cosmology which may have been derived from the immeasurable past. However, a certain sense of style and vitality which characterize the match itself seems to reflect the temperament of Edo citizens.[3] Unlike *silmu* (Korean wrestling) which decides the champion after five matches, in sumo the match is settled in one contest of only a few minutes. People seem to enjoy the contrast between the lengthy preparation for the bout and the rapidity of the battle itself; they also appreciate not only the decorative

aspects which surround sumo, but also its narrative structure. The core
of this narrative is the combat itself: it can be understood as a mythical
battle fought between the positive and negative elements of the cosmos
in which the former is always the winner and the latter the loser. The
game itself is held in a theatrical as well as a festive space, with
ceremonies to mark its beginning and end. Thus sumo resembles
kabuki theater: both allow people to transcend everyday life.

The theatricality of sumo

Few people would make the connection between kabuki theater and
sumo. Yet the similarities between the two explain why both sumo and
kabuki have regained popularity in postmodern Japan. First of all, both
have stuck to the fashions of the Edo period which makes them appear
timeless. This timelessness seems to have a great appeal in postmodern
culture.[4] Secondly, they both use highly stylized gestures to mark the
climax of their performances. In sumo there are forty-eight clearly
defined ways (or 48 te) in which the match can be won. The performance of sumo is identified with the image of a god playing in the ring,
but the deity can only be manifested in the body of the wrestlers (rikishi)
at the moment of winning, if the win is correctly performed. An
experienced spectator enjoys the style (kata) of the performance at the
very moment of winning. It is kata which is the ultimate concern of
sumo. That is why the yokozuna (the highest rank of wrestler) perform
the most essential kata during the dohyô-iri (a ritual performance,
literally meaning "entering the ring"); this ritual is thought to introduce
cosmic energy into the ring and hence into the world.[5]

The space in which the sumo match is held is carefully marked out
in shapes which have a religious significance. The "ring" (dohyô) is a
rectangle on the surface of which a circle is laid out with twisted straw
rope (shimenawa). The boundaries of the rectangle itself are marked
with straw sacks of the type normally used for storing rice. While
both straw rope and rice are important ritual materials in Shintô, these
two shapes symbolize the mandala which expresses cosmic totality in
Buddhism. This mixture of religious symbolism is typical of Japanese
religion before the separation of Buddhism and Shintoism during the
Meiji Restoration and is still found in some surprising places in postmodern Japan (see, for example, Gill in this volume).

Not only is the stylization of gestures and the marking out of
ceremonial space common to both sumo and kabuki, but both performances also feature ceremonial stamping. The stamping which takes
place in the sumo ring also occurs in various village sumo performances,
as well as in the Buddhist ceremonies such as the Nigatsudô (February

Hall) which takes place in the Tôdai temple of Nara. It is said that the stamping originally derived from the *onmyôdô* (secret) rituals of the Taoist tradition in esoteric religion. Although stamping also occurs in noh theater, it was in kabuki that this type of performance became highly stylized and was given a special name: *roppô*. *Roppô* is thought to be the strongest expression of the power of the deities. There are eighteen special plays in kabuki called the *jû hachiban* (eighteen pieces) which are filled with stamping actions and in which only Ichikawa Danjûrô (from the Ichikawa family)[6] can play the role of the protagonist. It is therefore possible to argue that the style including *roppô* is in a sense equivalent to the 48 *te* in sumo. They both mark privileged moments in which the divine is experienced by means of the powerful effects of the performance on both participants and observers.

Sound is another way in which sumo and kabuki mark out a different time and space. The clapping of wooden blocks by the summoner (*yobidashi*) is used to mark the changes in the program for sumo, and of scenes in kabuki. Drums were used in both performances as well. Although no longer a feature of kabuki, the *yagura-daiko* drum was beaten up on a separate high stage (*yagura*); this sort of drum is still used in sumo. The use of the *yagura-daiko* is a way to mediate between the deities and men.[7]

There are also similarities between the symbolism which surrounds and constitutes these two types of performances. Take, for example, the highly decorated apron worn by the *yokozuna*, which is thought to be a manifestation of divinity. Similarly in kabuki, the whole costume worn on stage is thought to be *yama*: the word meaning "mountain", thought to be the point of contact between the gods in heaven and men on earth. In the past the concept of *yama* came to be extended to anything that might suggest the presence of the divine. Therefore kabuki actors themselves came to be thought of as *yama*, wearing costumes which were believed to be the primary *yama*. This means that the actors in kabuki are meant to manipulate their costumes in such a way that they appear to be the movements of the gods. In sumo, these two elements (performer as *yama* and costume as *yama*) are usually kept separate during the match, but are united in the performance of the *dohyô-iri*, when the decorated apron (*keshô-mawashi*, lit. the apron for a horse), replaces the chain of black string normally hung around the wrestler's loincloth.

Now while these elements might give a particular decorative and esthetic pleasure to sumo and kabuki, they also are useful in producing and marking a festive space which is separate from everyday life. This becomes clear if we look at the historical geography of kabuki and sumo. During the Edo period, kabuki theaters and sumo stadiums –

along with pleasure towns (*hana-machi*, literally "flower towns") such as Yoshiwara – were all labeled "bad spaces" (*aku-basho*) and thus were literally set apart. So, for example, while the *rikishi* were not segregated from Tokyo social life, their stadiums (*kokugikan*) were in a special area called *Ryôgoku* which was understood to be located beyond this world. The actual location of *Ryôgoku* was just beyond the Sumida River which was historically the eastern boundary of Tokyo. The area beyond the river was thought to be the intermediary space between the living and the dead. It was a privileged space where fox ghosts might appear, even in daylight. There could be found thousands of booths not only for sumo, but for theatrical and other types of performances (just as in *Bartholomew Fair* in Jonson's London). Therefore it is significant that *the Kokugikan*, which was built towards the end of the nineteenth century, is still located beyond the Sumida River near Ekôin-ji, a temple which remains one of Tokyo's largest ceremonial centers for the dead.

The continued location of sumo performances in this area hints at the possibility that the modern (or postmodern) bouts are meant to be seen as a kind of freak show: battles between fantastic figures re-enacted on a theatrical stage. This distinguishes sumo from other modern sports in which statistics are sometimes more appreciated than their theatrical features. Aside from these features which, as already argued, mark sumo as somehow timeless, there is one more aspect of the sport which must be discussed before considering its current popularity: its relationship to the feudal courts and kingship or, for Japan, the emperorship.

Sumo and Japanese emperorship (*tennôsei*)

Since its beginning sumo has had deep associations with East Asian cosmology. The modern sumo match seems to have two sources: one is in rural villages, the other in court performances. The former seems to have been an indigenous performance; whereas the latter was a semi-ritual performance brought to the Japanese court in ancient times. This court sumo seems to have been introduced by thirty wrestlers who accompanied a Korean prince in his Japanese exile. The ancient court not only adopted, but re-formulated this wrestling so it became part of court ritual. Village sumo or wrestling was enjoyed as part of the cycle of seasonal rituals as well; usually it was included as part of the rituals at the village shrine after the harvest. Sumo was one of various competitive games played on such occasions which might also include tug-of-war or archery. Sometimes sumo contests were the occasion when village cosmology was re-created.[8] In such cases, the village was divided into two parts: the mountainside versus the river or seaside, east versus west, etc. These bouts were perceived as the symbolic battle between positive and negative cosmological forces. This is why the east and west are still important as the sides from which the *rikishi* mount the modern stage.

Moreover, the *dohyô* on which the combat takes place reflects the so-called *fû-sui* (wind and flowing water) cosmology which, with its various symbols (see diagram), is common throughout East Asia. This cosmology was (and sometimes still is) applied on various levels in society and the physical world: in the layout of a capital city, in house building and in the imperial court, as well as in rituals, such as in village sumo where the chief priest of the shrine would have to watch from the north side of the ring so that he would be facing south. This is the position allocated to the emperor in *fû-sui*.

Kyoto, which was built in the tenth century, is said to be designed on the basis of this East Asian cosmic model. The palace of the emperor was built in the northern part of the city, so that it faced south. During court audiences or ceremonies, the emperor had to sit facing the south. Even today, when the emperor watches sumo, he must sit on a special seat arranged for him in the northern quadrant of the stadium, facing south.

Fû-sui Cosmology

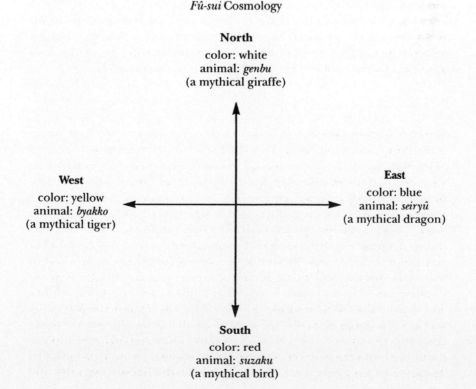

North
color: white
animal: *genbu*
(a mythical giraffe)

West
color: yellow
animal: *byakko*
(a mythical tiger)

East
color: blue
animal: *seiryû*
(a mythical dragon)

South
color: red
animal: *suzaku*
(a mythical bird)

As already noted, sumo today might seem a kind of freak show in which near-naked, gigantically fat men perform. This has always been part of the Japanese sport. However, this sort of spectacle became unacceptable in societies such as China and Korea, especially among the aristocratic classes, where Confucianism held sway.[9] In contrast, in Japan, sumo was supported mainly by local feudal lords during the Edo period. It is for this reason that it went into decline after the Meiji Restoration (1868), since these lords lost their power and domains. It was only in the 1970s when the then emperor visited the Tokyo *Kokugikan* that sumo began to regain popularity. Whether or not he was conscious of it, he was acknowledging the ancient cosmological role of the emperor and was thus enacting and reinforcing it. It now seems that the present emperor is continuing to fill this role as I shall discuss in the last section of this chapter.

Sumo and the mass media: *manga* (comic strips) and film

The representation of sumo in other forms of the mass media has reflected its ups and downs in popularity. Sumo wrestlers were popular heroes in traditional forms of mass media such as *ukiyoe* prints. These prints of *rikishi* were called *sumôe* or *rikishie* and were similar to the prints of adored kabuki actors (*kabukie*). When film became popular in Japan (after 1911), sumo became one of the favorite subjects of the new medium. The lives of wrestlers like Futabayama, a star of the 1930s and 1940s became part of formulaic success story films in which a young outsider struggles against great odds to achieve the dream of perfecting their art (a formula still used to portray the lives of modern wrestlers such as the star of the 1970s, Wakanohana).

There was another formulaic sumo theme, of which the story of Nayoroiwa is typical. He was not a great wrestler, never making it to *ôzeki* (the rank just below *yokozuna*), but he was famous for continually trying to achieve the ideal form in sumo. This moved audiences greatly.[10]

However, it is the true story of the wrestler Futabayama which is interesting for what it tells us about the relationship between sumo and the media before television created a resurgence in the popularity of the sport. After the Second World War, sumo was almost totally ignored by the Japanese. This was partly as a result of the retirement of the *rikishi* Futabayama, who had been a super-star since 1939. The Sumo Association owed a great deal to Futabayama. He had been instrumental in saving the Tokyo Association of Sumo from the decline it had entered in the Meiji era (1868–1911) when a number of *rikishi* had left and the number of spectators decreased. During these twilight years of sumo, it became easy for a talented young fighter such as Futabayama to mount the ladder to stardom with greater rapidity than would have been possible previously.

In an era when sumo was either heard on the radio or just glimpsed in newsreels shown two weeks after the event, the young super-star brought spectators back to the ringside. His sumo was so spectacular that people even enjoyed watching the delayed newsreels. Once he retired in the 1940s,[11] people lost interest in sumo, even though there were still great wrestlers, such as Akinoumi from the Western stables, and Haguroyama and Terukumi, both from the Eastern stables. This was a second period of decline for sumo, not helped at all by the association of the sport (as well as other sports, such as *kendô* and *jûdô*) with pre-war militarism.

Along with the renewal which sumo has achieved since the 1970s, *manga* (comics) have also grown in popularity. Just as in the past prints, films, newsreels, the radio and plays helped to popularize sumo, so now does *manga*. At first the heroes of the sports comics were baseball players, but *rikishi* have recently joined the ranks. Notari Matsutaro (slow-moving Matsutaro), for example, was the first of these heroes. He is an optimistic sort of wrestler who has ignored the traditions of sumo in his climb up the ranks; his claim that he did not feel nervous fascinated readers. The second *manga* in this area was *Aa, Harimanada*, whose protagonist, Harimanada, is a type of anti-hero. He also ignores rules when he feels it necessary to do so and sometimes appears on the *dohyô* wearing a mask to frighten his opponents. He becomes a source of scandal and must face the supreme boss of sumo who is called Futagoyama. Harimanada does not care at all. Since the world of sumo is characterized by the demand that the *rikishi* adhere strictly to its rules and etiquette, and thus reflects the workaday world in which they live, younger readers especially support these anti-heroes because they realize their hidden wish to be free. These *manga* which appear in both book form and on television, ensure the place of the sport in modern popular culture. But it is with the enhanced role of wrestlers as "stars" in public culture (see also Steffánson in this volume) that we can best see the continued connection between the theatrical, the emperor and the sport.

Sumo and emperorship in contemporary Japanese culture

The wedding of the Crown Prince seems to have been enthusiastically received by a majority of the population. The hitherto unknown story of the seven years' wait which the Crown Prince endured in the hope that Owada Masako would consent to marry him, moved the Japanese deeply. With this marriage, the royal family of Japan obtained the full support of nearly all the Japanese people, in contrast to the period just after the war, when not a small number of Japanese insisted on the abolition of the *tennô* (emperor) system. And it was with the marriage of the present emperor that the royal family began to regain the nation's support. The present Emperor Akihito's romance with his empress-to-be began on a tennis court, and fascinated people, who thought of it as a fairy tale.[12]

The fact that in the case of the current emperor so many potential brides – fearing isolation and bad treatment by courtiers – had refused even to consider marriage into the royal family, did give satisfaction to many people who wanted, to some extent, the degradation of the royal family because of the Emperor Shôwa's commitment to the war. In contrast, when the present Crown Prince again chose a bride from a commoner family, the wedding was welcomed as if this royal marriage was one taking place between Heaven and Earth. The mass media took full advantage of the occasion.

Part of the nation's joy may have been rooted in what had been a growing fear that, during his two-year stay in Oxford, the Prince might marry an English woman. This concern with the purity of Japanese blood and tradition can also be seen in the way in which the public strongly opposed the nomination of Konishiki (originally Sully, a Hawaiian) to the rank of *yokozuna*. On the other hand there was no resistance to the nomination of Akebono (a Samoan) to the same rank, because he behaved modestly and showed every sign of following the rules and lifestyle of the sumo world. The possibility of a British empress spoke to the same anxieties – would she conform? – and the Japanese were relieved when this never happened.

The marriage of the prince was also compared with the impending wedding of Takanohana, a twenty-two-year-old *rikishi*, to Miyazawa Rie, the most famous pop star in Japan.[13] Takanohana was considered to be like the Crown Prince at the time, because his father had been a top-ranking wrestler some fifteen years before and, as chairman of the Japanese Sumo Association, continued to be an important figure in sumo. If this "ideal" marriage between two young stars had taken place, the royal marriage would have lost some of its glamor.

Interestingly enough, Takanohana seems to have canceled his betrothal to Miyazawa not long after its announcement – an announcement which had promised a semi-royal wedding – for the sake of his career. He has been accused of sacrificing his love in order to follow the decision of the Sumo Association which wanted him to concentrate on his career. It is true that after the betrothal, Takanohana's record of wins was poor, apparently because of the vast media pressure. It seems clear that the Sumo Association won out over his love, because Takanohana regained his form, strength and concentration and even the wrestling of his older brother, Wakahanada, improved!

Takanohana's case is often contrasted with that of the Crown Prince because the latter endured a long wait and finally won his first love's hand in marriage. The withdrawal of Takanohana from his marriage seems to have promoted the prince's wedding. In short, people tolerated Takanohana's failure because the Crown Prince had succeeded. At the same time, the prince's wedding absorbed the glamor which would have endowed the wedding of the sumo super-star.

Conclusion

While discussing sumo as part of popular culture in Japan today, I have been referring to other institutions, such as the emperorship and kabuki, both of which have produced public idols. The creation of idols or "stars" can be considered one of the defining characteristics of popular culture. All three of these institutions are closely related, although the last section concentrated specifically on the relationship between sumo and the emperorship. The institutions are comparable for a variety of reasons: they are based on agricultural ritual and *fû-sui* cosmology. Chinese *fû-sui* has influenced different arenas of Japanese culture from the layout of cities in the Heian period (794–1185) to court music; from the setting-up of aristocratic households to use of the earth mound in sumo.

Both the emperorship and sumo are associated with the four seasons and related rituals. The New Year's ritual (*shihôhai*) and the first fruit offering (*kan'name-sai*) which takes place in the autumn are important markers in the rites that surround the emperor. In sumo there are four seasons of matches; this, however, is a new practice. In the past, it was at new year and at the harvest that bouts were held: sumo constituted part of a ritual complex that was called *sumô seihi*. These elements, the layout of space and the marking of time, clearly show how sumo and the emperorship are part of a large and much more comprehensive system.

Today, to return to the subject of idols, you can see on television how the audience on the side where wrestlers enter and leave the ring touch the wrestler's body as he goes by. When asked why they touch the *rikishi* as he leaves the ring, audience members have replied that they hope for his physical power to be transmitted to them. This is similar to the belief in the power emanating from physical contact with royalty which was common in many kingships. This sort of contact is, of course, impossible with the imperial family in Japan today, no matter how much more accessible they have become.

Thus, it is this sort of purely corporeal element, distinct from the esthetic pleasure of sumo, which has allowed the sport to regain its popularity. Although most contemporary audiences are not aware of it, sumo is marked by various ceremonial elements which are associated with power. This sort of dynamic energy is also to be found, so audiences seem to feel, in kabuki (in particular in the *jû hachiban*, as performed by the Ichikawa family) and in the emperor who is still too remote and powerful to be touched. The relationship between these three institutions, but especially between the emperor and sumo, is such that when the popularity of the emperor decreased, so did the audiences for the other two performances. In this way, I argue, we can see that the emperorship is inextricably tied to popular culture and not just to the more sophisticated arts of high culture.

Notes

1   Although the screening of sumo on British television no longer occurs, articles on the more exotic aspects of the sport continue to appear, most recently in Watts' article on women in sumo for the *Guardian* (1997).

2   See Watts, Chapter 10, for a discussion of consumption. For a more detailed argument see Miller 1987 and 1995.

3   Umehara Takeshi, a Japanese philosopher, has argued that sumo integrates two tendencies: the refined and stylized form of *Yayoi* culture with the crude dynamism of *Jômon* culture. Umehara's argument, based on the ancient *Jômon* and *Yayoi* pottery styles, while interesting cannot be discussed here.

4   *Editor's note*: The element of nostalgia should also not be ignored here and in this respect sumo and kabuki might both well be similar to the traveling theater companies described by Ivy (1995).

5   This notion (that the appearance of the deity allows positive energy to enter the world) is the core of many Shintô rituals in Japan (see Hori 1968).

6   The Ichikawa family is rather like a royal family in the world of kabuki. The name of Danjûro is inherited by each successor to the family headship.

7   The use of percussion instruments to mark states of transition occurs widely; for an interesting delineation see Needham 1967: 606–14.

8   See Bernier 1975 for an anthropological description of how this cosmology is re-created by village rituals.

9   In fact, the original Korean version of sumo, *silmu*, never became a court sport.

10   Another typical story along these lines was made into a successful play by the popular playwright Shin Hasegawa in the 1940s. *Ippongatana dohyô-iri* (*Dohyô-iri With a Sword*) told the story of an unsuccessful wrestler who goes home to see his mother, having written to her that he had been successful in attaining the rank of *yokozuna*, which was untrue. Fearful of her disappointment, the wrestler cannot, in the end, face his mother and leaves without seeing her, after performing a solitary *dohyô-iri* with a sword.

11   Futabayama continued to be in the limelight after his retirement. He became a follower of the new religion called Jikôson and was also arrested after a dramatic street fight. People had great sympathy for him, but this did not aid the Sumo Association.

12 Although the reality is that this meeting had been carefully planned and arranged by the late Professor Koizumi Shinzo, who was a professor at Keio University as well as the Crown Prince's private tutor.
13 Although I will briefly consider the case of the Crown Prince and Takanohana here, a longer discussion on the two engagements and the media coverage of both can be found in Chapter 8. In many ways, Steffánson agrees with my conclusion about the relationship between the imperial family and popular culture.

References

Bernier, B. 1975 *Breaking the cosmic circle, religion in a Japanese village.* Cornell University East Asia Papers no. 5. Ithaca, NY: China-Japan Program, Cornell University.

Hori, Ichiro 1968 *Folk religion in Japan: Continuity and change.* Chicago: University of Chicago Press.

Ivy, Marilyn 1995 *Discourses of the Vanishing: Modernity, phantasm, Japan.* Chicago: University of Chicago Press.

Miller, Daniel 1987 *Material Culture and Mass Consumption.* Oxford: Basil Blackwell.

——(ed.) 1995 *Acknowledging Consumption: A review of new studies.* London: Routledge.

Needham, Rodney 1967 "Percussion and Transition" in *Man* vol. 2(4): 606–14.

Takeuchi, Makoto (July) 1993 "Sumo that lived history in Japan" in *Geijitsu-sinchô*: 39–53.

Umehara, Takeshi (July) 1993 "Sumo, my secret love" in *Geijitsu-sinchô*: 30–38.

Watts, J. 1997 "Women in sumo". *Guardian*: p. 14.

Yamaguchi Masao 1987 "*Sumo ni okeru gireito uchûkan*" ("Symbolism and cosmology in sumo") in *Bulletin of the National Museum of History and Folklore,* vol. 15: 99–130.

PART II

The Male Domain

CHAPTER 2

Transformational Magic
Some Japanese super-heroes and monsters

TOM GILL

Introduction

In any culture, there are elements of change and elements of continuity (Ohnuki-Tierney 1987). The literature on Japan tends to overemphasize either change (such as in technology) or continuity (for example, cherry blossom viewing, haiku, sumo, etc.). In this chapter, I hope to show how cultural continuities may be found even in an area of popular culture which is subject to countless fast-changing influences: commercial television dramas for children.

The makers of these programs are under constant pressure to respond to changing tastes, to maintain audience ratings, and to sell advertising and spin-off products. Yet a look at the programs reveals recurrent themes which, in some cases, have their roots in supernatural beliefs dating back to antiquity.[1] In this chapter I shall discuss how some of these old beliefs find expression in the super-heroes and monsters of Japanese children's television. The very longevity of these themes and their shared symbolic similarities (as outlined below) suggest that they are of fundamental importance in Japanese culture.

Japan has seven national television networks, two public and five commercial, besides numerous local and satellite stations. At any given time there are likely to be some twenty to thirty assorted children's dramas in the viewing week, most of which disappear from the screens after a year or so, often to be replaced by something very similar. Nearly all of these programs air between the hours of 5 and 7.30 pm, and they typically last thirty minutes including three commercial breaks, some of which are devoted entirely to advertisements for spin-off products. In addition, most of the programs I discuss have spawned feature films which are shown during the school holidays. Perhaps two-thirds of the

programs are animated, but many of the most popular ones, and most of
those discussed here, are dramas performed by heavily costumed actors.

The small selection of programs mentioned here rely on pre-
schoolers, aged 3 to 6, for the bulk of their viewers, and are primarily
aimed at boys. There are fascinating super-hero programs for young
girls too, such as *Sailor Moon* and *Cutey Honey Flash*, but space is limited
so they will be left for others to discuss.[2]

Ultraman and *Superman*

Perhaps the most popular character ever to emerge from children's
television in Japan is Ultraman, a widely recognized icon, on a par
with Superman in American culture. *Ultraman*, a costume drama, was
launched on Mainichi/TBS TV in 1966 by Tsuburaya Productions; there
were no new series launched in Japan between 1980 and 1996, when
Tsuburaya ended a sixteen-year drought with *Ultraman Tiga* (1996–97).[3]

Like "Superman", the name "Ultraman" implies a man who exceeds
ordinary men. Both words have Latin roots: "super" meaning "above"
and "ultra" meaning "beyond". But there are significant differences.
Superman is the super-individualist: he flies solo; he never changes;
he has no Superdad and Supermum, no Supersiblings.[4] In contrast
Ultraman was once alone, but as each year passed the family grew
bigger, spawning series such as: *Ultra Seven* (1967), *Ultraman Jack* (1971),
Ultraman Ace (1972), *Ultraman Taro* (1973), *Ultraman Leo* (1974), an
animated version called *The Ultraman* (1979) and *Ultraman 80* (1980).
Along the way various other ultra-brothers appeared, such as Zoffy and
Julian; and also Father of Ultra and Mother of Ultra.

The commercial advantages of this big happy family of Ultramen, in
terms of dolls, suits, stickers and so on, are obvious. But it is probably
also fair to say that Ultraman was originally modeled on the solitary
Superman and developed his family because filial loyalty, fraternal
solidarity, camaraderie and teamwork were found to have more appeal
for Japanese children than the struggle of a lone individual.[5] In fact,
some of the former qualities went into the very creation of Ultraman,
since no one person can lay claim to the honor: *Ultraman* was designed
by a committee at the Tsuburaya Creative Department.

With one exception (discussed below), all Ultramen, and Mother of
Ultra, share the same basic color scheme: red suits with silver trim.
These two colors are combined in various patterns of Essoldo Cinema
curves and stripes. Why red and silver? I believe it is really a shiny
version of red and white, the traditional colors of celebration and good
luck in Japan.[6] Ultraman is thus a sort of good luck talisman: he brings
beneficial magic.[7]

Superman's predominant colors are red, yellow and blue – hinting, perhaps, at the American flag. He is a patriotic American created in the 1930s to fight for what the American 1950s television serial used to call "truth, justice and the American Way." Such nationalistic themes are much less evident in Japanese heroes than in their American counterparts. There is no Captain Nippon in Japan, while patriotism is fully embodied in the hero Captain America. Another contrast is that while Superman is incredibly strong and can fly, in other ways he is still a human being. Superman is human-sized and he lives on Earth; he may be superhuman, but he is also recognizably human.

Ultraman lives on Planet Ultra and has to commute to Earth. In fact he is not really human at all: he is as tall as the Tokyo Tower and weighs about 40,000 tons. He has a sort of brooch in the middle of the chest (or on his forehead in some versions), which changes color or flashes on and off when his energy reserves are running dangerously low. He has a pointy head with a ridge running down the middle of the face, and some versions have a residual dorsal fin. These attributes tell us that there is something of the fish in Ultraman. There is something of the insect, too. Some versions have bulging, multiplex eyes, for instance. None have eyeballs (though sometimes the pinholes for the actor to see through are rather obvious), nor eyelashes or any other hair. His brother Superman is a hairy man, but Ultraman is a smooth man.

Another contrast is in the use of language. Superman is laconic, but he has a way with words. He will tell villains that their game is up, he will make ironic quips in times of crisis. Ultraman, in most of his incarnations,[8] is completely inarticulate. He does not speak English or Japanese. The only word he utters is "SWATCH!," an onomatopoeic exclamation as he swishes into the sky once more after a mission. Nor does Ultraman share Superman's hidden emotions. He does not suffer teenage angst over any Japanese Lois Lane.[9]

While Superman holds up falling buildings, stops trains falling off cliffs and diverts death rays, Ultraman only does one thing: he fights monsters. He may use his specium ray to finish the job, but most of the action is hand-to-hand wrestling. A Japanese informant offered me the theory that Ultraman satisfied the psychological desire for violence and helped dispel the sense of impotent frustration which lingered on in Japan after the nation was beaten in the Pacific War and had to sign the American-authored constitution renouncing the aggressive use of arms.

Ultraman may be good at fighting, but he is not as overtly masculine as Superman. Superman is a big, American football-playing, sweaty locker-room-type hunk with big biceps and there is even a suggestive bulge in his all-American underpants. Ultraman is sexless, if not downright feminine. When we lived in Japan, my son, then a five-year-old fan, often described Ultraman's smooth, sculptured pectorals as *oppai* (breasts). There is no hint of any genitalia: he has a smooth, plastic crotch.[10] Again, whereas Superman is strong enough to win every battle, Ultramen, especially Ultraman Taro, often have to call for help from home. Taro is an apprentice Ultraman, an Ultralad. His rays do not always work properly; he needs monster-battling advice from Seven and Ace.

The monsters in the programs are so numerous that they appear to have been constructed from identi-kits generating variations on number of heads, number of eyes, shade of green, hairy/scaley, claws/tentacles, spines/goitres. The most famous is the Baltan Starman (*Barutan Seijin*), whose pair of gigantic claws associates him loosely with the lobster. Then there are the likes of Bemstar, Ereking, Mururoa, Kiira, and the Babaru, Metron and Hypolito Starmen. These beasts may trouble Ultraman Taro, but for an experienced Ultraman they usually pose no problem, for Ultraman is often bigger than the monster (imagine Superman big enough to rap King Kong on the cranium). After half an hour of complicated plotting and suspense-building, the monster is usually disposed of in a couple of minutes with a couple of Judô throws and karate chops.

Thus it can be argued that Superman is an American fantasy: strong, lonely, resourceful and independent. An immigrant to the US (as are most "Americans"), Superman left Planet Krypton behind long ago and today he lives inside Clark Kent. He could be said to represent the power contained within every human being: the hero within every ordinary man. Superman is one of many heroes common in the Judeo-Christian tradition: he possesses an inner strength which enables him to emerge victorious against overwhelming odds. Ultraman is a more reassuring, perhaps a more plausible fantasy: he can beat the monsters because he is bigger than they are and can call on his brothers to help if necessary. In relying on others, Ultraman could be said to be Japanese to the bone. Also worth noting is that Ultraman has never been internalized like Superman: he is external and gets called in, like the pest-extermination man, to get rid of those annoying slobbering monsters. This last attribute makes it possible to liken Ultraman to one Shintô god among many, who will miraculously appear from nowhere and intervene to save Japan: a *deus ex machina*, a divine wind, a *kamikaze*.[11]

Ultraman's popularity peaked in 1967, towards the end of the first series, when a single episode captured no less than 42.8 per cent of the viewing audience, equivalent to nearly 40 million people. It troughed with *Ultraman Leo*, who struggled to register 10 per cent in the ratings. *Ultraman 80* fared only slightly better, which accounts for Tsuburaya's lengthy hesitation before producing the new series. The lesson of *Leo* and *80* is that mediocre Ultramen will not sell: the popularity of the original Ultraman demands that something really good be attached to the name. Perhaps now, with the widespread perception that Japan is plagued once more by intractable social and economic problems, is the right time for Ultraman to return.

Ultraman cleansed: Gridman

One of *Ultraman's* modern descendants is *Gridman*. *Gridman* comes from the same stable as *Ultraman*, Tsuburaya Productions, and appeared on Mainichi/TBS television from 1993–4, pulling in a mainly pre-school audience of around 8 to 9 per cent. Gridman is decidedly similar to Ultraman, complete with red/silver coloring and energy brooch, but he looks more human: his heavy-jowled silver face suggests a crusty old brigadier. His lifestyle is completely different from Ultraman's: he inhabits a computer-generated parallel universe of clean, generic sky-scrapers. When monsters threaten, he merges with a small boy, who beams himself to Gridman's universe and enters Gridman's body by pressing a button on a magic amulet worn on the arm, called the Acceptor. Gridman is then observed on screen by two other children, a boy and a girl, who assist him by tapping away at their computer keyboards and sending in extra supplies of remote-controlled hardware to support him.

The plot pattern is also rather different from Ultraman: Gridman is *never* strong enough to win on his own. He gets lobbed over buildings and booted into the gutter by monsters considerably larger than himself. But once the additional hardware arrives, things soon change. A barrage of rockets to soften up the monster, then the robo-dragon goes in claws-first. Gridman merely has to finish off the shell-shocked beast with a quick burst of the Gridbeam. And these monsters do not splatter black blood and tentacles all over the screen as they would in *Ultraman*: they hygienically disappear in an electronic puff accompanied by a short bleeping noise. Gridman is Ultraman post-economic miracle, Ultraman for the electronic age.

Events in the computer world govern those in the real world: the end of the monster brings relief to some tricky situation in the lives of real people. In one episode, scientists excavating a *Tyrannosaurus Rex* skeleton are suddenly attacked by their own mechanical digger. The spirit of the old dinosaur has somehow got into the hydraulics. While it chases them around in a quarry, Gridman does battle with a *Tyrannosaurus Rex*-derived monster in his own boxed world. This monster has been sent by an evil schoolboy, who is under the sway of a Darth Vader-derived supervillain in some other universe.[12] In the end,

when Gridman finishes off the monster, the digger becomes inanimate
once more.

In another episode, a mother and child are trapped in a toy ware-
house by a platoon of marauding model tanks. Again, Gridman's victory
in his videogame battle exorcises the demons and the tanks grind to a
halt just in time. Sometimes the relation between the parallel universes
works the other way: in yet another episode, Gridman's failing power
supplies are topped up by energy generated by several flabby middle-
aged men working out on exercise machines in a gym and somehow
patched through to Gridman's world.

Magical rescue, rather than individual heroism, is the theme of
Ultraman and *Gridman* alike. But where Ultraman comes crashing into
the threatened world of frail mortals, Gridman does his business in a
separate, though connected, sphere controlled by child technocrats.
Aided by new skills and equipment, humankind has regained a degree
of control over nature in the latter version of the giant super-hero myth.

Color-coded gangs of five

Japanese television super-heroes fall into a quite limited number of
categories: one is the giant super-hero as described above; another is the
gang of five, a group of five pals, often mounted on motorbikes,
dedicated to defending justice and fighting evil. Every year the Tôei film
company produces a new version of the gang of five, usually airing at
5.30 pm on Fridays on TV Asahi. Some 80 per cent of its seven million
viewers are in the target age range of 3 to 7 years, and the producers
estimate that it is watched by 90 per cent of all 3-to-7-year-old Japanese
children. "It's one of the first things they see when they open their eyes,"
says one of the producers.

The 1993 version was the *Dai* (Great) *Renjâ*: four young men and
one token woman, who turn into super-heroes: *Ryû* Ranger (Dragon
Ranger, the leader in a red uniform), *Tenma* Ranger (Sacred Horse
Ranger in a blue uniform), *Kirin* Ranger (Fiery Horse Ranger in
yellow), *Shishi* Ranger (Lion Ranger in green) and *Hô* Ranger (Phoenix
Ranger, who is a girl in pink). These in turn gave way to the *Kaku*
(Hidden) *Renjâ* in 1994, and then to the *Ô* (Great, again) *Renjâ* in
1995.

The *Dai* Rangers are virtually identical to their many predecessors, as
the following list will show. It comes from a children's fanzine in which
portraits of the gangs are invariably posed to show a central/leading
figure, and usually the second and third tiers are clearly indicated too.
In the following translation (my own) I have used the positions of the
actors in the portraits accompanying the descriptions to link color with

status. Colors of the same status class are separated by commas; those in different classes by semi-colons.

Feb 1979: *Batorufîbâ J* (Battle Fever J)
"The Defense Ministry's strongest force, they fight with a dance action."
Red; blue; orange; green; white.

Feb 1980: *Denshi Sentai Denjiman* (Electronic Combat Unit Denjiman)
"Imbued with the science of the Denji Starmen, they destroyed the *Bêdâ* ([In]vader?) Clan."
Red; yellow, blue; pink/white, green.

Feb. 1981: *Taiyô Sentai Sanbarukan* (Sun Combat Unit Sun Vulcan)
"Three heroes with the power of the eagle, the shark and the leopard."
Red; blue, yellow.

Feb 1982: *Dai Sentai Gôguru Faibu* (Great Combat Unit Gogul 5)
"Five powerful warriors chosen by computer."
Red; black, blue; yellow, pink.

Feb 1983: *Kagaku Sentai Dainaman* (Scientific Combat Unit Dynaman)
"Five super-scientific heroes with monstrous fighting abilities."
Red; blue, black; pink, yellow.

Feb 1984: *Chôdenshi Baioman* (Super-electronic Bioman)
"Contain bio-particle energy from a bio-star in their bodies."
Red; pink, yellow; blue, black.

Feb 1985: *Dengeki Sentai Chenjiman* (Electric Attack Combat Unit Changeman)
"Five men who have been drenched in the earth force and have acquired its power."
Red; pink, white; blue, black.

March 1986: *Chôshinsei Furasshuman* (Ultra-New Star Flashman)
"Brought up in the Flash Nebula, they fight with star power."
Red; pink, yellow; blue, green.

Feb 1987: *Hikari Sentai Masukuman* (Shining Combat Unit Maskman)
"Warriors who forged their own bodies to use aura power."
Red; yellow, pink; black, blue.

Feb 1988: *Chôjû Sentai Faibuman* (Superbeast Fiveman)
"Five heroes with the power of wild beasts inside their suits."
Red; green, black; blue, yellow.

Feb 1989: *Kôsoku Sentai Tâbo-Renjâ* (High Speed Combat Unit Turbo Ranger)
"High school warriors who specialize in high-speed attacks."
Red; pink, yellow; blue, black.

Feb 1990: *Chikyû Sentai Faibuman* (World Combat Unit Five Man)
"A combat unit of 5 brothers possessed of many united powers."
Red, blue, black, pink, yellow.

Feb 1991: *Chôjin Sentai Jettoman* (Birdman Combat Unit Jet Man)
"With their 'birdnic waves', they acquired the abilities of birdmen."
Red (hawk); blue (swallow), white/pink (swan – female); black (condor), yellow (owl).

Feb 1992: *Kyôryû Sentai Jû-Renjâ* (Dinosaur Combat Unit Monster Ranger)
"Dinosaur warriors who woke up after 170 million years' sleep."
Red (tyrannosaurus rex); pink (pterodactyl – female), yellow (sabre-toothed tiger); blue (triceratops), black (mammoth).

Feb 1993: *Gosei Sentai Dai-Renjâ* (Five Star Combat Unit Great Ranger)
(See above)
Red (dragon); green (lion), pink (phoenix – female); blue (sacred horse), yellow (mythical fiery horse).

Feb 1994: *Ninja Sentai Kaku-Renjâ* (Ninja Combat Unit Hidden Ranger)
"Ordinary youths perform a double transformation: into hooded *ninja* with advanced fighting skills, and then into beasts from oriental mythology."
Red (monkey); white (crane – female), blue (wolf); black (toad), yellow (bear).

According to Toei, the series' popularity peaked in 1980, with *Denjiman*, which had an average rating of 16 per cent, against 7 per cent for the most recent versions. The program has tended to keep its preschool and early primary school audience, while losing older viewers: a common pattern with long-running entertainments in Japan. As the average viewing age has dropped, so has the significance of gender: audiences for early versions were 70 per cent male, whereas now the gender split is about fifty–fifty.

The gangs have shown remarkable consistency over the years in their use of the totemic theme and in number and color. The very first gang of five, *Battle Fever J*, had a political flavor: the red leader was called Battle Japan, and his followers included Battle Cossack,[13] Battle France and Miss America. Since then, however, nearly all the incarnations of the Ranger gang seem to have related the members of the gang to existing, prehistoric or mythical animals. This can be seen as a kind of modern totemism: the beasts are chosen for their positive attributes – usually strength, courage or cunning – and to differentiate the characters of the gang members. The use of birds to symbolize females has also become firmly established. As in Lévi-Strauss' (1962) famous critique of totemism, these animal species are clearly chosen because they are "good to think".

A second important point is that with one exception, *Sanbarukan* (1981), each unit has five members. Why five? Five is a number that signifies hierarchy. It is an odd number, which suggests a man in the middle, or in front, in short a leader. It is also the smallest number that allows for a plural middle class and a plural lower class as well as a singular leader. The gang of five is a miniature class system: each member has reasons to be content with his or her station, for each has a special set of skills; at the same time, it is always made perfectly clear who leads and who is led.

The strong Japanese tendency to divide the natural and human world into groups of five may be a further influence on the television gangs of five, members of which tend to have simple, clearly defined characters, elemental if you like, dominated by a single characteristic linked to their totemic beast. Japanese people do not think in terms of three primary colors, rather they recognize five cardinal colors (*goshiki*): red, blue, yellow, white, black.[14] These are the very colors of the five *Kaku* Rangers. It is obvious that some quite strong cultural chords are being struck here.

An alternative explanation comes from the producers at Tôei: the smallest number for a group drama is three (duos have never been very popular with Japanese children); but three is "lonely" (*sabishii*). No-one makes programs about gangs of four, because four is an unlucky number.[15]

A third point to note about these gangs is the use of color. Each unit's members appear virtually identical except for their color-coded suits.[16] Out of sixteen units, colors are as follows:

Red: 16;	Status: leader (16)
Blue: 16;	Status: middle (8) low (8)
Yellow: 14;	Status: middle (8) low (6)
Pink: 12;[17]	Status: middle (8) low (4)
Black: 10;	Status: middle (4) low (6)
Green: 6;	Status: middle (1) low (5)
Orange: 1;	Status: middle (1)
White: 1;	Status: middle (1)

It is obvious that there is always a red member who is always the leader. There were no purely white rangers until the summer of 1993 (see below), although all suits in all units use white trim to offset distinguishing colors. White also tends to be accentuated with pink uniforms, perhaps to remind us of *kamaboko* again (see note 6). These pink uniforms are, I believe, invariably worn by the token female in the gang (there is always at least one female, and on occasion two, but women have never been in the majority).

Red, blue, yellow and pink then are staples, with green and black disputing the fifth place. However, the overwhelming impression is of the unquestioned dominance of the color red. Why always red? Tôei conducts regular surveys on child color-consciousness, which consistently show that red is by far the most popular color with Japanese children. Its associations with blood and fire make it a powerful color in most cultures, and so it is in Japan. Fire is seen in great quantities in Ranger programs: sheets, gouts, eruptions, great balls of fire. There is a limit to how much blood can be shown on programs with a large

pre-school audience, but a fair amount of it drips from flesh wounds. I
would argue that the associations go something like this:

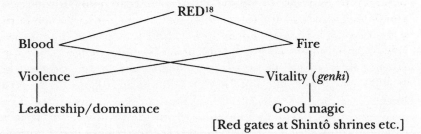

Blood

Violence

Leadership/dominance

RED[18]

Fire

Vitality (*genki*)

Good magic
[Red gates at Shintô shrines etc.]

The association between red and leadership has a well-documented
history. In the seventh and eighth centuries, one aspect of the Chinese
system of bureaucratic government adopted by the Japanese imperial
court was the five-rank (*gogyô*) hierarchy of civil servants. Each rank was
indicated by clothing of an appropriate color (*seishoku*). Red ranked
second only to purple, which enjoyed the same supremacy as Tyrian
purple in the ancient Roman empire, and for the same reason: the dye
was extremely difficult to make. In the Heian era (794–1185), these
status-indicating colors were strictly forbidden to the common people;
as dyeing techniques improved, the gorgeous reds of the madder
root, sappanwood and saffron became powerful symbols of the court
aristocracy (Saito 1988). Notwithstanding the absence of purple it is
tempting to speculate that the Ranger gangs might be remote descendants of the old five-rank court hierarchy.

Like Ultraman, the Ranger concept has recently been transplanted
to the United States. The 1992 model, *Jû-Renjâ*, was culturally adjusted,
re-shot with American actors and released on US television, and then
British television, as *Power Rangers*. The body-suits and motorcycle
helmets have been kept; likewise the red-pink-yellow-blue-black color
line-up, and the prehistoric theme, but there are one or two interesting
changes. Inevitably, the color system has taken on ethnic significance:
Black Ranger is played by an African American actor, Yellow Ranger by
an Asian American actress. This makes two girls in the team, since Pink
Ranger, inevitably, is female too. On the team line-up pictures, Black
Ranger has been moved up to the middle tier of the hierarchy in a
minor gesture towards affirmative action (yet at the expense of one of
the girls). The Red Ranger retains supremacy, and is played by a generic
white male hunk. The primitive magic of the Japanese version has gone;
instead, like most American heroes, the Rangers have been clumsily
politicized.[19]

It has been argued that Rangers inevitably come in packets of five, but
in recent years the five has tended to become six. In the *Jû-Renjâ* story

there is a sixth ranger, Dragon Ranger in the Japanese version, Green Ranger in the American version, who starts out hostile but is won over and joins the gang in the course of the series. The theme is repeated in the *Dai-Renjâ* series, with a small boy called Kô, imbued with the spirit of a snow leopard, who transforms into a white Ranger called *Kiba* (Fang) Ranger. A complex family history makes him an enemy, but as with Dragon Ranger he converts to the cause just in time for his figurine to be added to the set for the end-of-year gift-giving season. He takes up a position at the center of the gang, alongside *Ryû* Ranger (the red one) and only very slightly behind him. Once again, that powerful and significant red-white combination emerges. When the *Kaku-Renjâ* were launched the following year, one member – the female one – was clad all in white for the first time ever.

The five original *Dai* Rangers are all teenagers – the four males work in a Chinese restaurant, a pet shop, a boxing gym and a beauty parlor when off-duty (like Clark Kent, Rangers are often wimps when in civvies), and Hô is a Chinese student. In contrast, Kô, the newcomer, is much younger and smaller, but just as powerful when transformed, of course. The young child gaining acceptance among older, more mature children is another common Japanese theme. Interestingly, the American version replaces little Kô with another big, strapping teenager.

As in *Superman*, Rangers are of normal human size and hence easier to identify with than Ultramen. Their adversaries, too, are of the wicked humanoid variety rather than outsize monsters. They are called *yôkai* (bogeys; hobgoblins), whereas Ultraman and Gridman always fight *kaijû* (monsters). Quite often the *yôkai* are women. In the *Jû-Renjâ* series the main enemy is a witch-figure called "Bandora", a reference to Pandora's box. She fights the Rangers with grotesque gnomes and hunchbacks in her thrall.

The *Dai* Rangers also have a leering witch-foe, Colonel Gara (*Gara Chûsa*), who has two male accomplices: Colonel Shadam (a possible Gulf War reference) and Colonel Saidos. They all wear leather pilots' caps, monocles, with plenty of thongs, straps and studs, reminiscent of the *Mad Max* movies. They are a troika, the "three executives" of an evil empire called Goma, which is ruled over by the corpulent, pasty-faced King Goma XV. The troika commands an army of pathetic foot soldiers called *kottopotoro* ("putties" in the *Power Ranger* version) which are rubbished in large numbers by the *Dai* Rangers in most episodes. They are like the footbots in *Teenage Mutant Ninja Turtles*: humanoid, but sufficiently formalized and mechanical to be destroyed without humanistic qualms.[20]

As with Ultraman, the fighting scenes for which every viewer waits only occupy a few minutes towards the end of each half-hour episode. I lack space to analyze the material with which the rest of the episode is filled, but one theme which seems to recur very often, in this series and others, is that of loss of parents or alienation from them. Kô, the boy who becomes *Kiba* Ranger, had the mark of the leopard branded on him by his mother when still a child, and has frequent flash-backs, complete with howls of pain. Now he is living with a foster-mother, a young single woman who at one point in the series throws him out of the house for touching her breasts. At the end of the episode he is re-admitted on condition that there will be no more unauthorized fondling. Overtly sexual themes like this are quite common in Japanese entertainment for pre-schoolers.

Whether or not one regards such programs as significant cultural indicators, one cannot ascribe them simply to one man's idiosyncrasy: like Ultraman, the Rangers are designed and produced by a team whose personnel varies with the years. There is no single auteur to be discerned behind the mythology. It comes from the broader culture, and in turn illuminates it.

Purple heroes

We might ask why the leaders of Ranger gangs are always clad in red rather than purple, the traditional color of leadership. First, of course, because of the powerful associations of red outside its connection with old court hierarchies, discussed briefly above. Second, because although these red riders are leaders, they are not supremos. There usually seems to be an older man, a *sensei* (teacher/master) to whom they defer. The red rangers are field commanders, not generals.

So far I have only come across two purple heroes in the television culture. One is Ultraman King: the only Ultraman who is not red and silver. He is purple with silver trim and a silver beard. This makes perfect sense: purple is the imperial color. The other is Jan Pâ-son (TV Asahi/Asahi Communications/Tôei, 1993–4). The name is supposed to mean person, not parson. It seems to be a feeble attempt to substitute the "man" with which so many heroes' names end. Jan Pâson, who closely resembles the American Robocop, is a purple robot, whose weaponry includes the "Break Knuckle" (where his rocket-propelled fist flies off the arm) and a cannon concealed in his knee-cap. He has a comrade called Gun Gibson who touts a colossal bazooka called a "spindle cannon". JP (as he's affectionately known) drives the "Dark J Car" which is also purple and contains a detachable purple helicopter called the "Sky J Car". Gibson is a Wild West-like character. He rides a large motorbike called the "G. G. Slayer", festooned with tassels and silverware, and wears a cowboy hat.

These robots are emotional types. In an early episode some enemies kill Gibson's robot girlfriend, sending him into a frenzy of grief in which he wanders around randomly blowing people up. JP finally manages to console him and they bury the girlfriend's central microchip under a tree. This cements their friendship (and the following week Gibson dolls appeared next to JP dolls in the toy shops). JP himself is attracted to frail human women; in one episode he thanks a young lady for showing him what feelings are and tells her he is about to be "reborn". However, like Ultraman, he appears to lack the basic equipment for passionate relationships.

Again like Ultraman, JP started out as a lonely solo act (*"Hitori de doko e yuku?"* – "Where are you going all alone?" – asks the melancholy theme song), but rapidly acquired a large support group. As well as Gibson there are several human friends and a little flying robot with expressive eyebrows who melds with JP's "Jan Dejik" handgun to make a yet more powerful cannon. Japanese heroes never seem to be alone for long: merchandising, as much as culture, sees to that.

Jan Pâson aired on TV Asahi at 8 am on Sunday mornings, 1993–4. Early in 1994, he was replaced with an even more violent program called *Blue Swat*, about a SWAT team of two men and one woman who use highly sophisticated weaponry to destroy disgusting monsters. Despite the title, their uniforms are clearly purple.

Transformations and incorporations

Along with color, transformation (*henshin* or *henkei*) and incorporation/combination (*gattai*) must be examined, as they are staple themes of all children's SF adventures in Japan. The former literally means "change body" or "change form", the latter "combine bodies".[21] Transformation is a theme of folk tales and religions all over the world, and Japan is no exception. Significantly, a popular Japanese word for almost any kind of ghost or monster is *bakemono* (literally: a thing that changes). An alternative word for *yôkai* (hobgoblin) is *henge*, both the characters of which mean "change".

When the Allied occupying armies arrived in Japan at the end of World War II, they found (using what would now be seen as pejorative and ethnocentric labels) that "spirit or demonic possession, necromancy, black magic, witchcraft and purification rites are very common among the common people" (Bunce 1955: 113). Today these beliefs remain strong and find expression in the huge followings of certain charismatic religions (Astley n.d.; Davis 1980; Matsunaga n.d.). Human-animal and human-demon transformations are a stock theme of *ukiyoe* paintings: old women who cast the shadow of a fox; beautiful courtesans who are reflected as ferocious demons in the samurai's cup of sake. The original transforming goblins of Japanese folklore are still shown on television in *Nihon Mukashi-banashi* (*Japanese Tales of Long Ago*, Mainichi/TBS TV), a long-running animation which has won prizes for its educational content. The *tanuki* (raccoon dog) and *kappa* (water sprite) are two popular folkloric figures with the ability to transform themselves.[22]

Incorporation, by contrast, looks like a much more modern, machine-age myth. The two come together in most modern tales of super-heroes. Gridman can transform himself in a number of ways: he can expand, and become Gridman Big. When this is not enough, he can be merged with his peripheral hardware and be incorporated into Thunder Gridman. The tank merges with his abdomen, the robo-dragon folds itself round his shoulders. Only Gridman's head still protrudes from a far bigger, bulkier torso in which body and armor are one seamless mass. Somewhere inside all the armor and weaponry is Gridman, and somewhere inside Gridman is the small boy, the self in the middle of a nested Russian doll.

The theme of transformation is familiar from Marvel comics, of course, but the circumstances are significantly different. By and large, the American heroes bio-transform; the Japanese mecha-transform. The childhood incident which marks the hero out for the future is a common element in American comics: the atomic radiation, the spilled test-tube, the spider serum. These are the magic potions which give the transformatory power. Spiderman has got the knack of transforming on purpose; Batman and Superman are always powerful and only require a change of clothing. For the Incredible Hulk, the transformation is involuntary and convulsive; there is no uniform, just the torn remains of his working clothes. It could be said that the American heroes are variations on the Jekyll and Hyde theme: for Dr Jekyll the transformation is at first voluntary, then shades into involuntary; the Marvel men are stationed along the curve.

Japanese heroes do not usually transform biologically. The serum motif is missing from the mythology. A device is required. This is true even for Ultraman. I noted earlier that Ultraman is a helper who arrives from afar. That is basically so, but there is a half-hearted stab at the transformational theme: Ultramen must be summoned up, by one of a group of special policemen who wear rubber jump suits and motorcycle helmets. This is done by switching on a device resembling a Pifco torch with a red filter. The torch is waved in the air, and (an) Ultraman comes flying in. We are supposed to believe that he takes over the body of the policeman, but we never see this happen. The only proof we have is that the actor playing the policeman does not appear while Ultraman is on Earth, and that after Ultraman's departure we may see some tell-tale sign: typically a flesh wound on the same part of the body as where the monster got a claw into Ultraman. Gridman's Acceptor is a high-tech version of the Ultraman torch.

The transformation device used by the *Dai* Rangers is a small gadget called an "aura-changer". It consists of two parts, one with a slot and the other with a key, one worn on each wrist. Inserting the key into the slot produces the change. The *Kaku* Rangers have a very similar item called a "*doron*-changer".

The underlying difference between bio-transformation and mecha-transformation is clear enough: only people with special personal histories, exposed to radiation or serum, can bio-transform, whereas anybody, any child, can mecha-transform provided she or he has the appropriate kit. Compared with the American version, the Japanese is both more democratic and more commercially exploitable: Acceptors, aura-changers, etc., are readily available in the shops.

Transformational gadgets are enough of a cliché to be lampooned in the less po-faced cartoon series. In one episode of *Doraemon*,[23] the very long-running, very popular cartoon about a blue, atomic-powered robot cat, Doraemon fixes up his weakling friend Nobuta with a *Chikara Denchi* (Strength Battery), which allows him to become incredibly strong for very brief periods if he sits still and does nothing for a long time to charge up the battery. It is the sort of transformational machine that might have been "made in Britain".[24]

Mecha-transformation took off in the 1980s with the comic series *Mobile Suit Gundam*. The latest version, *G Gundam*, was recently still showing on Asahi TV, immediately before *Kaku-Renjâ*. The mobile suits are worn by children. They are colossal, exotic robots that fly through space and battle teams of similarly massive opponents. They can convert into tanks, rockets and so on. An entire new genre of toys has been spawned from this series: trucks and police cars that turn into robots; dinosaurs that turn into robots; ships that turn into robots; and the robots can in turn be merged with other robots to make bigger, better robots.

Which leads to the complementary motif of incorporation. I have already described the incorporation of Gridman into Thunder Gridman; similar events occur in practically every super-hero series of at least the last decade. Sometimes the nesting is truly elaborate. In the case of the *Dai* Rangers, we first have the transformation from child to Ranger, accomplished with the aura-changer; then each *Dai* Ranger has his own vehicle, into which he disappears and is effectively swallowed. Just occasionally we glimpse him at the controls of his hidden interior cockpit. The Blue and Yellow Rangers (Sacred Horse and Fiery Horse) both climb into vehicles resembling chess knights. The Green Ranger (Lion), pilots a vehicle resembling a lion, that covers the ground in great clanking leaps. The Pink Ranger (phoenix) flies around in a pink aeroplane resembling a bird, and the Red Ranger (dragon) controls a gigantic red robot called the *Ryû-Sei-Ô* (Dragon Star King). This robot in turn can transform into a vast flying dragon. It is clearly the best of the vehicles, another superior status marker.

The process of transformation and incorporation does not end there. If the Rangers find themselves up against an adversary too tough even for the *Ryû-Sei-Ô* and the other four vehicles, they amalgamate all five of them into a truly massive robot called the *Dai-Ren-Ô* (Great Connected King). The two chess knights attach themselves to the *Ryû-Sei-Ô*'s legs like huge boots; the lion vehicle divides into three parts to form the head and both arms; the bird wraps itself round the *Ryû-Sei-Ô*'s waist to form a kind of kilt. Thus the children of the gang have gone through three stages of transformation/incorporation: turning into Rangers, disappearing into vehicles, and combining vehicles.

Another interesting version of the transformation and incorporation theme appears in *Jay-Decker*, a cartoon which was launched by TV Asahi in 1994. This features three pieces of anthropomorphic construction equipment: they are clearly foreigners, for their names are Dumpson, McCrane and Power Joe. They are robots in the form of a dump truck, a crane and a power shovel, which then come together to create the "Build-Tiger", a huge robot/tiger. The idea builds on the fact that orange and black stripes are a popular color scheme for construction equipment. The mighty Build-Tiger is controlled by a very small boy called Yûta.

This recurrent popular fantasy might be read in two ways: first, as a mechanism for dealing with fear of adults. Adults are the real bogeymen of any child's imagination: they are huge, irrational and unpredictable, rather like monsters. How comforting then, to be bigger than them, to be a big person, concealed from the world by the anonymous crash helmet; better still, to be that big person hidden in the interior cockpit of a behemoth that could crush any adult to custard by simply putting its foot down.

Secondly, the child in the robot can be read as a metaphor for the spirit inside the body,[25] suggesting that an important theme is that of mind achieving control over the unruly body. This theme runs through Japanese culture: it is there in the popular obsession with *gaman* (endurance), for instance, and in the ascetic varieties of Zen Buddhism. The child in the robot, with his array of buttons and levers, and mastery of all manner of *hissatsu kôsen* (sure-to-kill rays) and *tokusen panchi* (special punches), is the self in full control – and fully hidden.

The Momotaro theme

In this chapter attention has been drawn to the important Japanese word *genki*, which signifies health, vigor and good spirits. It is familiar to anyone who has ever attempted to study the language from the customary greeting *genki desu-ka?* (literally: are you fit?).[26]

A *genki* person is one whose *ki* is flowing correctly, ensuring rude physical health.[27] There is also a link between bodily flows and emotional vitality. The body/mind link can run in either direction. Thus in Japanese folklore, small children whose thoughts and emotions are not corrupted by adult knowledge are thought to be particularly *genki* and capable of performing incredible feats of strength.

This brings us to another powerful figure in the Japanese popular pantheon: the small but incredibly powerful boy, depicted as chubby, rosy-cheeked and very *genki*. The most famous traditional versions are Momotaro, the Peach Boy, and Kintaro, the Golden Boy. Momotaro defeated ogres to retrieve a village's stolen treasure; Kintaro wrestled with bears. Smaller still was Issun-bôshi, the Japanese equivalent of Tom Thumb, who was only an inch high, but still rescued a princess from an ogre by stabbing the ogre in the eye with his pin-like sword.[28]

Today the super-strong little boy is alive and well in Japanese hero mythology. He re-emerged just seven years after the war ended, in 1952, in the person of *Atomu Taishi* (Ambassador Atom), later renamed *Tetsuwan Atomu* (Mighty Atom), and popularized in the English-speaking world as Astro Boy (Schodt 1983: 63–5). The Mighty Atom fought dinosaurs and robots and bad men with the old Momotaro spirit of *hisshô* (certain victory).[29]

This creation of the great comic artist Tezuka Osamu spawned a host of descendants. These include Son-Gohan and Trunks, a pair of tiny, incredibly powerful heroes in *Dragonball*, a very popular cartoon series from Toei which aired from 1986 to 1997 on Wednesdays at 7.30 pm on Fuji TV, commanding massive ratings (in the region of 20 per cent of the viewing audience). A large portion of this series is taken up with fights in which these tiny boys destroy gigantic ogre-like adversaries. Characters in *Dragonball* have so much *ki* energy that they literally glow, emit flames, float into the air and so on. Their creator, Toriyama Akira, knows his myths well: the original concept of magic balls which give control over dragons comes from Chinese mythology, and many characters are overtly linked to folkloric forebears: the name "Son-Gohan", for instance, is a jokey reference to Son-Gokû, the magic monkey of Chinese and Japanese tradition.

Another Momotaro-type hero who has been linked by his creators directly to the old folk magic is Yaiba, an animated cartoon character who was on TV Asahi from 1993 to 1994. Yaiba looks very similar to Son-Gohan: a very small boy, with stylized spikey hair pointing in seven directions, who is full of raw, bellicose energy. He shouts a lot, is dressed as a samurai, and carries a magic sword which emits water, ice, thunder, fire, etc. He is one of a gang of seven. The other members are a cute schoolgirl, a tall, one-eyed samurai, an irascible little old man with a long beard, a dinosaur dressed in armor, a cat and a vulture. Each carries a magic ball, color-coded of course. They lose energy if parted from their balls; but if they all put their balls together they can create greater energy than the sum of their powers. This theme of magic balls also features in the *Dai* Rangers. They put their balls together on the control panel of the *Dai-Ren-Ô* robot.

Yaiba's opponents are also derived from folk mythology. In one episode, he takes on an old hermit with the power to transform himself into an agile monkey and turn people to stone with magic darts fired from a blow-pipe. After a desperate battle, during which all his comrades are petrified, Yaiba succeeds in sucking the old man into the hilt of his sword, narrowly avoiding sucking himself in at the same time. Finally, there is even a baby hero called "Akachanman" (Babyman) who makes occasional appearances in the children's series *Anpanman*. He is a flying super-baby who returns to his cot and bottle after each daring mission.

Conclusion: the classificatory impulse

In hero-monster tales with plural heroes and monsters, the theme of classification always seems to be most important. When I ask Japanese children what they like about these programs, they come up with answers such as that the heroes are *kakko-ii* (smart, dashing) or that the monsters and fighting are *omoshiroi* (interesting). But when they talk among themselves, I notice, the main issue is mastery of classificatory knowledge: who can tell the difference between Gridman Big and Thunder Gridman; who can name the yellow one in the *Dai* Rangers; who can say whether a certain monster fought against Ultraman Great or Ultraman Powered, etc? Most of the fanzines which these children read have almost no stories in them: they are primarily catalogs, of heroes and monsters, classified by age (i.e. year of release), gender, genus, planet of origin, color of uniform, fighting technique, strength, status or posture.[30] For those who have read the plethora of material on socialization in Japan, these themes will be familiar: how the body is formed (Ben-Ari 1997); notions of appropriate gender behavior (Higuchi 1978); the importance of seniority (Hendry 1986); and the concept of Japaneseness or origin (Goodman 1989).

Despite the cultural specificity of the themes examined above, I believe this concern with classification may well be universal. Certainly British children find it deeply satisfying to know which Tracey brother pilots which Thunderbird.[31] Moreover I suspect that classificatory disputes may be heard in playgrounds all around the world. For as Edmund Leach (1982), among others, has argued, the human experience entails imposing a system of discontinuities on the seamless continuum perceived by the baby or animal. To the small child order, classification and taxonomy are not arid academic issues, but the key to security and confidence; to a sense of one's place in the world. Hence, I would suggest, the pervasiveness of the classificatory theme in children's television adventures in Japan and elsewhere. Evil villains and rampaging monsters both excite and alarm by holding out the intriguing yet disturbing possibility that the order of things may be re-shaped, or even hurled into chaos. But in every episode the heroes bring us back from the brink, restoring a familiar order which the young viewer will value more highly, having seen it under such evident threat.

Notes

1 For an interesting discussion of this see van Bremen 1995.
2 For a discussion of *Sailor Moon*, see Napier Chapter 5.
3 During Tsuburaya's sixteen-year hesitation over *Ultraman*, the old series grew in popularity around the world. Two new series were made in the US: *Ultraman Great* (1990) and *Ultraman Powered* (1993). In 1996 Tsuburaya released a movie version, *Ultraman ZEARTH*, which was followed by the new TV series, *Ultraman Tiga*.
4 Fans of Superman may question the accuracy of my account of Superman the loner. True, as Clark Kent he may have adopted earth parents and lived with his Aunt May, but when he becomes Superman he generally fights on his own. True, too, there have been fleeting appearances of Superboy, Supergirl and Superdog, but they were fellow citizens of Planet Krypton, not relatives; and the appearance of Marlon Brando as Superman's father in the film version, is, I would argue, a late and cynical commercial corruption. When a story runs for so long, thematic impurities will inevitably creep in. At any rate, Superman as icon is always depicted as fighting a lone struggle against evil and disaster.
5 It could be said that Ultraman is a case of a cultural figure who has been "re-made" in Japan (Tobin 1992).
6 For example, *sekihan*, the white rice cooked with red beans at weddings and other celebrations; the pink and white *kamaboko* (compressed fish meal), also considered felicitous; the red and white striped awnings and favors often seen at festivals, the red and white colors adopted by the two moieties of a Japanese school when competing against each other at the annual athletics tournament.
7 Japanese encyclopedias offer various theories as to why the red and white combination is so powerful: some derive it from the idealized beauty of the

Japanese plum and its blossom; others put the competitive association down to the colors worn by the Genji clan (white) and the Heike clan (red) during a clan war of 1180–85, highly reminiscent of the Wars of the Roses in England. I feel sure there are deeper underlying reasons as I discuss later.

8 In some of the later feature-length *Ultraman* films, the scriptwriters found it impossible to sustain interest without giving the inhabitants of planet Ultra some lines. But in the typical TV episode, Ultraman simply arrives near the end to fight the monster, without comment.

9 The only time I can recall Ultramen displaying emotion was in an episode of *Ultraman Taro*. A particularly dangerous monster had trapped Taro and four of his brothers in paralyzing ether cylinders. Father of Ultra – easily recognizable with his silver sideburns and splendid pair of Viking horns – had to come and get them out. He killed the monster and liberated the lads, but died in the attempt. The brothers of Ultra stood around the body with heads hung low, then bore the body back to Planet Ultra in a slow (mach 200) and solemn flying convoy. Later, in typical super-hero fashion, Father of Ultra was resurrected by a special machine.

10 It should be noted that since he is most often portrayed by an actor in a rubber Ultrasuit, distressing rubber wrinkles and folds inevitably do appear.

11 In this summoning of the hero we can see a similarity to the summoning of the divine, as Yamaguchi argues for sumo and kabuki in Chapter 1.

12 The evil schoolboy also has an unhealthy adolescent obsession with Yuka, the girl among the Grid-heroes. Although the viewers are overwhelmingly pre-pubescent, juvenile sexual frustration is a subtext in *Gridman*.

13 Battle Cossack is the only gang member ever to have worn orange; his color was supposed to signify Russia, but red had already been claimed by Battle Japan.

14 Note also that Japan has borrowed from Chinese culture the concept of five natural elements (*gogyô*) (rather than the four in European culture): fire, wood, earth, metal and water. The same word, *gogyô*, also signifies the five virtues of Buddhism: *fuse* (charity), *jikai* (obedience), *ninniku* (endurance), *shôjin* (diligence), and *shikan* (spiritual concentration). Japanese Buddhism recognizes five, rather than seven, sins: *sessho* (murder), *chûtô* (theft), *ja'in* (adultery), *môgo* (slander) and *onju* (drinking). Confucianism also recognizes five virtues deriving from five fundamental human relationships: justice between ruler and ruled; benevolence between parent and child; propriety between husband and wife; order between elder and younger; and sincerity between friends. Then, too, there are the five senses.

15 The Japanese word for four, *shi*, also means death.

16 For cross-cultural comparison, here is the color-coded line-up of the five Tracey brothers in *Thunderbirds*, as indicated by their sashes: Scott (TB1): pale blue. Virgil (TB2): pale yellow. Alan (TB3): off-white. Gordon (TB4): orange. John (TB5): lilac.

These are pretty insipid pastel shades. I would describe Alan's sash as very pale pink, but the above are the descriptions in the official *Thunderbirds* annual. They share the color-coding principle with the Japanese gangs of five, but the colors play a much less significant role. Not many British children could name all five sash colors – lilac? – but every Japanese child who follows *Dai-Renjâ* knows that *Ryû* Ranger is the red one, etc. All Japanese gang of five members wear bold, unambiguous colors, which I think symbolize robustness and vitality.

17 Including pink and white.

18 The makers of the Ranger series take the color red very seriously. Whereas most Japanese TV programs are shot on Fuji film, the Ranger series are always shot on Eastman/Kodak, which they say gives a better red.

19 Japan got its own back with the launch of the *Kaku-Renjâ* in 1994: Ninja Black is a Japanese-American boy who cannot speak Japanese, walks through earth, and is imbued with the spirit of the toad. Clearly he is a peculiar foreigner; note also the association of black with foreign, even when skin color does not match.

20 Otherwise, the Goma empire consists of a collection of very low-budget *yôkai* which are well into the realm of self-parody: *Hakaishi Shachô* (Gravestone President), who looks like a rubbery walking gravestone; *Tôfu Sennin* (Tofu Hermit) in a white suit with a one-eyed cube of tofu for his head; *Nokogiri Daisôjô* (Saw Archbishop) whose head is a couple of saw-blades nailed together with three eyes painted on them ... and so on.

Often these beasts are able to defeat individual rangers, or even the whole gang when they are at odds with each other and unable to concentrate their energies. But once the five are working in concert, they are soon victorious: the spiritual power of harmony and teamwork invariably brings success.

21 I have seen *gattai* used to signify sexual intercourse in other contexts.

22 One of the *Kaku* Rangers' foes is a modern *kappa*, bald on top as all *kappa* are, but with green rasta dreadlocks hanging from the sides of his head.

23 Created by Fujimoto Hitoshi and Abiko Motô; *Doraemon* has appeared in the comics of Shogakukan Inc. since 1969, and on Asahi TV since 1979.

24 For more on transformational gadgets in *Doraemon*, see Schilling 1993.

25 Japan, and indeed "the Orient" in general, is sometimes said to be characterized by a holistic way of thinking that does not make the Descartian dichotomy between mind and body – hence, for example, holistic oriental medicine, and the concept of mastering skills by repetition. Yet Japanese concepts of human behavior often seem to make a very clear mind/body distinction. Take *yakuza* (gangster) movies, for instance, with their recuring theme of the hero who maintains iron control of his body until losing it in the last reel in an explosion of righteous violence (see Buruma 1984: 167–95).

26 Roughly equivalent to "How are you?", the characters for *genki* are *gen* (origin) and *ki* (energy) which imply that one's life-spirit is flowing correctly. Illness or unhappiness are ascribed to poor circulation of *ki*, a concept borrowed from ancient Chinese philosophy which informs martial arts such as *judô* and karate and therapeutic techniques such as acupuncture and shiatsu massage.

27 This is reminiscent of the English Renaissance concept of the four humors: one whose blood, phlegm, black bile and yellow bile are in correct proportion will be healthy and emotionally balanced.

28 Dower (1986) has some fascinating material on how Momotaro was used in Japanese propaganda during World War II: the Allied forces were the ogres, of course, Momotaro the outnumbered but indomitable Japan. This belief in the ability of childish, innocent verve to overcome massive odds (which must surely rank alongside the equally optimistic belief about the Divine Wind – *kamikaze* – that would blow away invading fleets, embodied in the suicide pilots) was an underlying cultural reason for Japan's stubborn refusal to surrender until after Hiroshima and Nagasaki.

29 The characters for *hisshô* appear on the headbands of baseball supporters, exam candidates, etc. – again, that doggedly irrational optimism.
30 Posture is important to all heroes; each strikes his own distinctive fighting pose. Each Ultraman has a different arm/hand configuration for launching beams; knowing them is like gaining familiarity with masonic handshakes.
31 Many years ago, I battled with my brother over the Mole, the underground drilling machine featured in that series. My heretical brother insisted that the Mole was Thunderbird 6, since it appears on the title sequence immediately after Thunderbird 5. I pointed out that the Mole does not have a "6" painted on the side, and that if it were Thunderbird 6, this would ruin the symmetry between the five Tracey brothers and five Thunderbirds. Neither of us has changed his mind more than 20 years later. Meanwhile, the very same episodes of *Thunderbirds* are being argued over by yet another generation, just as Japanese children are still arguing over the classification of Ultramen and Rangers of the 1960s and 1970s, like tiny museum curators.

References

Astley, Trevor n.d. "A Happy Ending: *Kofutan no Kagaku* and the end of the world." Paper delivered at BAJS Conference 1996, Oxford Brookes University.

Ben-Ari, E. 1997 *Body Projects in Japanese Childcare: culture, organization and emotions in a preschool.* Richmond, Surrey: Curzon.

Bunce, William K. 1955 *Religions in Japan.* Rutland, Vermont and Tokyo: Charles E. Tuttle.

Buruma, Ian 1984 *Behind the Mask: On sexual demons, sacred mothers, transvestites, gangsters and other Japanese cultural heroes.* New York: Pantheon Books.

Davis, Winston 1980 *Dojo: Magic and Exorcism in Modern Japan.* Stanford, Ca: Stanford University Press.

Dower, John W. 1986 *War Without Mercy: Race and power in the Pacific War.* New York: Pantheon Books.

Goodman, R. 1989 *Japan's International Youth: The emergence of a new class of schoolchildren.* Oxford: Oxford University Press.

Hendry, J. 1986 *Becoming Japanese: the world of the pre-school child.* Manchester: Manchester University Press.

Higuchi Keiko 1978 *Onna no ko no sodatekata.* Tokyo: Bunka Shuppankyoku.

Leach, Edmund 1982 *Social Anthropology.* London: Fontana Press.

Lévi-Strauss, Claude 1962 *Totemism.* Harmondsworth: Penguin.

Matsunaga, Louella n.d. "Japanese New Religions Movements in the UK." Paper delivered at BAJS conference 1996, Oxford Brookes University.

Ohnuki-Tierney, Emiko 1987 *The Monkey as Mirror: Symbolic transformations in Japanese history and ritual.* Princeton: University of Princeton Press.

Said, Edward W. 1978 *Orientalism: Western conceptions of the Orient.* London: Routledge and Kegan Paul.

Saito, Seiji 1988 "*Nihon Bunka no Naka no Aka*" (*The Colour Red in Japanese Culture*) in *Sekai Dai Hyakka Jiten.* Tokyo: Heibonsha.

Schilling, Mark 1993 "Doraemon: Making dreams come true" in *Japan Quarterly* Vol. XXXX: 405–17. Tokyo: Asahi Shimbun.

Schodt, Frederik L. 1983 *Manga! Manga! The World of Japanese Comics*. Tokyo, New York and San Francisco: Kodansha International.

Tobin, Joseph J. 1992 "Introduction: Domesticating the West" in his edited *Re-made in Japan, Everyday Life and Consumer Taste in a Changing Society*. New Haven and London: Yale University Press.

van Bremen, Jan 1995 "Introduction" in *Ceremony and Ritual in Japan, Religion in an Industrialized Society* edited by Jan van Bremen and D. P. Martinez. London: Routledge.

CHAPTER 3

Akira, *Postmodernism and Resistance*

ISOLDE STANDISH

Contemporary urban style is empowering to the subordinate for it asserts their right to manipulate the signifiers of the dominant ideology in a way that frees them from that ideological practice and opens them up to the sub-cultural and oppositional uses. (Fiske 1991: 253)

Introduction

This chapter is concerned with a textual analysis of *Akira* (1988),[1] the highly successful cyberpunk film created by Otomo Katsuhiro. This analysis is an exploration of the complex systems of codes and practices employed by the film and the spectator[2] in the creation of meaning; however its main emphasis will be on the perspective of the spectator. As with most commercial films produced by the Japanese studio system, *Akira* (Tôhô Studios) is aimed at a specific audience: adolescent males who are fully conversant with the codes and cultural systems employed in the film.[3] Therefore, to reach an understanding of how a Japanese adolescent male creates meaning (and so derives pleasure) from *Akira* involves not only an understanding of the uses the film makes of other textual systems, but also an understanding of the position occupied by some adolescent males in Japanese society.

The aim of this chapter, then, is twofold: first, to come to an understanding of *Akira* from the point of view of its intertextuality; and second, to present an interpretation of the film as a point of convergence of the spectator-film-culture nexus. To this end, I intend to discuss two categories of textual systems developed by Allen and Gomery (1985): first, the "nonfilmic intertexts" which involve the film's use of conventions and codes from other systems of representations, such as the *bôsôzoku*[4] sub-culture and the *Akira manga* (comic) series;

and second, the "filmic intertext", that is, the film's use of conventions drawn from the *nagare-mono* or "drifter" films of the 1950s and 1960s, the science fiction/horror genre and other films, in particular the American film *Blade Runner* (Ridley Scott 1982).[5]

Through an examination of the *bôsôzoku* sub-culture as a cultural expression of a section of Japanese youth, the first part of this chapter will demonstrate how *Akira* uses *bôsôzoku* style to reflect a youth culture of resistance which exists alongside mainstream contemporary Japanese society. This raises many questions in relation to the myths of Japanese social and cultural homogeneity and the supposed classless nature of Japanese society.[6] For ethnographic detail I shall be largely drawing on Satô's (1991) study of the *bôsôzoku* and *yankî* (punk) youths. I shall then proceed with a structural analysis of *Akira* as a text which draws on a postmodernist pastiche of conventions to create a mise-en-scene which denotes chaos and corruption.

It should be noted that while Satô provides a useful ethnographic account of *bôsôzoku*, he fails to present the sub-culture adequately within its larger social, political and economic contexts and as a result he fails to answer the following questions which are crucial to understanding the underlying causes of the development and attraction of the sub-culture. First, why is the membership of *bôsôzoku* gangs predominantly made up of youths from manual working-class backgrounds? Second, why is their behavior in opposition to the norms and standards of Japanese society? On the other hand, Satô does refute the psychological "strain theory" which he states was the most common explanation cited by Japanese academics and the media during the 1970s for the occurrence of *bôsôzoku* activities and which he defines as

a behavioral expression of frustrated wants and needs, resulting from an incongruity between culturally induced aspirations and socially distributed legitimate means. (1991: 3)

Satô argues instead that *bôsôzoku* behavior is an expression of *asobi* (play) which forms part of a rite of passage marking the change from childhood to maturity.

Asobi is an important factor, but it is only one in a multiplicity of factors which are related to the occurrence of *bôsôzoku* activities. By emphasizing *asobi*, Satô fails to explain adequately the social and historical causes which lie behind the manifestation of this particular form of delinquent behavior. Therefore I intend to broaden the discussion by taking up these issues and by suggesting that at the social level, the factors listed below have contributed to the emergence of a generational consciousness which, despite myths of the classless nature of Japanese society, is linked to a post-war polarization based on occupational status. The development of the youth sub-cultures in the post-war period should be viewed as one of the expressions of this generational consciousness through its manifestation of style and behavior. The factors we need to consider are:

1 Post-war changes in the Japanese systems of education and work, part of which was a shift to a meritocracy and achievement-oriented social status;
2 changes in the structure of the family, especially the gradual decline of the extended family;
3 the proliferation of the mass media. Television was first broadcast in Japan in 1953. At that time there were 866 television sets, but by 1959 this number had jumped to two million and was increasing at a rate of 150,000 a month (Anderson and Richie 1959: 254);
4 the changes in the comparative ranking of work and leisure. Material affluence has also increased the importance of leisure and recreation in the lives of all Japanese. Technological innovations in industrial production and the demands of unions for fewer working hours have, since the early 1970s, reduced working time (Satô 1991: 184);
5 the emergence of adolescence as a socially constructed category which accompanied the increase in the spending power of Japanese youth and the growth of a market designed to exploit this surplus spending power.

Bôsôzoku sub-culture, seen as an outward manifestation of a new generational consciousness poses a direct challenge to the traditional "work ethic" and achievement-oriented ideology of the previous generation. *Bôsôzoku* have adapted and inverted images, styles and ideologies to construct an alternative identity, an otherness, which challenges the ideals of Japanese social and cultural homogeneity. Hence, the moral panic[7] which followed media reports of *bôsôzoku* activities in the mid-1980s may be explained in part as the fear of difference, "otherness".

Satô states that "the majority of those who participate in gang activities are from middle-class families" (1991: 2). There is a problem here as most Japanese define themselves as middle-class, despite economic and occupational differences. Thus Satô goes on to state that the majority of *bôsôzoku* youths come from "blue-collar" backgrounds, a point supported by DeVos in his psycho-cultural study of deviancy in Japanese society (1973).[8] Therefore, it would perhaps be more accurate to say that most *bôsôzoku* youths do not come from economically disadvantaged backgrounds, such as in the UK and the USA where academic studies have made the link between delinquency and economic deprivation, but from lower *status* groups who do not fit in with the Japanese ideal of the white-collar salaryman and his family. So despite the fact that the majority of Japanese consider themselves to be middle-class, it is clear that there is a polarity of occupational status in society which can be said to be divided along the lines of blue-collar/low status workers, and the salaryman/white-collar/high status workers. The polarity of occupation is determined by education and is reflected in the emergence of distinct youth cultures divided along these lines.

Traditional explanations of the classless nature of Japanese society are by and large dependent on the linking of income to class and do not take into account the status attached to certain occupations and denied to others.[9] They also tend to ignore the fact that social standards and norms are determined by dominant elites, filtering down through society to become the consensual view. A person's ability to achieve status depends upon the criteria of status applied by other people in the society (*seken*) in accordance with the consensual view (*seken-nami*), that is, the standards and norms individuals use in evaluating other people (Cohen 1955: 140).[10] This raises "status problems" for those who fail to achieve in a highly competitive education and employment system. Hence, the desire of the *bôsôzoku* youths to establish a set of status criteria outside the consensual view, in terms of which they can more easily succeed. *Bôsôzoku* discontent with mainstream society reflects the polarization between blue-collar and white-collar status groups whose position is determined by their children's access to education. The emergence of two distinct youth cultures divided along these same lines, the manual working-class youth, *bôsôzoku*, and the college students' *dokushin kizoku* (literally, unmarried aristocrats) youth culture reflects this contraposition. It is also evident in the geographical division of Tokyo into the Yamanote region, mostly populated by salarymen, and the Shitamachi area where blue-collar workers tend to congregate.[11]

From this perspective of occupation-determined status divisions, the reason for the emergence of *bôsôzoku* can be explained in Cohen's (1955) terms of "the compensatory function of juvenile gangs". He suggests that working-class youths who under-achieve at school and who are unable to conform to "respectable" society, often resort to deviant behavior as a solution to their problems:

> It is a plausible assumption ... that the working class boy whose status is low in middle-class terms *cares* about that status [and] that this status confronts him with a genuine problem of adjustment. To this problem of adjustment there are a variety of conceivable responses, of which participation in the creation and maintenance of the delinquent subculture is one. Each mode of response entails costs and yields gratifications of its own ... The hallmark of the delinquent subculture is the explicit and wholesale repudiation of middle-class standards and the adoption of their very antithesis. (Cohen 1955: 128–9)

This point is further supported by Satô when he states that

> while they may be faceless unskilled labourers or not very promising high school students in their everyday lives, they can become "somebody" with definite status through their universe of discourse. (1991: 69)

This "compensatory function" is crucial to an understanding of *Akira* and the *bôsôzoku* sub-culture as a whole. In the analysis of *Akira* which follows, it will be demonstrated how, by drawing on the imagery of *kôha* (hard type) as a defining feature of masculinity, the narrative performs Cohen's "compensatory function" which, I believe, is one of the reasons for *Akira*'s huge box-office success.

The meaning of *bôsôzoku* style

Having placed the occurrence of *bôsôzoku* behavior within the context of the emergence of a generational consciousness and the status divisions of labor in Japanese society, and linked this to Cohen's "compensatory function", it is possible to argue that *bôsôzoku* style is a form of resistance, which Fiske defines as "the refusal to accept the social identity proposed by the dominant ideology and the social control that goes with it" (1991: 241). From a reading of the imagery and symbols which make up the *bôsôzoku* style, it becomes evident that the *bôsôzoku* members are attempting to negotiate a "meaningful intermediate space" within the dominant work ethic and achievement-oriented ideology of modern Japanese society. This they have achieved through their particular behavior, such as the outright challenging of police authority, and through the creation of a unique style.

Bôsôzoku youths have appropriated historical and cultural objects and signs which are made to carry new, covert meanings. This violation of taken-for-granted meanings became a form of resistance to the dominant order: for example, the *bôsôzoku* phonetic use of Chinese characters, which are often complex, to express the names of their gangs. These work at two levels, the meanings created by the phonetic usage and the meanings inherent in the Chinese characters. For their clothing, they often wear *tokkôfuku*, the uniforms worn by the *kamikaze* pilots of World War II, or *sentôfuku*, military combat uniforms. They often wear *hachimaki* (head bands) with the rising sun or the imperial chrysanthemum crest in the center. These are all symbols usually associated with extreme right-wing political movements, including the *yakuza* (gangsters). Satô states that there is no real evidence to suggest that *bôsôzoku* youths are affiliated in any way with these organizations.[12] I would suggest that the right-wing symbols employed by the *bôsôzoku* have been inverted into threatening symbols of group solidarity as well as referring to the traditional "tragic hero" who has dominated Japanese popular culture since the *Chûshingura* (*Forty-seven Rônin*) story. These objects and symbols had already been imbued with new post-war meanings in war-retro films.[13] They have been re-positioned further within a *bôsôzoku* subcultural context, and part of their appeal and value is derived from their potential to shock. As Hebdige states, "violations of the authorized codes through which the social world is organized and experienced have considerable power to provoke and disturb" (1991: 91).

Fiske has argued that the pleasure "style" affords is its ability to empower the creator. He tells us that:

> ... it is a pleasure of control or empowerment, a carnivalesque concentration on the materiality of the signifiers and the consequent evasion of the subjectivity constructed by the more ideologically determined signifieds. (1991: 250)

He then goes on to demonstrate how Madonna, through style, "turns herself into a spectacle" (253) and in so doing denies the spectator the position of voyeur. She does this by "controlling the look", thereby inverting the normal power relations of looking just as in a carnival. It is interesting that in a questionnaire on pleasure and *bôsô* (mass vehicle rallies) activities, Satô found that "*Medatsu koto* (being seen) was ranked as important as the 'activity itself' among the reasons of one's enjoyment" (1991: 27).

This pleasure in *medatsu koto* is further evidenced by *bôsôzoku's* deliberate courting of the media, the staging of *bôsô* drives for the cameras and the writing of articles for magazines. Through the desire for *medatsu koto*, whether it is media coverage or inadvertent pedestrian spectators, it is the *bôsôzoku* youth who is in control of the look. A journalist clearly stated his sense of powerlessness when confronted by *bôsôzoku* youths:

> *Bôsôzoku* from all of Japan cooperate with our efforts to gather data. It is more than cooperation. They are almost aggressive. They phone the publisher night and day and demand to be interviewed. Some even come to the publisher's office driving motorbikes ... I am so overwhelmed by their *medachitagari seishin* (*medatsu*, spirit: desire to show off) that I feel like a sub-contractor who is working under orders for a magazine which might be called, say, *Monthly Bôsôzoku*. (quoted in Satô 1991: 93)

By creating a spectacle, in Fiske's "carnivalesque" sense of the word,[14] they are inverting the "look" as an expression of control and it is from this process of control that their pleasure derives, hence, the centrality of *medatsu koto* to that pleasure.

In summation, *bôsôzoku* youths have, through their style, sought control over their social identity in contemporary Japanese culture where, in a post-industrial consumer society, image and identity are no longer fixed, but open to be played with.[15] They have taken right-wing political symbolism out of its traditional political and historical discourse (the rise of ultra nationalistic right-wing movements and World War II), and have asserted their right to use it as a signifier of group identity and for the "tragic hero" of the *Chûshingura* tradition. They have created a "spectacular construction" of their own image which defines their "otherness" and, by extension, their resistance to the dominant culture. How did the film *Akira* fit into *bôsôzoku* culture?

Akira and postmodernism

Having discussed the *bôsôzoku* as a sub-culture apart from, and in opposition to, mainstream Japanese society, I shall now analyze the role of *Akira* as part of the patois of *bôsôzoku* sub-cultural language. *Akira* is a film which legitimates and mythologizes the position of *bôsôzoku* youth on the periphery of Japanese society and so becomes a sharp critique of contemporary corporate Japanese society.[16]

Akira is a text which simultaneously displays the two distinct characteristics of the postmodern which Fredric Jameson (1983) discussed: an effacement of boundaries, for instance between previously defined stylistic norms (Eastern and Western) and between past and present, resulting in pastiche and parody; and a schizophrenic treatment of time as "perpetual present". In *Akira*, this effacement of the boundaries between stylistic norms and between past and present does not manifest in an appeal to "nostalgia" as Jameson has argued it does in Western postmodernist films. For example, Scott's *Blade Runner* (1982), although set in a futuristic Los Angeles/Tokyo[17] cityscape in the year 2019, simultaneously plays on 1950s' conventions of *film noir*. The Raymond Chandler image of the hero detective (Harrison Ford), the emphasis on faded sepia family photographs and memories, establish a nostalgic humanness which is contrasted with the alien cyborgs who also inhabit the film's space. *Akira* similarly draws on the 1950s and 1960s conventions of a specific male genre based on the drifter film (*nagare-mono*)[18] in the construction of the character called Kaneda. Kaneda displays all the positive attributes of the outsider as represented by the actors Ishihara Yujirô and Takakura Ken, all of whose films are still widely available. The outsider is physically strong, but, above all else, he remains loyal to the code of brotherhood, regardless of personal cost. He is thus brought into direct opposition with the establishment, represented in the films by the scheming, self-interested politicians and the moguls of the military-industrial complex. As an archetypal outsider, Kaneda is not bound by any of the conventions of the "legitimate" society which, as the following discussion makes clear, is portrayed as corrupt and degenerate. *Akira* thus conforms to a central theme that runs through the films of the *nagare-mono* and the *yakuza* genres, that is, the clash between male codes of brotherhood and the constraints imposed on male freedom by the law and social institutions, such as the family. Hence the *nagare-mono* always exists on the margins of society, for it is only there that he can remain true to his moral code.[19]

Akira, while set in a futuristic present, takes four historical signifiers which are juxtaposed to underscore the corruption and degeneration of contemporary Japanese society, creating an historical "pastiche". The first historical signifier derives from the *kurai tani* (dark valley) period (1931–1941) of pre-war Japan when right-wing military factions combined with *zaibatsu* (industrialists) and vied with politicians for political control of the country. In *Akira*, the Colonel is symbolic of this sort of military faction. The film's representation of the Colonel is so constructed that he is easily identified with the portrayal of General Anami, the War Minister in Prime Minister Suzuki's cabinet of 1945, in the highly successful film *Japan's Longest Day* (*Nihon no ichiban nagai hi*, directed by Okamoto Kihachi, 1967).[20] The industrialists, with whom the Colonel is in collusion, are shown to have connections with the terrorists, while the politicians are depicted as weakened through internal conflicts.

The second historical signifier relates to the dropping of the atomic bombs on Hiroshima and Nagasaki. The opening credit sequence of the film is dominated by a silent white flash which destroys the cityscape leaving only the impact crater over which the title *Akira* appears in red letters. When they lose control of their power, Akira, the most powerful of the mutant children, and Tetsuo become metaphorical nuclear weapons. Takeshi, Kyoko and Masaru, the spectral children, are haunting images of post-nuclear mutants. They are the result of the obsession of the military scientists' research into the psyche and, at the end of the film, they will destroy the corrupt world as it is depicted in the first part of the film.

The third signifier relates to the Tokyo Olympics (1964) and the fourth to the political unrest and student demonstrations against the revision of the US-Japan Security Treaty (*Anpo*) in the 1960s. Kaneda and his *bôsôzoku* friends exist in a quintessential postmodern city, Neo Tokyo 2019, where the "evils" of each modern historical period coalesce into a post-atomic world-war futuristic present. The havoc and destruction of the past is being simultaneously criticized and contrasted with a future utopian society that will come about after the film.

Akira is, above all else, concerned with the esthetics of movement and destruction, subordinating any sense of narrative sequence to images of the spectacular; a point which was partially determined by the serial nature of the *manga* (comic) series from which *Akira* the film was derived. *Akira* the comic first appeared in *Young Magazine* in December 1982. The long-running serial structure of the *manga* narrative directly influenced the structure of the film version. Serial forms are influenced by several factors; first, serials are resistant to narrative closure and they have an extended middle. Traditional Hollywood realist narratives are generally constructed in the Todorovian sense, that is, the narrative begins with a stable situation which is disturbed by some force and, finally, there is a re-establishment of a second, but different equilibrium. The serial structure of a long-running *manga* is naturally resistant to the re-establishment of a final equilibrium.

Secondly, the serial form has multiple characters and sub-plots. Hence, the compression of this long-running *manga* serial into a feature-length film curtailed the development of the multiplicity of sub-plots which developed individual characterizations, enhancing the film's sense of fragmentation and disruption of narrative flow. For in *Akira*, there is no one central character; there are multiple characters who interact within a given set of circumstances, reducing the film to a montage of multiple patterns of action. The *bôsôzoku* youths, Tetsuo and Kaneda, form the catalyst around which these multiple patterns of action coalesce.

The fast editing, the dislocation of narrative sequence and the disruption of the diegesis produce the sensation of fragmentation of images where meanings are disjointed and referential. This emphasizes the sense of movement and the physical experience of "flow" and the sensuality of destruction. Satô links the concept of "flow" which refers to the "holistic sensation that people feel when they act with total involvement," to the physical sense of pleasure that *bôsôzoku* experience when they hold mass bike and car rallies. Satô quotes from Mihaly Csikszentmihalyi:

> In the flow state, action follows upon action according to an internal logic that seems to need no conscious intervention by the actor. He experiences it as a unified flowing from one movement to the next, in which he is in control of actions, and in which there is little distinction between self and environment, between stimulus and response, or between past, present and future. (1991: 18)

In fact, the whole structure of *Akira* is similar to that of a *bôsô* drive where there are periods of dare-devil driving which involve extreme concentration followed by rest periods at pre-arranged meeting places. These rest periods allow for stragglers to catch up with the main group and for the release of tension. In the film, there are periods of intense violence, destruction and physical movement punctuated by quiet periods when, for example, Kaneda is involved with his terrorist girlfriend Kei, or when the three mutant children converse. These quiet periods in the film allow the spectator to relax before the next sequence of violent and destructive images.

Through the techniques of fast editing and others listed above, the film reproduces the sense of "flow" in, for example, the bike chase at the beginning of the film when Kaneda and his gang have cornered the Clown gang on the freeway and are in pursuit. The animation is that of a camera following the chase, sometimes from aerial shots which highlight the bike's headlamps as they pierce the empty night sky, and at others from low-angle shots which emphasize the size and power of the bikes as the wheels rotate with a whirring sound. When the gang members do engage in combat, the camera speed changes to slow motion as a biker is thrown over the handle-bars, and as soon as he hits the tarmac, the camera reverts to normal speed, maximizing the sensation of the bike's movement as it speeds away leaving the victim instantly miles behind. These images, by emphasizing the sensual experience of movement, are not in any sense representations of the "real"; they are images of what Baudrillard (1988) has called the "hyper-real". The "hyperreal" effaces the "contradictions between the real and the imaginary"; the "sensuous imperative" of these images becomes our experience of the event depicted and our site of pleasure (Baudrillard 1988: 143–7). The sequence of the bike chase replicates, in the sensation of hallucinatory and hyperreal images, the "flow" as experienced by actual *bôsôzoku* and described by Satô. The sound track further enhances the "sensual imperative" of the images as the low key mechanical "post-rock" music pulsates in time with the bike engines throughout the chase, complementing the metallic sparks that fly forth as bike hits tarmac and bodies fall to the ground with a thud. Satô noted the elaborate modifications *bôsôzoku* made to their vehicle exhaust systems and the importance of massed engine sounds to their pleasure in a *bôsô* drive. This pleasure is reproduced in the film through the sound track.

Baudrillard's concept of the "hyperreal" also applies to the historical signifiers listed above. As stated earlier, *Akira* was targeted at a particular audience: adolescent males, who could relate to the *bôsôzoku* sub-cultural images and styles which pervade the film. These targeted spectators are at least one generation removed from the actual experiences of the historical events and so their knowledge of the "dark valley" period and the political unrest of the 1960s is already indirect and fragmentary, a point the film exploits in its structuring of the images of demonstrations and the violence and degeneration of this cybernatized society.

The film reproduces futuristic images of a city in the age of simulation, where signs now bear no relationship to reality and the definition of the real becomes, in Baudrillard's words, "*that for which it is possible to provide an equivalent representation* ... the real becomes not only that which can be reproduced, but that which is always already reproduced: the hyperreal" (his emphasis; 1988: 145–6). As already noted, theNeo Tokyo cityscapes that punctuate the film are drawing on the iconography of *Blade Runner's* Los Angeles/Tokyo in the year 2019, which has become a metaphor for urban decay. The warm orange colors which Otomo uses in the night scenes are taken directly from the polluted haze of *Blade Runner*. *Akira's* Neo Tokyo is a "critical dystopia" in that it projects images of a futuristic city which perpetuates the worst features of advanced corporate capitalism: urban decay, commodification and authoritarian policing. High-rise buildings representing corporate wealth exist alongside the dark decaying streets of the old town, highlighting the divisive nature of the society. Colored neon signs and holographs dominate the skyline, signifying com-mercialization. They also provide the dominant source of light for the night scenes, complementing the motorcycle headlights of the *bôsôzoku*.

The cityscapes thus represent an esthetic of postmodern decay, as well as revealing the dark side of scientific experimentation and technology. The uniqueness of architecture to a specific place, culture and time has been lost in Neo Tokyo. These images of a cityscape could be taken from any late capitalist city, such as New York, London. There is nothing in the scenes to link these images specifically to Tokyo.

As also has been noted, the film makes no attempt to place the images of violence and destruction within any logical form of cause-and-effect narrative. The images exist alone, relying on the shared cultural knowledge of the audience to produce meaning. The only assistance the audience is given is through a double mediation of news reports, which are either distorted background voice-over, as in the opening sequence, or television news flashes, complete with commercials, that echo forth from multiple video monitors in shop windows during riot scenes. The effect of this technique is to encourage the spectator to identify with Kaneda whose knowledge of the causes of the chaotic world in which he exists is at best fragmentary. It also works to foreground Kaneda and the Colonel who are, apart from Tetsuo and the three mutant children, the only characters given a semblance of a narrative flow in the film.

Both Kaneda and the Colonel are *kôha* types, the embodiment of a hard masculinity to which actual *bôsôzoku* youths aspire. Satô defines *kôha* as "the hard type [that] is a traditional image of adolescent masculinity which combines violence, valour, and bravado with stoicism and chivalry" (1991: 86). The *kôha* type of masculinity is contrasted with the *nanpa*, or soft type: "a skirt chaser or ladies' man" (Satô 1991: 86). The college student/*dokushin kizoku* belong to this latter group. The *kôha* school of masculinity also carries with it connotations of *makoto* (purity of motive) which is very much evident in the characters of Kaneda and the Colonel. Neither have been taken in by the corruption that characterizes the degenerate society in which they live. Their use of violence is legitimated by their purity of motive and so, despite his extremely violent behavior, Kaneda is the real hero of the film.[21]

In Japanese popular culture, *makoto* takes precedence over efficiency as an esteemed cultural value, hence the Japanese predilection for the "tragic hero" who proves his purity of spirit in death. However, Kaneda is also "efficient". He is loyal as well, another highly valued characteristic in Japanese Confucian-based society. The flash-backs to the orphanage, where he first met Tetsuo, reinforce these characteristics while simultaneously exposing Tetsuo's deepening dependence on him. These flash-backs have two functions: first, they are constructed to arouse a sense of sympathy in the spectator for Kaneda and Tetsuo; and thereby they reinforce the simplistic media-perpetuated view that the break-down of the traditional family is to blame for adolescent delinquent behavior. But more importantly for their young audience, the flash-backs are liberating, picking up on the conventions of the *nagare-mono*[22] and reflecting a trend in recent films targeted at the young, for example *Kitchen* and *Kimi wa boku o suki ni naru* (*You Are Going to Fall in Love with Me*), in which young adults (*dokushin kizoku*) are portrayed as being without the emotional clutter of the traditional extended family.

Kaneda's qualities of *makoto*, efficiency and loyalty are continually compared to the bumbling of the other "bad" characters in the film, particularly with Tetsuo, his one-time friend who, through his own personal weakness and as a result of experiments carried out on him by a scientist, metamorphoses into a destructive mass of protoplasm and metal.[23] Tetsuo's character is carefully structured in one of the multiple character sub-plots (fully developed in the *manga* series, but only hinted at in the film through flash-backs) to provide a foil for Kaneda. As children they lived in the same orphanage and Tetsuo came to rely on Kaneda's superior strength. But Tetsuo's envy of Kaneda was the weakness which inadvertently led him to become a test case for scientific experiments, after which his nascent psychic powers make him go on the rampage, killing the barman from the gang's local haunt and

Yamagata, another gang member. These incidents provide Kaneda with the legitimation necessary to confront the power that Tetsuo has become in the final climactic half of the film, for Tetsuo is no longer himself. As Yamagata asks just before his death, "Are you really Tetsuo?".

Kaneda, a *bôsôzoku* youth, through his academic failure, has been placed on the margins of this corrupt and emotionally empty society. His qualities of efficiency and loyalty, combined with his failure at school and his ignorance, make him the film's embodiment of innocence and purity. Therefore he is qualified to become the founder of a new utopian society that will be formed after the old society has been purged through cataclysmic destruction.[24] In the final scenes, Akira and the other three mutant children, the gods of the post-atomic war age, sacrifice themselves (as would have the traditional "tragic hero") so that a new society can come into being with Kaneda as its progenitor. Apart from Kaneda, his girlfriend Kei and one other junior gang member, the Colonel is the only other survivor. He has also shown attributes of efficiency and sincerity of purpose, but more importantly, he is in control of artifacts, such as helicopters, advanced scientific weapons, etc. As Sontag states, in science fiction films things

> ... are the locus of values because we experience them, rather than people, as the sources of power. According to science fiction films, man is naked without his artifacts. (1979: 494)

Since the Colonel and Kaneda are both representations of the *kôha* school and are shown to be efficient, loyal and competent in their use and control of artifacts, they are obvious survivors in a film which seeks to promote this image of masculinity.

The core values of *makoto* and loyalty which the film promotes give the characters (particularly Kaneda and the Colonel) a sense of historical continuity, as these are themes which, as I have already argued, go back through *yakuza*, *nagare-mono* and war-retro films to the *jidai-geki* (period/historical films) and *Chûshingura* story. This historical continuity is brought into sharp contrast with the fragmented time-frame and postmodernist mise-en-scène of the film. These values of the *kôha* hero are seen to override the postmodern social conditions which, according to the film, will self-destruct. Only those few, the *bôsôzoku*, who refuse to conform to the values of the corrupt world and who were forced to live on the margins of society, will survive to form a new and – by definition – a better world. The characters in *Akira* are spared the psychological struggle that Deckard experiences in *Blade Runner* over questions of how humanness is defined in a world of "simulacrum". It is the *bôsôzoku*'s ignorance which shields them. Kaneda has no doubt about his basic humanness, his core values of *makoto* and loyalty, his "morality", are never questioned in the film. As Harvey explains:

> The depressing side of the film [*Blade Runner*] is precisely that, in the end, the difference between the replicant [cyborgs] and the human becomes so unrecognizable that they indeed fall in love ... The power of the simulacrum is everywhere. (1992: 313)

Akira, on the other hand, becomes a re-affirmation of recognized core values of traditional Confucian society and so provides a continuity of "morality" which is felt to be lacking in the outside "de-industrializing" world where traditional values are threatening to disintegrate.

Conclusion

Through an analysis of the meanings of the *bôsôzoku* sub-culture of style, the conventions of the *nagare-mono* film, and an examination of the determining role of the *manga* series on the narrative structure of the film, as well as a discussion of the adoption of images of a postmodern society inspired by *Blade Runner*, this chapter has attempted to demonstrate the importance of intertextual signifying systems in the creation of meaning in *Akira*. It has also sought to demonstrate how *Akira*, as a science fiction/horror film, "is [primarily] concerned with the aesthetics of destruction, with the peculiar beauties to be found in wreaking havoc, making a mess" (Sontag 1979: 491). Moreover, through the fragmentation of images and lack of narrative flow, the film makes disjointed references to politically unstable historical periods to create a view of a dystopic future.

Existing on the margins of this society are the *bôsôzoku* youths whose self-esteem is enhanced through the mythologizing of their role in opposition to mainstream society, which is portrayed as corrupt and degenerate. This aspect of the film brings us back full circle to Cohen's "compensatory function" and explains in part the tremendous success in Japan, first of the *manga* series and subsequently of the film. Yet what of its popularity with youths from high occupational status groups who presumably do not need this emotional "compensation"? I would suggest that the film's appeal lies in part in its "nostalgic" portrayal of the outsider, free from the social constraints which force individuals to compromise. This is certainly the case with the *nagare-mono* films of the 1950s and 1960s, whose principal audiences were salarymen, those Japanese who Tayama describes as "being enmeshed in society" and "living secure lives" (1966).

Notes

1 The film, *Akira*, grew out of a best-selling *manga* (comic) series of the mid-1980s.

2 This chapter will attempt to explore the culturally specific codes and practices which a Japanese spectator employs to create meaning and derive pleasure from *Akira*. (Obviously, Western audiences will apply different – non-Japanese – codes and practices in their construction of meaning, thus leading to a different interpretation of the film, an issue not dealt with here.)

3 In Japan, *manga* and animation films tend to be gender-specific. There is very little cross-readership and cross-spectatorship. In bookshops signs clearly indicate which comics are for girls and which for boys, as does the color-coding of the comic jackets: dark hard colors, blacks and blues, for boys and soft pastel shades of pink for girls. I suspect that at home siblings might engage in a degree of cross-gender readership; however, the industry itself appears to be structured so as to discourage this, despite the fact that thematically gender-specific *manga* and *anime* are often similar. At the time of writing (1996) the two top-rated series for boys and girls, *Dragon Ball Z* and *Sailor Moon* (see Napier, Chapter 5) are, despite plot differences, thematically similar.

   In 1988, at about the same time that *Akira* was released, *Hana no Asuka-gumi* (*The Flower of the Asuka Gang*) was also released. This film is also set in a post-World War III dystopic society where gangs rule the streets, the principal differences being that the main gang members and leaders are adolescent girls.

4 *Bôsôzoku* literally means "tribe of running violently" (*bô* is violent, *sô* is to run, *zoku* is tribe); *bôsô* is more commonly defined as "reckless driving", so the term might best be translated as "gang of reckless drivers"; it is used to refer to members of motorcycle and car gangs. This term is perhaps best rendered in English as "speed tribes" (Greenfeld 1994). In the late 1970s and 1980s, members of these gangs formed a socially cohesive section of Japanese youth.

5 *Blade Runner* was ranked 25th in Japan's *Kinema Junpo* Best Foreign Films for 1982. This film had an obvious influence on *Akira*, as is made clear by the fact that both films are set in the year 2019. However, it could be said that this is a superficial similarity as the sub-texts of the films are quite different.

6 For a detailed exposition of the myths surrounding Japanese cultural and social homogeneity see Dale (1988), Mouer and Sugimoto (1990) and Weiner (1997).

7 A film that plays on this "moral panic" is *Sono otoko kyôbô ni tsuki* [*Because that Guy is Tough*, released in the UK as *Violent Cop*] 1988, starring Kitano (Beat) Takeshi in which he plays a tough policeman fighting corruption inside the police force on the one hand, and drug pushers on the other. The film feeds on fears of the degeneration of Japanese youth and of wanton violence. For example, the film opens with a group of relatively young high school boys beating up a tramp in a park. This is closely followed by a scene in which a group of young primary school boys (wearing yellow caps) are seen throwing cans from a bridge at a boatman passing below.

8   Mouer and Sugimoto also cite Japanese studies which confirm that
     "juvenile delinquency ... occurs more frequently among young people
     whose parents are in blue-collar occupations and self-employed ..." and
     that "... education is not unrelated to the occupational hierarchy. Those
     with higher levels of education are much less likely to commit crimes,
     particularly those of a violent nature. Juvenile delinquency is tied to the
     parents' level of education. Delinquency is lowest among those whose
     parents have had a university education, regardless of their occupation"
     (1990: 352-3).

9   The ideal is also based on how Japanese answer questions about their class
     position – not a very reliable way of assessing status evaluations.

10   For a more detailed discussion of the role of *seken* and its relationship to the
     formation of subjectivity, see Sugiyama-Lebra (1992).

11   This division is also seen in the film industry which targets films to specific
     youth audiences: for example, *Bîbappu Haisukûru* (*Bebop High School*) is a
     classic example of the *yankî*-style animation film which glorifies the school
     under-achiever in much the same way as the more complex *Akira* elevates
     the *bôsôzoku*. At the other end of the scale are the more sophisticated films
     such as *Kitchin* (based on the novel by Banana Yoshimoto) which are
     targeted at the *dokushin kizoku* end of the market.

12   However, there is some debate about this; Greenfeld (1994) suggests that
     this is not the case, as in fact *yakuza* do draw on the *bôsôzoku* gangs for
     recruits.

13   Here I am referring to films such as *Kumo nagaruru hateni* (*Beyond the
     Clouds*) 1953, *Ningen gyorai kaiten* (*The Sacrifice of the Human Torpedoes*) 1955,
     and *Ningen gyorai shutsugeki su* (*The Human Torpedoes' Sortie*) 1956.

14   It is interesting to note that Satô's informants frequently used the words
     matsuri (festival) and *kânibaru* (carnival) to describe the atmosphere of a
     bôsô drive. See Watts in this volume for a description of how soccer matches
     have developed a *matsuri*-like atmosphere as well.

15   In contemporary capitalist societies, there has been a marked shift in the
     role of commodities – a move from use-value to sign-value (cf. Watts in this
     volume for further discussion of this). This has resulted in the fragmen-
     tation of the traditional (in the Western sense of the word) working classes,
     where people now choose their identity through commodities and style:

     In both the cases of architecture and clothing, the shift has not just been
     one from mass-ness to specialization, but also from focus on function to
     a concern with style. In clothing, these characteristics in conjunction with
     the newer aesthetics of the shocking (and even the ugly) have justified
     the label of postmodern. (Lash 1991: 39)

16   *Akira* does not have a narrative structure in the traditional Hollywood style,
     therefore, a plot summary is not very practical. However, the Collectors'
     Edition Double Pack Video released in Britain provides a file on the
     principal characters to assist non-Japanese viewers. Here is a brief summary
     from the tape:
     Introduction

     Akira ... awakened to his hidden powers, powers that he could not
     control; powers that swept the megalopolis of Tokyo and the world in the
     maelstrom of World War III. Our stage is Neo Tokyo, the super techno
     city of 2019, thirty years after the holocaust – a ravaged city and one
     totally unaware of the cause of its misery ...

Characters – Data File

KANEDA: AGE 16.

An outsider who is far from obedient and cooperative. He is known to act before thinking things out. The leader and organizer of a bike gang, he is perceived by his fellow students as more than a little egotistical.

TETSUO: AGE 15.

The youngest member of Kaneda's gang. Known to have an inferiority complex because he is thought to be weak and immature. He is also thought to be extremely introverted.

KAY: AGE 16.

Government assigned code name, her real name remains classified. Joined and became active in a terrorist group shortly after her brother died in prison. Strong willed yet sensitive.

THE COLONEL: AGE 42.

Career military, on special assignment in Neo Tokyo. Father was a member of the Self-Defence Forces and participated in the original Akira Project prior to the start of World War III. The Colonel knows the secret of Akira.

KYOKO.

Sequestered by government. Realized extra-sensory powers at age 9; adept at telepathy and clairvoyance. Number 25 in the top secret Akira Project.

TAKESHI

Sequestered by government. Realized extra-sensory powers at age 8. Especially adept at psycho-kinesis. Number 26 in the top secret Akira experiment.

MASARU

Sequestered by government. Paralyzed from the waist down by polio age 6. Realized extra-sensory powers at age 8. Especially adept at second sight and psycho-kinesis.

AKIRA

28th and most successful ESP experiment.

File access restricted.

17 The designer of *Blade Runner* was inspired by the Californian designer Syd Mead who works for Bandai, a Japanese games company, where he designs futuristic images for Japanese computer games. It is more than a little ironic that *Blade Runner*'s cityscape was influenced by Tokyo and then that Otomo Katsuhiro should reproduce it once again, drawing on *Blade Runner*'s 2019 Los Angeles to create his 2019 Tokyo.

18 The *nagare-mono* film has its antecedents in the *matatabi-mono* (the wandering samurai/*yakuza*) genre. In the post-war period the actor Ishihara Yujirô came to prominence as an archetypal outsider in films such as *Ore wa matteruzo* (*I'll Wait*) 1957, and *Arashi o yobu otoko* (*The Man Who Calls the Storm*) 1957. However, Tayama, a Japanese critic writing in 1966, argued that by the early 1960s Ishihara had become entrenched in the establishment by appearing on television variety and talk shows. According to Tayama, this destroyed his *nagare-mono* persona, at which time the actor Takakura Ken took over the persona with his success in the highly popular *Abashiri bangaichi* (*Abashiri Wastelands*) series.

19 In the *nagare-mono* films of the 1960s, this code is referred to as *jingi*, which translates as "humanity and justice". However, in this case, "justice" is not to

be confused with the Western juridical-based definitions, but forms part of a nativist Confucian ethic (see also Gill in this volume). This term is also used extensively in *yakuza* films from the 1970s on, for example, the *Jingi naki tatakai* (*War without Morality*) series.

Akira, as a cybernatized version of the *nagare-mono* film, is primarily concerned with male/male relationships and the strains imposed on those relations by modern society. Female characters are marginalized, their principal function being to shore up the heterosexual imperative of the film.

20 This was ranked third in the *Kinema Junpô* Top Ten Films for 1967 and is still widely available on video.

21 As television studies on police dramas have shown in the West, the "main difference between heroes and villains is the greater efficiency of the heroes and the sympathy with which they are presented. Otherwise, there are few clear-cut distinctions, particularly in morality or method" (Fiske and Hartley 1989: 29).

22 In the first film of the *Abashiri bangaichi* series (1965), Tachibana's (the main character, played by Takakura Ken) unhappy childhood is depicted in flash-backs that show him and his mother being abused by his stepfather. This leads to a climactic clash and with Tachibana being thrown out of the house. The earlier films of Ishihara Yujirô are all similarly structured around generational conflict.

23 Tetsuo's very name is a play on his changing status in the film, as it means "iron man".

24 Here we have a re-working of a dominant theme of the war-retro genre of the early post-war period in which, through World War II, Japan is purified by destruction only to emerge stronger in the post-war period. This theme is evident in films such as *Daitôyô Sensô to Kokusai Saiban* (*The Pacific War and the International Tribunal*) 1959, and *Japan's Longest Day*, 1967.

References

Allen, R. C. and Douglas Gomery 1985 *Film History, Theory and Practice*. London: McGraw-Hill.

Anderson, J. T. and D. Richie 1959 *The Japanese Film, Art and Industry*. Tokyo: Charles Tuttle.

Baudrillard, Jean 1988 "Symbolic Exchange and Death" in *Jean Baudrillard, selected writings* edited by Mark Poster. Cambridge: Polity Press.

Cohen, A. K. 1955 *Deliquent Boys: The culture of the gang*. Glencoe, Ill.: The Free Press.

Dale, P. 1988 *The Myth of Japanese Uniqueness*. London: Nissan Institute/ Routledge Japanese Studies Series.

DeVos, George 1973 *Socialization for Achievement, Essays on the Cultural Psychology of the Japanese*. Berkeley and Los Angeles: University of California Press.

Fiske, J. and John Hartley 1989 *Reading Television*. London: Routledge.

Fiske, J. 1991 *Television*. London: Routledge.

Greenfeld, Karl Taro 1994 *Speed Tribes: children of the Japanese bubble*. London: Boxtree.

Harvey, David 1989 *The Condition of Postmodernity, an Enquiry into the Origins of Cultural Change.* Oxford: Basil Blackwell.

Hebdige, Dick 1991 *Subculture, the meaning of style.* London: Routledge.

Jameson, Fredric 1983 "Postmodernism and the Consumer Society" in *The Anti-Aesthetic, Essays on Postmodern Culture* edited by Hal Foster. Port Townsend, W.A.: Bay Press.

Lash, Scott 1991 *Sociology of Postmodernism.* London: Routledge.

Mouer, R. and Sugimoto Yoshio 1990 *Images of Japanese Society: A study in the social construction of reality.* London: Kegan Paul International.

Otomo, Katsuhiro n.d. *Akira* (orginal screenplay in Japanese).

Satô Ikuya 1991 *Kamikaze Biker, Parody and Anomy in Affluent Japan.* London and Chicago: University of Chicago Press.

Sontag, Susan 1979 "The Imagination of Disaster" in *Film Theory and Criticism, Introductory Readings* edited by Gerald Mast and Marshall Cohen. Oxford: Oxford University Press.

Sugiyama-Lebra, E. 1992 "Self in Japanese Culture" in *The Japanese Sense of Self* edited by Nancy R. Rosenberger. Cambridge: Cambridge University Press.

Tayama R. 1966 "*Abishiri Bangaichi: Nagare-mono no Erejii*" in *Shinario* (October): 134–7.

Weiner, M. (ed.) 1997 *Japan's Minorities: The illusion of homogeneity.* London: Routledge.

CHAPTER 4

Japan's Empty Orchestras
Echoes of Japanese culture
in the performance of karaoke

BILL KELLY

When things seem sufficiently enlivened, the chief raps on the table for attention and suggests that singing begin. Everyone claps in agreement, and someone calls out Mr. Ono's name. Clapping erupts again, and he stands, sings a brief folk song, and then sits down amidst much applause. The chief calls next on Kato, another of the younger men, who because he is a bit of a wiseacre, is regarded as the black sheep of the group. Kato makes an excuse, drinks a full glass in one swallow, makes more excuses, but fails to stand and sing as requested. An awkward silence follows. Everyone sympathizes with Kato's embarrassment, but he must sing like the rest, for the solo performance is an integral part of office parties ... finally ready he hurries through a popular song and sits down amid thunderous applause, obviously relieved. Then everyone in the group takes his or her turn singing a solo. With much giggling and handholding two women pair off in a duet. One young man sings a song filled with taboo sex words disguised rather transparently as puns in the midst of an otherwise innocent story. Another offers a rendition of a soulful ballad. The deputy who told the funny story ties his necktie around his head in the homespun manner of folk dancers and proceeds to sing and dance an exaggerated rendition of an old folk song ... Finally, the chief, in a polished and charming manner, sings a traditional song and then its modern counterpart. (Rohlen 1974: 99)

This opening passage is from Thomas Rohlen, based on fieldwork conducted prior to the birth of karaoke in 1968–69, and I have chosen to quote it at length because it illustrates elements of the way in which karaoke is performed in Japan. The fact that this earlier activity indicates a concern with a "way" suggests both a historical basis for karaoke, as well as a connection with an ethos perhaps characteristic of Japanese society. This ethos informs both contemporary leisure activities and those considered to be traditional; and it is these aspects of the performance that are a source of karaoke's distinctiveness in Japan and, in fact, of its Japaneseness.

Karaoke first emerged in the entertainment districts of Kansai[1] twenty years ago and the phenomenon has never enjoyed greater popularity in Japan than it does in the 1990s. A survey released by the Cultural Affairs Agency in November, 1993, cited karaoke as the most common cultural activity in which the nation participated. Of respondents who claimed to have participated in cultural activities in that year,

> karaoke ranked at the top with 43 percent, followed by traditional hobbies like tea ceremony, flower arrangement and horticulture with 32 percent, and creative arts such as drawing, photography and sculpture with 24 percent. (*Japan Times*, 4 November 1993)

According to an agency official quoted in an editorial which followed this report, "this year's white paper is probably the first document submitted for Cabinet approval to ever mention karaoke" (*Japan Times*, 7 November 1993).

A global phenomenon which has been successfully marketed throughout Southeast Asia, Australia, New Zealand, North America and many parts of Europe, karaoke is a rare (and perhaps the only) example of a modern leisure activity "made in Japan" and transplanted overseas.[2] As a Japanese cultural commodity, it is the object – the karaoke machine – and not so much the culture, as defined by its use in a particular social context, which has been exported. Just as karaoke's success abroad depends on the local culture in which it is either taken up or rejected,[3] so too the phenomenal success of karaoke in Japan can only be understood with reference to the wider context of Japanese society.

This is not to suggest that karaoke in Japan is an undifferentiated activity in a homogeneous land. On the contrary, vigorous efforts by an extremely competitive industry to promote karaoke to every sector of the Japanese population, combined with a complex history of interaction between technological innovation and social context since the phenomenon's "invention",[4] have resulted in a wide variety of karaoke venues. These include the multitude of drinking places which can be found packed together, honeycomb-like, in urban entertainment quarters: nightclubs, lounges, *sunakku* (snack) bars, shot bars, hostess clubs catering primarily for men, the much more rare host clubs; and places specific to minority or marginal communities such as gay, lesbian, Korean and illegal immigrant bars; as well as karaoke boxes,[5] coffee shops, restaurants, hotels, love hotels and the home. All of these collectively make karaoke available to nearly every sector of Japan's population. Even for a specific type of venue, there is great diversity, depending on factors such as age, status and income. Not only has karaoke been integrated into the hierarchy of night spots which are differentiated according to the income and status of their clientele (as reflected in their cost), but even karaoke boxes range from those run as small family enterprises in local neighborhoods, in which a karaoke-equipped room can be rented for less than one thousand yen per hour, to the spacious karaoke salons in one of Osaka's finest hotels which, elegantly decorated, furnished in European style and bearing names such as Athena or Muse, might cost five to ten times as much to rent by the hour. This diversity of both venue and social context, combined with differences in individual responses towards participation in karaoke, accounts for what might be termed the heterogeneity of the phenomenon.

This chapter begins with a critique of explanations most often cited in accounting for karaoke's popularity in Japan, followed by an analysis of several elements of its performance. This is then followed by an attempt to unravel those aspects of the phenomenon which reflect variation between individuals or particular sectors of Japanese society in their responses to karaoke from those aspects which, transcending such variation, are more sociologically satisfying in coming to terms with the particular character[6] of karaoke within its many Japanese contexts.

After establishing a cultural basis for the practice of karaoke in Japan, the question of changing perceptions of the phenomenon among the Japanese, culminating in its recent acceptance as a cultural activity, is addressed. Finally, it is suggested that karaoke, which reflects in some of its aspects heterogeneity, in others the homogeneity of Japanese society, might serve as a case in which the mediation of these concepts can be discussed.

Karaoke theories

Analyses of karaoke in the press and more recently in Japanese academic discourse have produced a multitude of explanations for karaoke's popularity. Among those most often cited for the phenomenon's huge success in Japan are that karaoke:

1 satisfies a widespread love of singing;
2 satisfies a desire to emulate favorite singing stars and is thus a means of fantasy fulfillment;
3 is an effective way to relieve stress;
4 serves as a forum in which individuals act strategically for their own political ends; and
5 is a medium for communication or, as one informant explained, a social lubricator among people who find conversation and the discussion of issues difficult.

These can all be said to be true of some individuals in Japan or to be more valid for certain sectors of the population compared to others (see, for example, Kelly 1997; Linhart 1986; Ogawa 1990).

A love of singing may be cited as a possible reason for karaoke's global appeal, but does not elucidate its particular manifestations in Japanese society; nor does it account for the many who, despite an aversion to singing in front of others, nevertheless take their turn at the microphone. Star-emulation has been more a motivation among the young, a phenomenon which one Japanese sociologist attributes to the idolization of pop singing stars (Ogawa 1990) (known in Japanese as *aidoru*, or idols)[7] among this sector. The recent increase in specialized karaoke studios which, catering specifically to the young, are equipped to produce promotional videos of singers, suggests that the desire to be like a star is particularly pronounced among the young. According to one article published in the Japanese magazine *Dime* (16 April 1987), such establishments were particularly popular among teenage girls who cited the dream of becoming a star as their primary reason for patronizing them.[8]

Although karaoke may serve as a panacea for stress release or as a forum for self-expression for many participants, those shy or embarrassed about singing karaoke may find it more of a source of stress and anxiety. For those who enjoy singing, have a propensity to perform in front of others, or who otherwise implicitly accept having to sing within a particular context, karaoke may serve as an arena for self-expression, but even in such instances it is a forum which is socially prescribed. To borrow Tagawa Tadasu's words "... the hero may think he is flying, but in fact all his great deeds take place on the palm of Buddha's hand" (1979: 363). For those less predisposed to perform publicly, the prospect of singing in front of an audience, namely co-workers, may provoke fear and even terror, but seldom an outright refusal to sing. They too are "on the palm of Buddha's hand" and would, in most cases, opt for the momentary humiliation and embarrassment caused by having to sing rather than upset what sociologist Daisaburo Hashizume has termed the "superiority of togetherness" (interview with H. Ogawa, 17 April 1991).

Karaoke's role as a means by which a man can influence allies and rally political support has been confirmed by one informant. A young businessman in Tokyo noted that when, what and how well one sings, how one responds to the singing of others and, perhaps more importantly, where one sits with respect to colleagues and seniors as individuals circulate to and from the karaoke stage, can serve to enhance one's political effectiveness on such occasions. However, such strategic maneuvering seems to be limited to those so inclined and is but one aspect, rather than a generalized, distinguishing feature, of karaoke.

Finally, as a medium for communication, karaoke serves as a somewhat formalized forum, the rules of which are understood by all, for the mediation of interactions between participants. Singing is roughly in turn, each person usually choosing a song which they feel reasonably competent to perform and which may somehow reflect their musical preferences. The singing of a song already sung by another person in the group, or which has already become associated with them, is taboo and is avoided. Although attention may not appear to be focussed on the performer during most of the performance, there are prescribed pauses – generally between verses and at the beginning and end of the song – during which the "audience" acknowledges the performer's efforts with applause and encouragement. The result is highly predictable but, most importantly, a comfortable forum for social interaction in which recognition of and adherence to the implicit rules serves to preserve a non-threatening atmosphere. It is therefore a "safe" activity which poses little or no threat to the "harmony" of relationships between individuals or between individuals and the rest. In this sense, it conforms to the needs of the occasion by providing a democratic forum in which each member is expected to do her or his part and, in so doing, to confirm his or her commitment to the collectivity. However, karaoke detractors argue that karaoke effectively stifles communication by formalizing any interaction. The noise level, combined with the time spent choosing songs, singing and acknowledging the efforts of others relegates conversation to the periphery.[9]

Although such explanations, which highlight the diversity of the phenomenon in Japan, are useful in understanding the opinions, motivations and attitudes of some with respect to participation in karaoke, they are only partial explanations. As they fail to transcend this variability, they are ultimately sociologically unsatisfying in understanding the phenomenon as a manifestation of Japanese society. In order to more clearly explain karaoke's connection with the society in which it was generated, it is necessary to turn to the performance itself, elements of which are a source of karaoke's consistency in Japan.

Performances

As illustrated in the opening quotation, one of the most distinguishing aspects of entertainment in this context is the solo performance. As Rohlen also points out

> ... it is no easy thing to stand before a group and sing. Trembling hands, shaking voices, and nervous faces reveal the stress many experience at the moment they are selected. (1974: 109)

However, regardless of the performance quality, participants are invariably met with a sympathetic and encouraging response from others in the group for their efforts. As Rohlen goes on to describe:

> When the ordeal is over, it is normal for the performer to experience a rush of relief and a feeling of gratitude to the others for their help. From that point ... he is deep into the group emotionally for he has revealed his humanity and been accepted by the others ... (1974: 109)

The willingness of an individual to perform in turn despite a reluctance, or even an abhorrence of doing so, is an indication of her or his dedication and commitment to the goals and aims of the collective whole. The solo performance within this context is an implicit acknowledgement by the performer that the objectives of the collectivity, and the relationships upon which achieving these objectives depend, transcend personal fears and insecurities with respect to singing. Through singing, the individual expresses to others in her or his circle that they are people – not individually, but collectively – among whom personal sacrifices can (and must) be made, and individual weaknesses exposed.

An activity in which all can participate, karaoke is perhaps more vitally one in which all participants can improve their performance. An important aspect of the solo performance is the implicit expectation that some degree of preparation and effort will be invested by the performer into polishing his or her act.[10] Whereas participation in karaoke or other forms of amateur singing in the United States or England might depend on talent – a good voice for example, particularly if an audience is involved – in Japan, anybody, regardless of ability, is provided the opportunity to do their best and is generally accorded patience and even encouragement along the way. Furthermore, there seems to exist a standard of singing, a sort of ideal model, set by professional pop or *enka* (ballad) singers, which participants can strive to emulate and against which their relative ability can be gauged. There has thus developed a "way of karaoke" (*karaoke-dô*)[11] which, with discipline and practice, enables one to perfect a chosen piece, performing it with a minimum of effort when the occasion arises.

Among karaoke practitioners, and here it is important to note that many in Japan do not like karaoke and avoid it whenever possible, it is standard practice to develop a repertoire of songs which have been sufficiently mastered to ensure a fairly consistent performance. This repertoire might consist of more than one hundred songs. Even non-enthusiasts who must, by virtue of their employment or other affiliation, occasionally take part, have at least one song, referred to as an *ohako* or *jû hachiban* (number eighteen).[12] Within the context of one's primary association, an office section, a group of school friends, or a club or organization, this song becomes associated with individual singers, becoming "their song", an idea which is historically related to the *enkaigei* (party trick), a song, magic trick, dance or humorous routine, which has been a feature of drinking parties since at least the Tokugawa period.[13] Both the *ohako* and its precursor, the *enkaigei*, represent the integration of individuality with the group context through the establishment of a sort of group-sanctioned identity. To violate this by singing another person's song would be unthinkable.[14]

Guidance for mastering "the way of karaoke" can be found in magazines and on television. Articles outline the finer points of karaoke technique, such as positioning and gesturing on stage before, during and after singing, the ideal distance between microphone and mouth, appropriate poise and etiquette vis-a-vis the audience, all of which depend on the style of the song or the gender of the singer. *Nodo jiman*, a popular weekly amateur singing program on NHK features professional guest *enka* singers, a man and a woman, who are called on to advise contestants on how to improve their delivery and performance. Performances are judged with one, two, or a cascade of bells indicating a weak, moderate, or successful effort and contestants are either congratulated or advised by the host to keep working at it and thanked for their efforts before the next contestant is invited on stage. Finally, karaoke enthusiasts can enrol in one of the many courses which teach everything from stage presence to singing technique. One might hear two middle-aged women waiting on a station platform discussing the way to sing a particular line of a particular *enka* song while referring to the words enclosed with a karaoke cassette tape.

Kazuko Hohki, founding member of a duo known as the Frank Chickens which performed a karaoke variety act in London clubs and who briefly hosted a chat show featuring karaoke on British television, summarized the difference between the use of karaoke in Japan and the United Kingdom by suggesting that the Japanese take karaoke seriously, whereas for the British, it is all in good fun.[15] This perception of karaoke's seriousness derives from the formalization of its performance in Japan; the existence of a standard to which participants can aspire, the widely-perceived necessity of mastering at least one or two songs to a level which is in keeping with this standard and the emphasis on the developing of a performance technique. The result is an activity in which a person's ability to perform can be improved and perhaps even mastered with respect to an ideal type.

In this sense, the performance of karaoke can be linked (as indeed it has been in the government report cited at the beginning of this chapter) with the more austere and esoteric disciplines such as tea. This

implies that there exists "a way" of performing the everyday and the
mundane – preparing and drinking tea or singing karaoke – which
reflects "a cult founded on the adoration of the beautiful among the
sordid facts of everyday existence" (Okakura 1992: 3). Furthermore, *dô*,
whether with respect to tea, karaoke, or the martial arts, is characterized
by accessibility. Participation is open to all, regardless of class, status or
"natural" ability. Reflecting more erudite and established cultural forms,
karaoke, like tea, "represents the true spirit of Eastern democracy by
making all its votaries aristocrats in taste" (Okakura 1992: 4). This is not
to suggest that karaoke should be conceived as or categorized with more
traditional arts, and most Japanese certainly would not equate the two,
but rather to emphasize that the practice or use of karaoke in Japan,
like the practice of other recent or imported activities such as baseball (Whiting 1990) and tennis, is colored by the same esthetic and
philosophical principles which are the essence of the traditional arts.

Although the predominance of the solo performance within the
context of the group and the emphasis on form as manifested in the
development of a *dô* of performing are several aspects of karaoke which
provide a cultural basis for the activity, only recently has it been officially
acknowledged as representative of Japanese culture. Once frequently
derided in the mass media as a kind of societal blemish, embodying the
worst aspects of the "after hours" world into which it had become
integrated, several factors may have contributed to the whitening of
karaoke's reputation. For one thing, its enthusiastic acceptance abroad
has not only increased karaoke's value as a commodity for export but,
more significantly, as an acceptable envoy of things Japanese to the
world. Although some in Japan might find the idea of karaoke as a
national symbol or lone cultural export more a source of embarrassment than pride, its success overseas, along with the resulting economic
ramifications, are likely to have contributed, at least in some sectors, to
the enhancement of karaoke's symbolic value at home.[16]

Karaoke's spread from the drinking establishments within which it
was first established to the karaoke boxes and studios which are now its
dominant manifestation has also contributed to the gradual improve-
ment of its image. Once associated with the "zones of evaporation"
(Linhart 1986) into which company workers, the so-called *sarariman*
(salaryman) and possibly his[17] colleagues, might disappear to indulge in
personal pleasures such as drinking, gambling, socializing, and
associating with women free from pressures of both the workplace and
home, karaoke had been associated with the seediness of the *sakariba*
(drinking districts). References to karaoke as a social ill and national
scourge, or the culture for a generation of "lost souls" were not un-
common in early accounts. Associated with the vice and self-indulgence

of entertainment districts largely operated by the *yakuza*, karaoke was embedded in a world which, although well-established in Japan and accepted, was nevertheless perceived to exist on the margins of legality and morality. As such, karaoke was treated as symptomatic of the lifestyle, increasingly perceived to be unhealthy and undesirable, of an overworked and underdeveloped company man.

The development of the karaoke box, and its subsequent and very rapid spread throughout Japan, vastly increased karaoke's accessibility by providing a low-cost, often alcohol-free, environment better suited to the young. Particularly popular among teenagers and young adults,[18] but also with young couples and even families, the karaoke box has displaced the karaoke bar as the dominant form, thus liberating the activity from many of its early and somewhat unsavory associations. As karaoke's popularity has soared among these sectors of the population, the prevailing musical genre has shifted from *enka*, with its sad and nostalgic themes (which often included references to night, sake, and the sympathetic figure of the mama-san,[19] all elements of the *sakariba*) to *poppusu* (pop), with its more frivolous, lighthearted themes and upbeat rhythm. Having largely shed its former image as an expressive outlet for the overwrought company man, karaoke has come to be perceived as a more wholesome form of leisure to be enjoyed by couples, friends and family and, as such, may be deemed more suit-able for inclusion under the rubric of "cultural activity" than was its predecessor.

As this brief analysis suggests, karaoke in Japan is not a uniform phenomenon, but one which reflects a degree of uniformity across different arenas. It is these different contexts, and particularly the nature of the relationships between participants within a given context, which is one source of variation. Where relations are highly formalized and hierarchical, for example between colleagues of a large company, this is reflected in the performance of karaoke, just as it would be in any other sphere in which the same individuals were gathered together. Thus, young office ladies (OLs) may be quick to accompany their male bosses in a duet upon request and may even invest some time and effort in preparing themselves for such an eventuality. Their choice of songs and style of performance may also be regulated in a way which reflects a demeanor and degree of modesty appropriate to their position. Similar measures might be expected of the other participants, as appropriate to their position. In such a situation, karaoke provides a forum for developing and nurturing the relationships upon which the effectiveness of the work unit, a company section for example, depends. As the karaoke box caters to groups in which the relationships between members are characteristically less hierarchical and more casual – a

group of school or university classmates for example – this too is
reflected in the performance.[20]

Conclusion

Although there may be considerable variation in individual opinion
about and feeling towards participation in karaoke within a particular
context, this often has little bearing on the act of participation itself
which, as Rohlen confirms for earlier performances, is seldom felt to be
optional. However, more than an abandonment of individual dignity
and personal desires, participation expresses a willingness to socialize
with fellow group members on an equal basis and is an expression on
the part of performers that their own needs are met through their
inclusion in the group. To put it in Takeo Doi's (1989) terms, singing
expresses a willingness, or at least an acceptance of the necessity, to
demonstrate a dependence on the benevolence of others within the
collective unit or, to put it in Japanese, to *amae*. With respect to karaoke
it is not a group's response to the medium per se which determines
behavior, but rather the response of group members to one another.
Karaoke is so widespread in Japan because it is well suited to the way in
which individuals interrelate within the context of their primary
affiliations. Karaoke is therefore a technological innovation which
provides a new medium for the expression of an established tradition of
performing in front of others, as a means of demonstrating – not
consciously but implicitly – an individual's membership within a
collectivity. At the same time it may also fulfill the needs, desires and
fantasies of the individual.

As a window into the range of relationships between individuals and
between the individual and the context of their primary affiliation (be
it the workplace, a social or athletic club, or a group of friends or
neighbors), karaoke serves as a useful case study in understanding
Japanese society, for it is these relationships upon which so much in
Japan depends. This provides evidence for heterogeneity in Japanese
society through the diversity of both context and individual opinion
towards participation within a given context. Not only that, but it is co-
existent with an historically evolved solo performance which provides a
sort of grammar for mediating the singing of karaoke in all of its
Japanese contexts and a concern with form as manifested through the
development of a way (or perhaps ways) of mastering one's karaoke
performance. Of course, the seriousness with which this way is taken up
depends very much on individual inclination and necessity, as
determined by social context.

The "unique" character of the karaoke performance in Japan does
not therefore suggest any kind of consensus of opinion or blanket

homogeneity, but rather historical continuity with a performance "tradition" which is embedded within the realm of *tsukiai*.[21] However, as Atsumi Reiko (1979) has described in an insightful paper on the subject, although such activities often involve – by definition – an element of obligation, an individual actor's maneuvering within such constraints is by no means completely prescribed, but may be negotiated with respect to her or his status within the collectivity and the nature of the collectivity itself. As a reflection on the discourse of the homogeneity versus the heterogeneity in Japanese society, the case of karaoke therefore supports an integrated view, suggesting that the framing of phenomena in such polarized terms may reveal more about its interpreters than about the object of interpretation. As Harootunian has pointed out, "Japanese culture has always been characterized by the avoidance of binary oppositions" (1989: 80).

Notes

1 Kansai (lit. western gate) refers to the region of western Japan which includes the cities of Osaka, Kyoto and Kobe.
2 This is not to imply a simple and uncomplicated transmission from Japan to the world; in practice, the process seems to have been quite complex.
3 For a discussion of this with specific reference to the United Kingdom, see Kelly 1998.
4 Perhaps a misleading term given the ambiguity of karaoke's origins. Rather than being the brainchild of a single inventor (as some claim), several versions of a karaoke-like machine seem to have been generated independently in different places at about the same time. (For a more detailed discussion see Kelly 1998.)
5 First fashioned in Okayama prefecture by outfitting old cargo containers with a karaoke machine and a few basic furnishings, the karaoke box (sometimes referred to as karaoke room or karaoke studio in urban areas) quickly spread throughout Japan, becoming the phenomenon's most popular manifestation.
6 I do not wish to overemphasize karaoke's uniqueness in Japan, but rather to suggest that there are aspects of its performance in Japan which reflect what Plath (1964) has termed an "articulation of traits" (and not the nature of the traits themselves) which might distinguish karaoke performance there.
7 See Stefánsson, Chapter 8, for a discussion of idols at a much more elite level.
8 During a recent period of field research, such establishments did not figure prominently on the karaoke landscape, suggesting that their popularity may have decreased in recent years.
9 According to one Japanese acquaintance, the way in which karaoke facilitates communication is by providing a forum in which friends and colleagues can meet and be (spend time) together, a function which may be more important than the act or content of discussion.

10   Although the degree of effort invested in mastering a song or polishing an
     act may vary considerably, depending on individual inclination and the
     context in which one is likely to sing; one university student (a woman)
     explained that the general tendency results from a feeling of "self-pride",
     suggesting that singing karaoke is, after all, the presentation of self.

11   The suffix *dô*, meaning "way of", is usually a component of words referring
     to the martial arts (jûdô, kendô) or other "traditional" arts, such as *shodô*
     (Japanese calligraphy). In a larger sense, as in the case of karaoke, it is used
     to refer to the fact that the performance must be highly stylized, that there
     is a proper and correct way of doing things. Thus, although some might
     feel that the use of *dô* to refer to something as frivolous as karaoke is
     inappropriate, this is how some of its practictioners describe the art of
     singing a song.

12   Although not entirely familiar with the etymology of this term, it is
     borrowed from kabuki and refers, in this context to a favorite karaoke song,
     usually chosen in part for its singability (see Chapter 1).

13   The sociologist Ogawa Hiroshi, a specialist in Japanese popular culture, has
     suggested that the *enkaigei* has been largely displaced by the *ohako* as a
     vehicle for individual performance in Japan (1990).

14   Although this seems to be a generalized feature of karaoke in Japan, the
     specific rules governing when, how, and what one sings are rather com-
     plicated, depending both on the context and the individual's status therein.

15   This is not to suggest that karaoke is not perceived as fun by many of
     its Japanese participants, but that this sense of fun is somewhat socially
     prescribed, perhaps echoing Chamberlain's turn-of-the-century obser-
     vation that "Serious ideas do for export. A nation's fun is for home con-
     sumption only: – it would evaporate before it could be conveyed across the
     border." (1992: 195).

16   Halldór Stefánsson first suggested the link between karaoke's increasing
     popularity overseas and its acceptance as a cultural activity in Japan (per.
     comm.).

17   This pronoun is used to indicate what was and continues to be primarily,
     although not exclusively, a male realm. During the late 1980s *oyajigyaru* (a
     compound combining a Japanese term for middle-aged man [*oyaji*] with a
     word derived from the English girl [*gyaru*]) was coined to describe the type
     of young company woman whose ambitious and career-oriented outlook
     and behavior is like that of her male colleagues. Using her femininity to
     negotiate her way through a male-dominated world, she is often portrayed
     in *manga* (comics) as threatening to the status quo.

18   Although popular with both young men and women, statistics gathered
     while conducting research at a karaoke box indicate that more women then
     men patronize such establishments (see Kelly 1997).

19   A term referring to the female proprietress (or perhaps the wife of the
     proprietor) of drinking establishments whose protective role in providing a
     warm, nurturing, and generally sympathetic environment into which
     patrons can escape to relax, drink and sing songs has obvious associations
     with the mother.

20   However, where the egalitarianism of relationships is crosscut, for example
     in the case of university clubs where stratification based on *senpai* (senior)
     and *kôhai* (junior) links may be pronounced, this may be reflected in
     the karaoke performance and perhaps in individual feelings towards
     participation.

21 Literally meaning "to keep company with", as well as being a noun referring to "friendship" or "acquaintance", this term is also used to refer to the obligatory after-hours drinking and socializing amongst colleagues which is deemed indispensable to the development and maintenance of good working relations.

References

Atsumi Reiko 1979 "*Tsukiai* – Obligatory Personal Relationships of Japanese White-collar Company Employees" in *Human Organization* vol. 38: 63–70.
Chamberlain, Basil Hall 1992 [1939] *Things Japanese.* Tokyo: Charles E. Tuttle.
Clarion Company, Ltd. 1990 (June) *White Paper on Karaoke.*
Doi Takeo 1989 *The Anatomy of Dependence.* Tokyo: Kodansha.
Harootunian, H. D. 1989 "Visible Discourses/Invisible Ideologies" in *Postmodernism and Japan* edited by M. Miyoshi and H. D. Harootunian. Chicago: University of Chicago Press.
Hendry, J. and Webber, J. (eds) 1986 *Interpreting Japanese Society, Anthropological Approaches* (JASO Occasional Papers no. 5). Oxford: JASO.
Japan Times 4 November 1993 "Culture-oriented goals urged: focus should be on creativity not work: White Paper", page 2.
——7 November 1993 "Culture means more than karaoke", page 16.
Kelly, William 1998a "The adaptability of Karaoke in the United Kingdom" in *Karaoke Around the World* edited by Tôru Mitsui and Shûhei Hosokawa. London: Routledge.
——1998b "Empty Orchestras: an anthropological analysis of karaoke in Japan". Unpublished DPhil thesis, Oxford University.
Linhart, Sepp 1986 "Sakariba: zone of evaporation between work and home?" in *Interpreting Japanese Society* edited by J. Hendry and J. Webber, pp. 198–210.
Ogawa Hiroshi 1990 "'Idol industry' hits the skids" in *Pacific Friend* 18(1): 32.
Okakura Kakuzo 1992 *The Book of Tea.* Tokyo: Charles E. Tuttle.
Plath, David 1964 *The After Hours: Modern Japan and the search for enjoyment.* Berkeley: University of California Press.
Rohlen, Thomas 1974 *For Harmony and Strength.* Berkeley: University of California Press.
Tagawa Tadasu 1979 "Artistically impoverished popular music" in *Japan Quarterly* 26 (July–September): 359–64.
Whiting, Robert 1990 *You Gotta Have* Wa. New York: Vintage.

PART III

The Female Domain

Vampires, Psychic Girls, Flying Women and Sailor Scouts
Four faces of the young female in Japanese popular culture

SUSAN J. NAPIER

Introduction

Nowhere is the dizzying rate of change in post-war Japan more apparent than in the shifting and varied identities of the modern Japanese woman. Well into the 1960s, the average woman in her thirties was almost sure to be a housewife and a mother. Today, while this lifestyle is still widely chosen, the percentage of married women who work outside the home is actually higher than those who stayed home thirty years ago. In addition, an increasing percentage of women prefer to put off marriage or remain childless, or both. While many women still opt for traditional secretarial work, others, such as the new Crown Princess before her marriage, have opted for high powered and high pressure careers.

What role does popular culture play in relation to the enormous changes undergone by Japanese women over the last several decades? In fact it has played an important, and even an exciting one, functioning both to reflect these changes and to inspire them. Ranging in variety from the *haha mono* or "mother movies" of the 1950s to the "flying women" image used in ad campaigns in the 1980s, images of women in popular culture have served on the one hand to re-inscribe traditional roles into post-war Japanese society and, on the other, to offer visions of escape from them. In fact, as we shall see, certain texts of popular culture not only implicitly resist the ideology of the patriarchal Japanese super-state, but actually work to problematize it, if not to actively subvert it.

Obviously, the two topics of women's roles and popular culture are wide ones, and cannot begin to be encompassed in a single essay. This chapter will examine one of the most intriguing of female identities in

Japan, the *shôjo*, or young girl, an image of far-reaching importance in popular culture, including advertising, television and popular music, and, in print media, the best-selling works of two "grown up" *shôjo*, the novels of Banana Yoshimoto and the popular poetry of Tawara Machi. In the hopes of limiting this discussion to a manageable textual territory, however, the material I will be drawing conclusions from is largely *manga*, the extraordinarily popular comic and cartoon narratives which pervade Japanese culture, and *manga*'s related *anime*, or animated films.

I selected *manga* for a number of reasons: first, because of their enormous popularity. As Soeda Yoshiya says, "manga are the dominant force in Japanese pop culture" (quoted by Sabin 1993: 208), or as John Lent puts it simply: "[t]he hugeness of the Japanese comic art industry has no parallel in the world" (1989: 230). Although actual readership figures are hard to establish, due to the fact that many copies are passed around from reader to reader, it seems clear that virtually everybody in Japan has had some exposure to *manga*, not only in childhood, but in many stages of their adolescent and adult life. The subject matter of *manga* is immense, including pornography, science fiction, sports careers, and even basic economics! Although critics and intellectuals decry this boom, seeing it as a symptom, if not a cause, of Japan's "decaying" high culture (see Oe 1989: 189), they cannot deny the pervasiveness and importance of *manga*'s influence. Whether one approves of them or not, popular culture images have enormous power, serving to "create and rework archetypes that eventually become the central mythology of our time" (Irons 1992: xxiii).[1]

A second reason why I chose *manga* has to do with the interesting relation between women and comics in Japan. In contrast to American and English comic culture which, even today, tends to be largely male, in terms of both creators and readers (see Sabin 1993: 222–34), Japanese *manga* have experienced a rising trend in the number of female readers and writers since the 1970s when the woman writer Riyoko Ikeda's *shôjo*-oriented *The Rose of Versailles* (1972–74) became a nation-wide best-seller.[2] Since that time, women writers such as Rumiko Takahashi have become some of the most important and well paid in the industry. The variety and range of women's *manga* range widely from clearly children's stories full of cuddly creatures to the erotica aimed at teenagers and housewives, and even, recently, to an increasing number of tales concerning professional career women. However, for the purposes of this chapter one of the most interesting trends in comics in the 1980s has been the association of women or girls and the occult, as shown in such famous and extremely popular works as *Devil Hunter Yoko* (*Mamono Hanta-Yoko*), *Mai the Psychic Girl* and *Vampire Princess Miyu*

(*Kyû setsuki Miyûa*). In the nineties, the association between women and the occult has continued and also broadened to include women with an enormous variety of superhuman powers plus a sub-category which might be called "cyborg women": women (and young girls) who are linked with some sort of high tech or futuristic science fiction technology.

This strong association of women with fantasy and science fiction brings me to my third reason for choosing to examine their role in *manga*. This is the fact that, unlike representational media such as television or film which rely on realism, the union of art and words which produces *manga*, both in comic and video, allows for a particularly wide variety of story formats and characters, often of a notably fantastic variety. It is my contention, as we will see, that it is in the genre of the fantastic that the numerous changes in contemporary Japanese woman's conception of her identity are most vividly presented, either literally or metaphorically, from the telekinetic destructiveness of *Mai the Psychic Girl* to the heroine's soaring flights in *Nausicaä*.

The equation of women and special powers was made most obvious in Oba Minako's 1976 classic *The Smiles of the Mountain Witch* (*Yamauba no bishô*), in which the fantastic powers of the witch were implicitly equated with that of any everywoman who must use "occult" powers in order to create a pleasing persona. While *Smiles* is a work of "pure literature" (*jun-bungaku*) rather than popular culture, this notion of woman's basic femininity as somehow occult is one which, I believe, is an unconscious sub-text in many fantasy *manga*.

Thus, the four female protagonists who will be discussed in this chapter all possess some form of psychic or occult power, which can be read as both wish-fulfilling fantasies of empowerment, at the same time as they can also be seen as intimately related with a young girl's normal femininity. Even more intriguingly, while fantasies of psychic powers are a staple of adolescence,[3] what is particularly interesting here, is that two of the four protagonists have ambivalent or simply negative feelings about these powers.

I would suggest that these works capture the young Japanese girl at a time of great change or uncertainty, perhaps the greatest period of change in Japanese female history. Of course, it should be noted that a sense of flux may be true for young Japanese males as well (see Napier 1993). Indeed, Scott Lash and Jonathan Friedman argue that "postmodernism [in general] is much more aware of identity choice" (1992: 2),[4] and it is certainly the case that the post-post-war generation worldwide seems caught up in an array of changing identities. But it is possible to speculate that, precisely because the Japanese female role was traditionally so circumscribed, the dizzying changes now confronting them have caused even more ambivalence in the female than in the male.

Face one: *Shôjo* as vampire

I would like to focus my exploration of the four faces of the young female in Japanese culture with a discussion of three 1980s texts centering around *shôjo* with extraordinary or occult powers: *Mai the Psychic Girl, Vampire Princess Miyu,* and *Nausicaä,* and ending with some commentary on the 1990s *shôjo* classic *Sailor Moon.* The first three works were written by men, but were immensely popular with both sexes in both their book and, (in the case of *Miyu* and *Nausicaä*), animated forms. Although quite different one from the other in style and subject matter, the texts may be seen as works which use the fantastic or the occult, especially in relation to their heroines' abilities, to explore a variety of *shôjo* identities, from traditional/conservative in terms of *Vampire Princess* and *Psychic Girl* to the surprisingly "liberated" protagonist of *Nausicaä,* and the powerful yet childlike heroines of *Sailor Moon.*

An initial definition of the word *shôjo* might be helpful to the discussion. As John Treat argues, the word *shôjo* is almost impossible to translate into English, since the most nearly literal translation, "young woman", "implies a kind of sexual maturity clearly forbidden to *shôjo*" (1993: 364). Allied with such signifiers of immaturity/innocence as stuffed animals, fluffy dresses, and an overall "cute" (*kawaii*) image, the *shôjo* seems to signify the girl who never grows up – a metaphorical attribute which, as will be seen, is given literal representation in *Vampire Princess.* As I have argued elsewhere, the *shôjo,* and her alter ego the *burikko* (the cute girl), is the perfect non-threatening female, the idealized daughter/younger sister whose femininity is essentially sexless (Napier 1981).

Although cultures throughout the world and throughout history have valorized virginity, it should be noted that the *shôjo* image is of a pervasiveness and importance that is arguably unique to Japan. Growing out of the increasing number of protected young ladies of good standing in pre-war Japan, the post-war *shôjo* is even more omnipresent, and significantly related to modern Japan's consumer culture, as Treat also points out (1993: 363–5).[5] Needless to say, the *manga* is one of the most ubiquitous products of consumer culture; and the *shôjo manga* (comic both for and about *shôjo*) is an important part of the industry. It should be noted however that the *manga* which I will be discussing in this chapter reach well beyond the *shôjo* sub-culture.

I begin with a discussion of the changing *shôjo* identity with *Vampire Princess Miyu* which, although fashionably occult and even quite violent, is actually the most overtly traditional of the four texts selected. Drawn and later animated in a style which might be called "Japanese Gothic", *Vampire Princess* uses many of the conventions of the Western vampire tradition, such as old dark houses, hooded figures and ancient curses, with one important difference: the vampires are all female.[6] Thus the two most important protagonists in the narrative are both women: Himiko, a young woman medium who is called in to help a little girl apparently attacked by a vampire; and Miyu, the actual "vampire princess", a thirteen-year-old *shôjo* who is the last of a long line of female vampires who suck their victims' blood at the same time as endowing them with eternal, zombie-like life. The narrative action revolves around a series of encounters between Himiko and Miyu, all of which take place at picturesque sites in the ancient Japanese capital cities of Kyoto and Kamakura, while the psychological action involves two major realizations on the part of Himiko. The first is her dawning understanding that Miyu's fate is a tragic one; not only does the young girl not wish to be a vampire, but she is frozen eternally at the age of thirteen, never able to grow up or to change in any way. The second psychological development is Himiko's own realization that she too may be a vampire, or perhaps a vampire's victim, and can escape this fate no more than Miyu. Throughout the work Himiko has felt strangely drawn to Miyu and, at the work's end it becomes clear that Miyu had once sucked Himiko's blood when she was still a small child.

Whether or not Himiko really is a vampire or a victim, the fact that both of these females are endowed with unusual and, in Miyu's case clearly anti-social psychic traits, initially suggests a degree of feminine empowerment and resistance against the dominant culture. Indeed, the very quality that characterizes a vampire, its liminality and marginality due to its undead state, seems to suggest an affinity with marginalized females. Or, as Jackson says, equating the vampire with other marginals, "the shadow on the edges of bourgeois culture is variously identified as [demonic] ... deviant, crippled or (when sexually assertive) female" (1981: 121). In fact, as Jackson also points out the vampire myth is also in many ways a fundamentally conservative fantasy. In the action of blood-sucking Jackson sees an attempted return to the presymbolic state of infancy, while the vampire's obsessional collecting of victims "centralizes the problem of power", to "prove the power of possession to try to establish a total self-supporting system" (1981: 59). This system, I might also point out, is an unchanging and eternal one, resistant to all efforts at subversion.

In Miyu's case, we do see her attempting to resist the frozen nature of the system, at least initially. Thus, in a revelatory flash-back, Miyu stands by the ocean side with her father and tells him how much she likes the constant changing of the sea. He, on the other hand, tells her how he

loves the permanence of a painting.[7] To make this contrast even more
explicit, at the end of the scene the father informs her that she can
never grow up or change because it is her destiny to be a vampire. Not
only is Miyu destined to be a vampire, we also learn at the end of the
video version that she must stay forever thirteen years old as part of
a pact that she is forced to make with the *shinma* (new demons) who
control both Miyu and her parents.

Ultimately the young vampire comes across as a pathetic rather than
frightening figure. Even when behaving at her most stereotypically
vampirical, disappearing and then reappearing with an evil laugh, Miyu
always wears a hair ribbon, and her laughter is actually the patently cute
giggle of a young Japanese girl.

Furthermore, it is not only Miyu who is frozen in time. The "Japanese
Gothic" aspects of the illustrations suggest a Japan far removed from the
changing real world. Thus, most of the encounters between Miyu and
Himiko take place against ostentatiously traditional backgrounds such
as the temples of Kyoto, or an old farmhouse in Kamakura; places
which, even to contemporary Japanese, are no longer familiar parts of
daily life. Interestingly, these encounters in the video are often accompanied by eerie Noh chants, reinforcing the traditional Otherness of the
narrative. In another note unusual for contemporary Japan, many
characters in the work also wear kimono. Even Himiko, who initially
appears to be a modern career woman, is revealed as having perhaps the
most ancient of all Japanese female professions, that of the medium, a
female role which goes back to the shamanesses of prehistoric Japan.

In the final analysis, then, is *Vampire Princess* a conservative or a
subversive work? In some ways it is both. Although the setting, the
narrative framework and Miyu's ultimately resigned acceptance of her
fate suggest a fundamentally conservative structure, there are many
hints of resistance throughout the text. Although not always explicitly,
the work problematizes, through the fantastic figure of the vampire, a
number of issues of particular relevance to contemporary Japanese
women: the weight of tradition and its resistance to change; the two-
edged aspect of woman's feminine identity, one which both limits and
empowers; and finally the attraction/revulsion inscribed within the
complex and enduring figure of the *shôjo* herself, a figure that is as
"demonic" as it is "cute". Moreover, as the text makes clear, this ambiguous *shôjo* identity is forced upon Miyu from outside.

Thus although *Vampire Princess* foregrounds two kinds of traditions
– the national tradition of Japanese culture and the traditional
female/vampirical powers – in fact it subtly undermines those traditions
by showing both Miyu's and Himiko's resistance to their enforced
"vampirization". In this regard, the presumed identification of the

female with the vampire is interesting. Although Miyu rebels against her enforced "vampirization", she never really forces the issue, finally accepting that, as she says, "I am possessed of a power different from other people".

Looked at from a critical standpoint, however, we might suggest that these powers are simply the more basic aspects of the feminine, made to appear special to rationalize her own essential imprisonment. Just as in Oba Minako's story, where female was equated with mountain witch, in this work female is implicitly being equated with vampire.

This brings up another issue related to the fact that all the vampires in this work are female. In part this may relate to the erotic sub-text throughout the work. The vampire princess is drawn to the beautiful young boys and, in one scene where Miyu competes with another vampire for a young man's affections, the erotic (and yet strangely sexless) rivalry is clearly foregrounded. Himiko and Miyu's own relationship is also ambiguous, suggesting both a kind of doppelgänger role for Himiko and also, perhaps a homoerotic attraction as well.[8]

In *Our Vampires, Ourselves* (1995), Auerbach traces the homoerotic sub-texts of the vampire literature in the West, finding them both in the nineteenth century and in post-war fiction. Auerbach points to "the intimacy, the sharing, (and) the maternal suffusion" (1995: 59) of the nineteenth-century vampire's allure, aspects which *Vampire Princess Miyu* seems to embody as well. Even the dark tunnel-like architecture of many of *Miyu's* settings connotes the female body and thus augments the sense of a largely female world in which same-sex relationships are most important.

Vampirism is not only a form of erotic coding; in this work, at least, it is profoundly related to issues of time, change, family, and the female role. Miyu's vampirism, for example, is handed down from her mother, just as all feminine arts are traditionally handed down from mother to daughter. In fact, one scene shows Miyu unknowingly drinking her mother's blood, symbolizing the fact that she is doomed to becoming a vampire.

Mention of blood brings me to a related point of interest here and that is the connection between blood, femininity and vampirism. Given that Miyu becomes a vampire at the age of thirteen, there can be little doubt that a connection between menstruation and vampirism is being drawn. In a sense, it is because she menstruates, that is, is female like her mother, that Miyu becomes a vampire. Body and tradition thus work together to imprison the *shôjo* for ever.[9]

Finally, the actual drinking of another's blood is intriguing as well. Traditional Japanese folklore is full of demonic females, and there seems at least a suggestion here that Miyu is following in that tradition,

becoming a creature who inherently needs to feed on others. Although
the obvious correlation in this case is with erotic relationships, one
might also speculate about the Japanese mother, whose all-sacrificing
image has dominated both popular and so-called high culture for
decades, if not centuries. Given that it is Miyu's mother who forces her
into her vampirism, is there some suggestion here that motherhood
itself is vampiric? Perhaps that is going too far, but it seems reasonable
to suggest that *Vampire Princess Miyu* is a text which shows a provocative
ambivalence towards both femininity and tradition.

Face two: Psychic girl(s)

While *Vampire Princess Miyu* initially seems traditional but in the long run
questions that tradition through what might be termed a "damaged" or
even "perverted" *shôjo* perspective, the next work to be considered, *Mai
the Psychic Girl*, at the outset appears to be highly contemporary but, in
fact, is less questioning and fundamentally more conservative than
Vampire Princess. A fourteen-year-old girl whose mother is dead, *Psychic
Girl*'s heroine, Mai, possesses awesome telekinetic powers which make
her capable of immense destruction. She herself is unaware of these
powers until she is discovered by a sinister international organization
known as the Wisdom Alliance which attempts to capture her for its own
purposes. The remainder of the narrative consists of her ultimately
successful attempts to elude and outwit the forces of the Alliance at the
same time as she searches for her father, who was almost killed in the
Alliance's first attempt to capture her. Despite many temptations to use
her powers for destruction, Mai refuses to employ them, fearing their
dreadful potential and insisting that she would rather be "just like
normal people".

Mai's insistent desire to be "normal" and her refusal to make use of
her powers is clearly shown to be a sign of unusual maturity and
strength. Thus, despite the textual celebration of the awesome powers of
telekinesis, in terms of a number of carefully drawn scenes of Mai's
psychic powers in action, the sub-textual message is that "normality" is
infinitely to be preferred. Mai's powers do not really threaten the
established order by conferring on her any new kind of identity. Instead
they make her long for her regular *shôjo* identity even more.

Indeed, in many ways Mai is even more stereotypically a *shôjo* than is
Miyu. Her appearance and her non-telekinetic activities are almost
classically those of a *shôjo*. In one scene, for example, we see her in a
Snoopy apron cooking dinner for a group of male students. Another
instance shows her in school uniform having tea with some giggling
schoolgirl friends. Perhaps, most appealing of all, she early on befriends
a puppy who accompanies her throughout the rest of the narrative.

In general, Mai is passive. In many incidents she is rescued by a male, for example a handsome young student named Intetsu. The few times Mai does take action on her own, it is usually for self-sacrificing reasons: at one point, for instance, she runs away from Intetsu rather than put him into danger. Most importantly, the only time she will ever use her psychic powers is to protect someone weaker, such as the little puppy she has rescued, or her amnesiac father.

One other case where Mai does take action is perhaps particularly revealing. This is in competition with her rival, another psychic girl, a beautiful blond East German named Turm Garten who is brought to Japan by the Alliance to destroy Mai. I would like to focus on the differences between the presentation of Mai and Turm because a comparison between the two reveals not only the problematic relationship between psychic powers and femininity, but also between the representations of Japanese and Western females. While *Vampire Princess* clearly brought up a traditional ideal of femininity, *Psychic Girl* puts forth a more modern ideal of femininity which is still quite a conservative one in relation to its Western equivalent.

Mai is obviously meant to represent an ordinary Japanese schoolgirl who just happens to have incredible psychic powers, but Turm, her blond rival, with her sinister lust for power is almost paradoxically Teutonic. Tall, arrogant, and dressed in far more adult fashion than Mai, Turm plays two functions. On the one hand, she fulfills certain wishful *shôjo* fantasies, allowing the reader to briefly identify with a blond, big-eyed "princess". Thus, in one scene which takes place at a reception at the East German embassy, Turm is shown in a stunning ball gown studded with roses, her long hair flowing around her while photographers avidly snap away. On the other hand, she is also consistently presented as cruel, selfish and greedy, as when she carelessly murders five men simply to display her psychic powers.

Turm's powers appear meant to be viewed by the readers as "out of control". Whereas Mai only wants to be normal, and exercises great restraint in her behavior, Turm glories in her difference from others, insisting to Mai that they are like gods, and boasting that she is the descendant of a German god. This consistently negative portrayal of Turm as vain and self-aggrandizing, both qualities unlikely to be prized among most contemporary Japanese of either sex, allows Japanese readers to turn back to Mai for their primary identification, secure that they would not really want to be like the East German girl, even if they admire her hair and clothes. It also teaches the reader an important subliminal lesson, that too many powers are dangerous, both to others, and to the possessor.

The contrast between Turm and Mai is limned most obviously in a number of confrontations between them in which the comic book panel shows only their eyes, through which their psychic energy is focussed. Turm's eyes are pale and heavily lashed, with sultry curved eyebrows. Mai's eyes, although still quite Western in appearance, are darker, with straight thick eyebrows, and seem to gaze out at the reader in a more direct and honest way. Clearly, Turm is meant to be somehow demonic, a dangerous representative of Western Otherness while Mai, even while exercising her powers, remains wholesome, and reassuringly "Japanese".[10]

It is also interesting to compare Mai with another Western "psychic girl", the heroine of Stephen King's horror classic, *Carrie* (1974). The moody, adolescent protagonist of King's novel would also very much like to be "normal", despite her frightening telekinetic powers, but the novel's tragic structure, and perhaps more realistic vision, does not allow for such a fairytale form of closure. Instead, Carrie is increasingly provoked by her sadistic classmates to the point where she destroys them all in a bloody telekinetic massacre on Prom Night, proving, once and for all, that "normality" is not an easy goal.

While the American psychic girl ultimately acknowledges her difference in an orgy of blood, Mai steadfastly believes that her psychic powers do not really cause a rift between her and the rest of society. This somewhat unrealistically optimistic vision is in some ways the mirror image of *Vampire Girl*, where the isolation inherent in difference was firmly emphasized. Mai's story is thus, as I have suggested, the more conservative and more conventional of the two. As such, she allows her readers to play out the favorite adolescent fantasy of psychic empowerment in a fundamentally reassuring form. As opposed to Miyu, Turm, or Carrie, Mai is not really "different". The powers she has seem alien to her personality and she works to contain them within a safe emotional context, one of sympathy and concern for others. Consequently, her powers are ultimately non-threatening, appropriate to the *shôjo* identity which she avidly seeks to embrace.

Face three: *Nausicaä* – from flying girl to flying woman?

Psychic stories are incredibly popular among Japanese *shôjo manga* readers. Indeed, while readership of *shôjo manga* has recently fallen overall, interest in the sub-categories of fantasy, suspense and horror has become increasingly prominent (Otsuka 1991: 53). Other kinds of empowerment, beyond the psychic, exist as well. One of the best examples of a truly "empowered" female is Hayao Miyazaki's heroine Nausicaä.

Nausicaä, the eponymous protagonist of our third text possesses elements of the self-sacrificing sexlessness of Mai, but combines them with an active and resolute personality to create a remarkably powerful and yet fundamentally feminine heroine. By far the most complex and imaginative of the works profiled here, the *manga* itself is an entertaining and engrossing fantasy which genuinely deserves the description Tolkien-esque. Set in a dystopian far future where the earth has decayed almost entirely, due to the noxious poisons in the air, *Nausicaä* is an allegory of post-nuclear disaster which still manages to be not oppressively moralizing or grim.[11]

Part of its appeal is undoubtably in the refreshing steadfastness with which the work's protagonist, Nausicaä, confronts this grim future world. A young princess, daughter of the King of the Valley of Winds, a pastoral world still untainted by the miasma of corruption from outside, Nausicaä is a complex and appealing heroine. She is first shown as a brilliant air warrior, able to ride the winds above her poisonous world on a small craft she calls a *maeve*. She is also an excellent swordswoman and is willing to shed blood, if absolutely necessary. But Nausicaä's skills are not only military; she also displays scientific acumen in the experiments she performs with vegetation from the poisonous forest, in an attempt to find a way to escape from the steadily encroaching poisonous miasma.

Despite these intellectual and physical accomplishments, usually the mark of the male in more conventional fantasies, Nausicaä is also extremely feminine, although with the requisite *shôjo* sexlessness. Thus, at one point she is shown comforting the children of the Valley of Winds in an overtly maternal fashion, while at other times she makes clear her horror of unnecessary bloodshed. Nausicaä, in fact, appears to lack any dark side which might make her personality more interesting to older readers. Compared, however, to the rather one-dimensional heroines of many Disney animations, (with the exception, perhaps, of the resolute Belle of *Beauty and the Beast*), she adds up to an impressive feminine role model.[12] Perhaps most interesting in terms of feminine empowerment, are two related aspects of Nausicaä's personality or powers. The first is her extraordinary, almost telepathic, ability with animals and insects, an ability which stands her in good stead in the post-holocaust world where insects have grown gigantic and threaten to take over the earth.

Thus, some of the work's most powerful scenes revolve around Nausicaä's ability to turn back a threatened invasion of Omu, gigantic insects whose movements could ultimately destroy the world. Nausicaä overcomes this problem without violence, through a combination of empathy and strategy. Unlike the male protagonists, she talks to the

Omu, apologizing for any anger they may feel, and trying to make them want to turn back of their own accord.

In the climactic scene of the *anime* version, Nausicaä is successful in turning back the Omu and saving her fellow humans from destruction, but only at what initially appears to be the cost of her life. This brings me to the second aspect of Nausicaä's personality, which is her consistent willingness to give everything of herself for others. Although utterly brave and willing to go where no man or woman has gone before, Nausicaä is also totally self-sacrificing; in a significant early scene, for example, she makes friends with a small fox-squirrel by letting it bite her and patiently bearing the pain and blood, until it realizes that she is not hostile. In other scenes she is shown as consistently willing to risk her life for anyone from her valley and in the video she is, of course, shown as happily sacrificing herself for the good of the human race. Indeed, in both comic and *anime* there is an explicit equation of Nausicaä with a godlike figure from ages past who will come to save the world.

Nausicaä is seen as having virtually godlike powers, as do Mai and Miyu. However, Nausicaä's powers are viewed in very different ways from those of the other two characters. First, they are consistently used for the common good in a way that Miyu's vampirism and Mai's destructive telekinesis could never be. Secondly, and perhaps more interestingly, it is obvious that Nausicaä is comfortable with and even thoroughly enjoys her powers. Unlike the *shôjo* in the other works, being "different" is shown as being "better", not only from the point of view of society, but from one's own perspective as well.

By Western standards, Nausicaä may not be seen as a totally liberated heroine. She fights in a man's world, but uses men's weapons only as a last resort, preferring the softer arts of persuasion and gentle reproof. But this aspect of her persona is not necessarily a negative one. Indeed compared to the "women warriors" of Western popular culture hits such as *Alien, Superwoman* and *Sheena*, where women are "liberated" in terms of the fact that they are given equal opportunities (Kellner 1992: 155), Nausicaä comes across as a far more positive role model.

Furthermore, although her personality may seem somewhat cloying, she more than holds her own in terms of independence and initiative even when compared with such equivalent Western heroines as Belle in *Beauty and the Beast* and Ariel in *The Little Mermaid*. She resembles both of these Disney heroines in that Nausicaä is motherless and deeply attached to her father, an almost archetypal element of the female protagonist in many fairy tales. But, unlike the traditional fairy tale structure in which both *Little Mermaid* and *Beauty and the Beast* partake, Nausicaä's story is not that of replacing one father figure for another. Instead, her tale conforms remarkably well to the traditional male protagonist's quest for identity (the *Bildungsroman*). Nausicaä's journey is a spiritual one, but it is also a journey outward, a quest into self-discovery that is both traditional and excitingly different.[13]

In this regard, the motif of flying is an interesting one. Although it may be coincidental, the "flying woman" (*tonde iru onna*) became a popular image in the early 1980s, exactly the time when Nausicaä was being written. The image originated in Erica Jong's best-selling novel about female sexual emancipation, *Fear of Flying* (1973), but in Japan the expression soon picked up overtones of more general independence and autonomy. Thus, Nausicaä is certainly not sexually empowered, but there is a strong suggestion in the work that flying is indeed a coded expression for psychic freedom, a metaphorical leap towards independence that only fantasy can illustrate effectively.

Face four: *Sailor Moon*

The fantasy element, both in terms of wish fulfillment and in terms of setting, is prominent in *Sailor Moon* (*Sērā mūn*), the last text to be discussed here. A broadly comic adventure story revolving around a group of junior high school girls with fantastic powers, *Sailor Moon* differs from the previous three texts in two important ways. First it was created in the 1990s and thus embodies some of the changes that have occurred in depictions of women in general in *manga* over the last few years. Second, it is more oriented toward the young child than the other three *manga* were. In fact, in its animated form as a popular television series, *Sailor Moon* seemed strongly oriented towards *selling* series-related products to the young child, thus making it also the most overtly commercial of all the works discussed.

In regard to the first difference, *Sailor Moon* seems to pick up on a number of trends of the early nineties. One is what Otsuka (1991) characterizes as a loss of "interiority" on the part of *shōjo manga* overall. The characters have much less of the psychological depth of Mai or Nausicaä, or even Miyu, a loss which is replaced by an emphasis on sheer narrative pace. Thus, none of the "Sailor Scouts" (as they are called in the English language version) have any time to agonize over their strange powers. They are far too busy saving the world from a group of non-human evil-doers or finding boyfriends for themselves and their friends, or both. This combination of an essentially pre-pubescent romantic strain with a basic fantasy action drama is amusing, if somewhat incongruous. To an adult reader/viewer the girls' lack of appreciation of their marvelous powers can be frustrating.

What they lack in psychological depth, however, the Sailor Scouts more than make up for in action adventure. Precisely because they no longer hesitate or agonize, the series is able to show them in a variety of active and, arguably, powerful stances. Since this is a children's *manga*, the plots are relatively simple, but they do usually involve the Sailor Scouts changing from typical schoolgirls into energetic and successful fantasy warriors. In this regard, they echo an important trend in adult fantasy *manga* in which heroines such as Angel Alita or the females in *Project A-ko* or the protagonist of *Ghost in the Shell* are powerful, independent and often extraordinarily violent fighters.

The commercial/child-oriented aspect of *Sailor Moon* also makes an important contrast to the other works discussed here. Although *Nausicaä* had commercial tie-ins as well, both the volume and variety of *Sailor Moon* products advertised on the Japanese version of the television show are mind-boggling. Most important of the products are the Sailor Moon dolls. Although in both the comic and the animated version the Sailor Scouts are given differing personalities (brainy Sailor Mars versus klutzy Sailor Moon, for example), the dolls subsume differences of character into differences of hairstyle and fashion.[14] Furthermore, both dolls and *manga* heroines are characterized at least as much by their fantasy accoutrements, such as Sailor Moon's "moon wand" (available for purchase of course) than for any psychological or intellectual traits; in this fashion they are the female counterparts to the toys described by Gill in Chapter 2.

The combination of dolls with fantasy technology returns us to the image of the "cyborg woman" which has risen to such prominence in the 1990s. These aggressive, violent, often quite dominating women (including the young girls of *Sailor Moon*) are an impressive contrast to the stereotypical image of passive Japanese womanhood that has existed for so long. And yet it must be said that they are far less interesting as characters than the heroines of the eighties discussed in the first part of this chapter. Although this undoubtably suggests that Japanese women in reality are becoming increasingly outwardly active and assertive, it also suggests that this change is accompanied by a loss of interior complexity, a change which some might lament.

Furthermore, the relationship between women and technology problematized in the figure of the cyborg woman is also a provocative one. Where in most cultures, women and technology have long been seen as having an antithetical relationship, this recent trend is almost a celebration of woman in combination with the machine. Newitz has explored this trend and suggested that "(f)emale bodies are therefore best suited to *mecha* ... precisely because it is related to reproduction and giving birth" (1995: 9). Although this is a fascinating hypothesis, I find the image of Nausicaä working both with technology and her own intuitive powers to be a more inspiring one.

Conclusion

Disturbing though the cyborg trend may be, it still seems clear that it is in science fiction and fantasy that we can find some of the most exciting and creative explorations of the female in Japanese society. Indeed, it is interesting that the non-fantastic *manga* aimed at older female readers seem to be far less inventive and imaginative than the *shôjo* fantasies. Although an increasing number of *manga* highlight what might be called "career women" stories, the grown-up women characters in these texts are infinitely more prosaic. Thus, the popular series *Hotel*, which features an attractive unmarried female doctor, dwells as much on the minute details of her professional career as on her dreams or romances, and certainly does not allow the character any romantic flights of fancy. Obviously, these career women *manga* perform a useful function in exploring some of the real-life problems of the contemporary Japanese woman, but they are less narratively exciting than the fantastic *manga*, since they do not really take advantage of any of the possibilities of the *manga* format.

It is also interesting to note that there seem to be relatively few *manga* concerning middle-aged women or mothers in contemporary Japan. Indeed, the most popular *manga* mother, the gently humorous Sazaesan, dates back to the 1950s. It is possible that mothers are the section of the population with the least time to read *manga* and therefore there is less likely to be innovation in any work directed at them. But it is also possible to speculate that is the role of mothers, even more than *shôjo*, that is still frozen in time in Japan.[15]

Intriguingly, it is only with late middle age and old age that *manga* representations of women seem to regain some of their former vigor. For example, the inventively nasty figure of *Ijiwaru bâsan* (*Naughty Granny*) is still quite popular. Even more entertaining, in a scurrilous sort of way, is the *Obatarian* series, an extremely funny and quite vicious parody of women of late middle age. Represented as four panel slices of life of the Obatalian (a pun based on "*zombies*" and "*old women*"), a supposedly neutral commentary describes such "typical" middle-aged women's activities as the ceaseless and vicious pursuit for respect, consumer goods, and a place to sit down on a train. *Obatalian* is inventive satire which reaches a kind of parodic hyperreality, a grotesque world in which all middle-aged women poke at all vegetables all the time. While funny and original, therefore, it is arguable that the series in some ways limits rather than expands female horizons.

And yet, it must be said that the Obatalian, despite their cantankerousness and narrowness are still both vigorous and vivid. One may deplore their stereotyping, but at the same time one cannot help

admitting that all aspects of the female persona have a far wider play in
Japanese popular culture than they do in the West. In particular, the
varied combinations of psychic powers and femininity which we have
discussed in this chapter seem to offer some intriguing alternatives to
Western fantasy females, suggesting, at least in Nausicaä's case, that
empowerment and femininity can come in many forms.

Notes

1 Or, as Glenwood Irons puts it later in the same introduction, "The study of
   popular literature is as useful and interesting as the study of the literary
   canon – perhaps because pop narrative readily panders to the masses with
   sensationalism, sexual titillation, fantasy and improbable adventure"
   (xxviii).
2 A translation of *Beryusai no bara* (*The Rose of Versailles*) and a brief biography
   of Riyoko Ikeda may be found in F. Schodt (1983).
3 This is not, obviously, a purely Japanese association. For examples of
   analyses of the female and occult powers in Western literature see, for
   example, Freud (1919), Rosemary Jackson (1981) and Kathryn Hume
   (1984).
4 See Chapter 3 for an analysis of how some young men choose identities in
   postmodern Japan.
5 See Chapters 6 and 10 for a discussion of young women as consumers.
6 Interestingly, I have yet to find any examples in either high or popular
   culture of male Japanese vampires. This may have to do with the logical
   association of women with blood which I come to later, or it may also be
   related to the traditionally female vampires of Western literature. But it is
   also arguable that vampire-esque creatures in traditional Japanese culture
   have been female as well. The most obvious example of this sort is the
   yukio-nna, or snow woman, who sucks the life out of travelers lost in the
   snow. Other, more literary manifestations, might include the woman in
   Izumi Kyoka's fantasy classic *Koya hijiri* (1990). Although she turns men into
   beasts rather than suck the blood out of them, she is implicitly associated
   with leeches, creatures whose actions of penetration and subsequent blood-
   sucking clearly mimic those of the vampire. More recently the *junbungaku*
   (pure literature) writer Kurahashi Yumiko has written a clever satire, *The
   Vampire Club* (*Bampiru no kai*), in which a group of modish female vampires
   meet once a month at a fashionable French restaurant where they drink
   blood red wine in a private room. At one point they are so overcome with
   the attractiveness of the restaurant's handsome male waiter that they end
   up attacking him and sucking his blood in an appropriately vampire-like
   fashion. In this work Kurahashi seems to be both satirizing women's
   sexuality and the omnivorous consumption of goods that highlighted the
   1980s.
7 This scene reminds me fascinatingly of a scene from the turn-of-the-century
   classic *Sanshirô* (1909) by Soseki Natsume, one of Japan's greatest writers.
   In this scene, an older man dreams a dream of his youth in which a girl he
   once loved appears to him, completely unchanged, as if in a painting.

When he asks her why she has not changed, she explains that this was her favorite time, the time when she first met him. He, on the other hand, acknowledges that he "must go on changing". At the end as they part, he tells her "you are a painting", and she tells him, "you are a poem". Although *Sanshiro* was written decades before *Vampire Princess*, the desire to keep the woman the same, as a kind of oasis of security in a constantly changing world, is expressed in both works. The main difference between the two is that in *Vampire Princess* this desire is now treated, on the part of the female characters at least, with ambivalence and even resistance.

8   In another scene between Miyu and a female school chum who offers her neck for Miyu's delectation, the lesbian sub-text seems quite obvious.

9   The polluting power of blood, and especially menstrual blood, is well documented for pre-modern Japan (see, for example, Smyers 1983 and Yoshida 1990).

10 The negative portrayal of Turm is particularly interesting when we consider how, even today in Japan, Westerners are still often portrayed as attractive, superior Others. This is especially true in more conventional *shôjo manga* which abound in Western-looking characters with huge, dewy eyes and long blond hair. The aforementioned mega-hit, *The Rose of Versailles*, is a particularly good example of idealized Western Otherness, holding up the eighteenth-century French court as a model of beauty and exotic fascination. In contrast Turm is the exotic Other represented negatively: an overbearing, overaggressive and dangerous fish out of water.

Interestingly, *Psychic Girl* also contains a portrait of a mixed-up American psychic boy whom Mai regretfully has to destroy, and a young Vietnamese psychic boy who ultimately turns against the Alliance in order to help Mai, impressed by her kindness and gentleness. This use of an international cast of dysfunctional psychic characters further works to reinforce Mai's basic wholesomeness and superiority.

11 At the same time, it might also be mentioned that in contrast to *Akira* (Chapter 3), Nausicaä's "world" is a remarkably organic, even perhaps, feminine one. The organic structures of the forest she explores, and the shifting amorphous quality of the clouds through which she makes her way, are all beautifully presented and strangely attractive. More than either of the other two heroines, Nausicaä *belongs* in her world, dystopian though it technically is.

12 In fact it could be said that Nausicaä has a "dark side" in the form of Princess Kushana, a doppelgänger, who first appears making war on the innocent people of the Valley of Wind. Like Nausicaä, Kushana is highly intelligent and a superb military strategist. Unlike Nausicaä, however, Kushana is presented without any alleviating "feminine" virtues, such as compassion or sympathy, and in the animated version of the work, she comes across as a clichéd villainess. The book version of *Nausicaä*, however, allows for a more complex and sympathetic, perhaps even genuinely "feminist" representation of Kushana. Thus, in various flashbacks, the reader learns that Kushana is the only surviving child of her father the king's first wife. Although her mother is still alive, she has been rendered insane by drinking a cup of poison meant for Kushana.

Kushana herself lives in daily fear of more plots against her and, as a result, has been forced to develop an aggressively hard exterior, particularly in dealing with her male rivals. It would be interesting to see how the "intellectual" Kushana's character develops throughout the story but unfortunately we can only speculate. As it is, Kushana shows signs of being a particularly interesting female character.

13   It is interesting that the heroine of one of Japan's first fairy tales, the shining princess of *Taketori Monogatari* (*The Tale of the Bamboo Cutter*) also ends up taking a journey outwards, or rather upwards, to the moon, leaving behind her both her grieving parents and her grieving suitors. But an even closer parallel to Nausicaä exists. The creator of Nausicaä has himself mentioned his indebtedness to another early Japanese folktale, *The Lady Who Loves Insects*, an unusual story about an independent young woman who horrifies the court by her love of insects.

14   Compare this with the Oguricap toys in Chapter 9, which, as Nagashima notes, while similar, allow their female owners to imbue them with individualized qualities which reflect various women's needs.

15   Or is it that motherhood is being viewed with increasing negativity? Although I do not have enough material on this to assert a trend, I would like to mention one particularly negative portrayal of motherhood in another occult *manga*, *Devil Hunter Yoko*. In this popular *anime* the grandmother and granddaughter, Yoko, are seen aligned against the aggressively careerist, modern mother. It is only the grandmother and Yoko, the film implies, who understand the real importance of tradition, in terms of demon hunting, at least.

References

Auerbach, Nina 1995 *Our Vampires, Ourselves*. Chicago, University of Chicago Press.

Freud, S. 1919 *Totem and Taboo: Resemblances between the psychic lives of savages and neurotics*, trans by A. A. Brill. London: G. Routledge.

Hume, Kathryn 1984 *Fantasy and Mimesis, responses to reality in western literature*. New York: Methuen.

Ikeda Riyoko 1972–74 *The Rose of Versailles*.

Irons, Glenwood 1992 "Introduction" in his edited *Gender, Language and Myth: Essays on popular narrative*. Toronto: University of Toronto Press.

Izumi Kyoka 1990 *Kôya Hijiri* (*The Saint of Mount Koya*), trans. by Stephen W. Kohl. Kanazawa: Izumi Kyoka Sakuhin Honyaku Shuppankai.

Jackson, Rosemary 1981 *Fantasy: The literature of subversion*. London: Methuen.

Jong, Erica 1973 *Fear of Flying*. New York: Signet.

Kellner, D. 1992 "Popular culture and the construction of postmodern identities" in *Modernity and Identity* edited by S. Lash and J. Friedman, Oxford: Blackwell.

King, Stephen 1974 *Carrie*. London: New English Library.

Kurahashi Yumiko 1985 "*Bampiru no kai*" (*The Vampire Club*) in *Kurahashi Yumiko no Kaikishohen*. Tokyo: Kodansha.

Lash, Scott and Friedman, Jonathan 1992 "Introduction" to their edited *Modernity and Identity*. Oxford: Blackwell.

Lent, John 1989 "Japanese Comics" in *Handbook of Japanese Popular Culture* edited by R. Powers and H. Kato. Westport, Conn: Greenwood Press.

Napier, Susan 1981 (April) "*Burikko to tonde iru onna: Nihon no josei no futatsu no mujunteki na imeji*" in *Asahi Business*.

——1993 "Panic Sites: The Japanese imagination of disaster from *Godzilla* to *Akira*" in *Contemporary Japan and Popular Culture* edited by J. Treat. Honolulu: University of Hawaii Press.

Newitz, A. 1995 "Magical Girls and Atomic Bomb Sperm: Japanese Animation in America" in *Film Quarterly*. Dec. 1–15, p. 9.

Oba Minako 1976 *Yamauba no bishô* (*Smiles of the Mountain Witch*).

Oe Kenzaburo 1989 "Japan's Dual Identity: A writer's lament" in *Postmodernism and Japanese Culture* edited by Najita and Miyoshi. Duke University Press.

Otsuka Eiji 1991 "*Naimen no soshitsu e kaiki*" in *Imago* vol. 2(10): 48–54.

Sabin, Roger 1993 *Adult Comics*. London: Routledge.

Schodt, F. 1983 *Manga! Manga! The world of Japanese Comics*. Tokyo: Kodansha.

Smyers, Karen A. 1983 "Women and Shinto: The relations between purity and pollution" in *Japanese Religions* 12(4): 7–18.

Soseki Natsume 1909 "Sanshiro" in *Soseki Zenchô*, vol. 4. Tokyo: Iwanami Shôten.

Treat, John Whittier 1993 "Yoshimoto Banana Writes Home: Shôjo culture and the nostalgic subject" in *Journal of Japanese Studies*, vol. 19(2): 353–88.

Yoshida Teigo 1990 "The feminine in Japanese folk religion: Polluted or divine" in *Unwrapping Japan* edited by Eyal Ben-Ari et al. Manchester: Manchester University Press.

CHAPTER 6

Japanese Women's Magazines
the language of aspiration

KEIKO TANAKA

Introduction

A strong unifying theme that runs through Japanese women's magazines is the prescriptive approach which they adopt towards their readers. This is much more striking than the attention to detail in features which Shimanaka Yukio (n.d.) notes, or the descriptive and pedestrian list of characteristics common to magazines in general which Kawai Ryosuke provides (1987). In this chapter special attention will be paid to linguistic questions, the frequency of certain expressions, keywords, and so forth. It is hoped that by examining these aspects of magazines for young women light can be shed on the contemporary lifestyles and aspirations of these women in Japan.

Women's magazines

Japanese women's magazines have changed greatly in character during this century. According to Shimanaka (n.d.) the first of six distinct periods, which spanned the years from 1900 to the end of the Second World War, was represented by monthly magazines such as *Fujin Gahô* (*Illustrated Women's Gazette* 1905), *Fujin Kôron* (*Women's Opinion* 1916), *Shufu* (*Housewife*), and *Shufu no Tomo* (*Housewife's Friend* 1917), *Fujin Kurabu* (*Women's Club* 1920) and *Sôen* (*Jardin de Mode* 1926). The principal policy common to these five magazines was "enlightened educationalism", expressed through essays on subjects such as "women's liberation", "liberalism" and the "attainment of female suffrage".[1]

The second period extended only from 1946 to the first half of the 1950s, when Japan experienced rapid economic recovery after defeat in the Second World War, partly due to the Korean War. *Shufu to Seikatsu* (*Housewives and Life* 1946), *Fujin Seikatsu* (*Women's Life* 1946), *Doresu*

110

Mêkingu (*Dressmaking* 1950) represent this period. In contrast with the theoretically inclined approaches taken by the earlier magazines, the new ones focussed on providing practical advice on various aspects of household-management, with an increasing use of photography. The "Big Four" in women's magazines were *Shufu to Seikatsu* and *Fujin Seikatsu*, together with *Shufu no Tomo* and *Fujin Kurabu*, survivors from the pre-war period (Koide 1992: 85).

Continuing economic growth marked the second half of the 1950s through to the late 1960s, and this third era witnessed the launch of larger women's magazines, which purveyed dreams of a richer life, magazines such as *Katei Gahô* (*Illustrated Home Gazette* 1958), *Misesu* (*Mrs*), *Madamu* (*Madame*), and *Hai Fasshion* (*High Fashion*). Shimanaka points out that foreign titles started to gain popularity around this time. It is worth noting that women's weekly magazines which were "devoted to the quotidian activities of pop stars and actresses" (Tasker 1987: 139) were first published during this era.

Koide contrasts the magazines launched in the first two of Shimanaka's periods and those launched during the third era (1992: 93). The magazines which appeared around 1955, whether theoretical or practical, were about how to be a "good wife and wise mother" (*ryô-sai-ken-bo*), whereas the magazines introduced later showed readers how to enjoy life. He neatly highlights the contrast by pointing out that while those in the first category typically carried features on how to make dresses, the later ones emphasise buying them.

Shimanaka's fourth period begins in the 1970s, when Japan went through a time of high economic growth. This period saw the launch of magazines such as *An An, Non-No, MORE,* and *Croissant;* these magazines, particularly *An An* and *Non-No,* are characterized by features not only relating to fashion, but also to tourism and food. He notes that titles using foreign words became even more popular, with a wider range of European languages being used. Koide marks the 1970s as the beginning of the consumer culture in Japan (1992: 92). The number of women going out to work increased dramatically and women's disposable income grew with it.

Koide further notes that the 1970s was the era when traditional categories for women began to break down. He claims that there were no longer dichotomies between the ideas and lifestyles of married women and unmarried women, working women and housewives, women who lived in metropolitan centers and those who lived in the provinces. The fact that social class is not mentioned by Koide, in common with other writers on this topic, may indicate a belief in the essential homogenization of Japan's population in terms of income and related phenomena.

In this new context, *Croissant,* launched in April 1977, was the first of a set of "new family magazines". The term "new family", first used by Marui, a money-lending company, in its advertising campaign, referred to the generation born after the war, the "baby boom generation" (*dankai no sedai*). The members of this generation were then in their late twenties and were expected to form a new kind of family, undifferentiated according to geographical origin or marital status. Publishers catering to women in their late twenties and early thirties therefore launched a variety of magazines with expensive publicity campaigns. After *Croissant* (Heibon Publishers) came *MORE* (Shuei Limited), *Angle* (Shufu to Seikatsu Limited), and *Aruru,* in rapid succession.

However, the last two magazines were discontinued within a year and a half and Koide (1992) suggests that this was because the definitions of the target audiences were too "vague". He further observes that those magazines which managed to keep going, notably *Croissant* and *MORE,* did so by changing their style. This explanation is somewhat lame. It can be argued that the attempt on the part of the publishers to cater for a newly uniform market was based on false premises. Traditional categories relating to women may well have been changing, but new cleavages were appearing, making the market *more* rather than *less* differentiated.

For his part, Shimanaka argues that *Croissant* represented a second wave of feminism which emerged in the second half of the 1970s. The expression "flying woman", derived from the title of the American best-seller *Fear of Flying* by Erica Jong, was frequently used by the media around this time to refer to unmarried, career-minded women (*kyaria ûman*). *Croissant,* in particular, is regarded as having encouraged such women. But J. Matsubara, in *Croissant shôkôgun* (*Croissant Syndrome*) (1988), considered that these were not independent women, but rather "lonely, middle-aged, unmarried women". In other words, the failure of this new kind of magazine may also be attributed to the publishers accepting exaggerated claims of a new feminism.

The fifth period of magazine development, from 1980 to 1985, is noted for the launch of Japanese editions of Western magazines such as *Cosmopolitan* in 1980, and both *Elle* and *Marie Claire* in 1982 (Shimanaka n.d.). The Japanese titles published during these years include *25 ans* (1980), *Lee* (1983), *ViVi* (1983), *Classy* (1984), *Sophia* (1984), *Éf* (1984), all with European-sounding titles. Shimanaka notes that a characteristic of this period is the emergence of market segmentation according to the age of the target audience. Perhaps the publishers had learned their lesson in the earlier years and were better prepared to cater for various niches in the market.

The last period in Shimanaka's schema covers 1985 to 1989. These years, he argues, are first characterized by the launch of magazines – namely *Orange Page* (1986) and *Lettuce Club* (1986) – published by retailers, such as Daiei and Seiyu, and sold through their supermarket outlets. They tended to be cheaper than their competitors (both retailing at 200 yen as of June 1994). Second, they focussed on practical information to do with running a household, rather like the magazines which emerged after the Second World War. They were a major threat to the existing, general magazines for housewives. Indeed *Fujin Seikatsu* and *Fujin Kurabu* were discontinued, the former in 1987 and the latter in 1988 (Kindai Josei Bunka-shi Kenkyû-kai 1989: 1).

The second notable event in the last period in Shimanaka's scheme was the emergence of a new magazine entitled *Hanako*. This magazine provided information on shops, restaurants and theatres in the Tokyo area and was sold exclusively in the metropolitan area. It could thus be said to be the equivalent of London's *Time Out*, but *Hanako* is specifically intended for women, as its title suggests, for Hanako is a popular girl's name.

The contemporary mass market for magazines

In this last period, the importance of magazines within Japan's publishing industry as a whole has never been greater. According to Kiyota, the key phrase which describes the current state of the Japanese publishing world, one of the world's largest, is "magazine high; book low" (*zak-kô-sho-tei*) (1987: 154). While sales of books have fallen since 1945, sales of magazines have continued to rise. Since the beginning of the 1980s the magazine turnover has constantly exceeded that of books, and the gap has grown steadily. As many as thirteen hundred new magazines were launched or re-launched between 1980 and 1985.[2]

Kiyota points to the parallel growth in popularity of pocket-size books, paperbacks and comic strips (1987: 136). Major publishers in Japan produce series in pocket-sized paperbacks (*bunko-shinsho*), such as the *Iwanami Bunko* and *Iwanami Shinsho* series, which, according to Bowring and Kornicki (1993), constitute about half of all books published. The 1984 edition of the *Publishing Year Book* talks of publishing as going through a "*bunko* boom". Various series of new "cultural paperbacks" (*kyôyô shinsho*) were launched in 1996, representing the "magazinisation" of the publishing industry.[3]

Kiyota (1987) explains the background to magazines of these years (*zasshi no jidai*) by saying that people in general, and the young in particular, prefer magazines to books. Magazines are described as "light-hearted", whereas books are "stifling" (*katakurushii*).[4] Winship cites Moore on the accessibility of magazines over books:

Unlike books, magazines can be used in a whole number of ways – there is no
correct order we have to follow in order to obtain meaning. (1992: 96–7)

Kiyota (1987) goes on to argue that these phenomena reflect "the age of
'light, thin, short, small'" (*kei-haku-tan-shô jidai*), when things which can
be described in these terms are preferred to those described as "heavy,
thick, long, and big". In contrast, Kawai stresses that magazines are large
(1987: 155), but it could be argued that size and thickness are not so
significant, as long as they are light-hearted in approach.

Kawai (1987) contends that the success of magazines over books is
due not only to popular demand, but also to the strategies of publishers
and their advertisers. For a publishing company, popular magazines are
particularly attractive because of advertising fees. For advertisers,
magazines are a desirable medium in an age when interests have become increasingly diversified and markets, in consequence, ever more
segmented. Magazines have the further advantage for publishers that
income from sales is more regular and predictable than that from
books.

Koide argues that the increased advertising content is the result
of severe competition amongst magazines (1992). There was a rush to
launch new weekly magazines in the late 1950s and the market continued to grow more competitive in the 1960s, particularly for women's
magazines. They became larger and thicker and, with a higher proportion of color pages, production costs increased. At the same time,
marketing costs also rose, due to severe competition. Faced with these
costs, the publishers sought to increase advertising revenue.

It was thus during the 1970s that the advertisement content increased
drastically: by 1979 the total number of advertisements in the main 78
magazines exceeded a hundred thousand pages (Koide 1992). Koide
also notes that the Heibon Publishers (today known as Magazine House)
set this trend by launching *An An* in 1970. *An An*'s success was followed
by that of *Non-No*, published by Shuei Limited in 1971. Shufu to Seikatsu
Limited then brought out *Junon* in 1973, followed by Kobun Limited's *JJ*
in 1975. Between 1976 and 1985, advertising revenue grew 2.46 times,
while that from the sale of magazines grew only 1.86 times. Of the total
revenue of magazines, income from advertising was 12.7 per cent in 1976
and 16.25 per cent in 1985. Thus we can see that the dependency of
magazine publishers on advertisements has grown significantly.

This trend accords with Bestor's claim that "most forms of popular
culture are associated with commercialized mass production and
consumption" (1989: 2). The lifestyle of the 1980s which Bestor describes is crystallized in the novel *Nantonaku kurisutaru* (*Somewhat Crystal*)
by Tanaka Yasuo (1981) which depicts the lives of the young and

comfortably-off residents of Tokyo, who have since been nick-named the "crystal tribe" (*kurisutaru-zoku*). Bestor (1989) remarks on Tanaka's 442 footnotes which identify food, drink, clothes, sports equipment, and other consumer goods, for the benefit of unfamiliar readers.[5] Other studies of 1980s consumerism in Japan reinforce this picture of increased consumption (see Field 1983 and 1989). There is thus a clear relationship between the "pervasive middle-class affluence of the 1980s" (Bestor 1989: 12) and changing trends in magazines which need to be further explored.

Contemporary women's magazines

This section focusses on magazines for young women which put the emphasis on fashion, gourmet food, travel and romance. Six women's magazines have been selected for analysis: *An An, Non-No, JJ, MORE, 25 ans* and *With*. Except for *An An*, which is published weekly and *Non-No* which comes out fortnightly, these are monthly magazines. They were all launched between 1970 and 1981 and they have survived successfully to date, despite a rush of new publications in the 1980s. Their print run ranges from 180,000 (*25 ans*) to 1,300,000 copies (*Non-No*), the total monthly print run of the six magazines coming to over 7.6 million copies.

These six magazines share the five points which Kawai lists as common to today's magazines in Japan; they are large (indeed generally larger than their Western counterparts);[6] their visual aspect is important; they have foreign-sounding titles;[7] they are a major advertising medium; and their focus is on consumerism, hedonism, and practical matters (1987: 155). The table below indicates the percentage of the total number of pages dedicated to advertisements:

Proportion of Advertisements in Selected Magazines[8]

Magazine	1980	1986
An An	48.0%	54.4%
Non-No	40.2%	39.4%
MORE	38.1%	37.0%
With	36.7% (1983)	37.2%
25 ans	15.5% (1983)	24.6%
JJ	n.a.	42.4%*

Source: Koide 1992:106; except for * which is from Inoue et al. 1989: 51

In a study of British magazines, Ellen McCracken (1993) asserts that it is important to both publishers and advertisers that part of the latter should be disguised so that magazines appear to have a balance between advertising and editorial matter. This assertion is somewhat undermined, however, by her claim that the publishers of *Vogue* consider that most of their readers buy their magazine primarily to read the advertisements. McCracken further argues for the importance of "covert advertising" which is defined as "promotions disguised as editorial material or hidden in some other form so that they appear to be non-advertising", as opposed to advertisements which are "overt" and "purchased" (1993: 38–40). Since covert advertising is not paid for by the advertisers it is not accounted for in the figures for advertising content.

In Japanese women's magazines, Koide (1992) claims, crucial to the dramatic increase in advertising content is what have become known as "tie-up" advertisements which are paid for by the advertisers, and are thus included in the advertising content figures given above. Koide also notes that publishers assert that contemporary readers are not "allergic" to advertisements and that they recognise "tie-up" material as such. Koide questions this, but does not pursue the matter.

The target audience of these magazines varies slightly, notably in terms of age, which accords with corporate strategies dividing the market into segments which are accommodated by different magazines published by the same company. For example, according to *Zasshi shimbun sô katarogu 1984* (*Comprehensive Catalogue of Magazines and Newspapers 1984*), 88 per cent of *An An*'s readership is between 16 and 25 years old, with 43 per cent in the 16–20 bracket, and 45 per cent between 21 and 25 years. Some 85 per cent of this age group is unmarried. *Non-No* is aimed at a slightly wider range of women, from senior high school students (16 years and upwards) to young housewives. Although this makes the target audience of *An An* and *Non-No* similar, their approach is different, in that *An An* targets readers who "aim to behave as more mature women (*adaruto-shikô*)" (Shu 1984). *JJ* is read by female senior high school students, junior college and university students, as well as "office ladies". *MORE*'s target readership is women in their 20s. *With* is more specific, aiming at women between 23 and 28. *25 ans*, as its title suggests, target women around the age of 25.[9]

These magazines, notably *An An* and *Non-No*, have been held responsible for an increase in domestic and overseas travel among women, giving rise to the term *An-Non zoku* (Shimanaka n.d.). When *An An* and *Non-No* were launched (in 1970 and 1971 respectively) it was usual for a magazine to carry detailed illustrated tourist maps of such cities as Kyoto, the old Japanese capital, and Karuizawa, a summer resort. Around 1975, they started doing the same for foreign cities such as

London, Paris and New York. It is not clear, however, whether the magazines were a cause of the travel boom among young women, or whether they were simply responding to increased demand. However, there is no denying that the timing coincided with a rapid increase of the number of Japanese going overseas. In 1970 the number of people travelling abroad was only 0.7 million; in 1975 it rose to nearly 2.5 million, and in 1990 and 1991 there were more than 10 million a year (Nikon Jôhô kyô iku kenkyû-kai 1993).

The above example of changing patterns of travel illustrates the complex relationship between magazine articles and altered lifestyles, and the direction of causality is hard to establish. Other major changes in society, such as the proportion of women in employment and the size of their disposable income, need to be taken into consideration. It may be that Shimanaka, coming from a publishing family and himself a director of a publishing house (Chôûkôron), attributes a greater influence to magazines over people's lives than can be substantiated. It remains, however, of considerable interest to tease out how women's magazines may attempt to influence the lifestyles of their readers.

The prescriptive character of contemporary women's magazines

The prescriptiveness of the language employed in women's magazines is a striking characteristic. The tone of many of the features is blunt and hectoring, a curious point, given the alleged Japanese concern with politeness and the avoidance of confrontation (for instance, Lakoff 1973). Even when not directly ordering readers about, the magazines draw lessons for young women from a surprising variety of events.

By arguing that there is a characteristic common to magazines, I do not intend to suggest homogeneity among magazines or their readership. Homogeneity has been much discussed in the existing literature on Japanese culture, without considering the heterogeneity of the society as noted above.[10] Reischauer (1985) argues that Japanese society shows an "extraordinary cultural homogeneity" and that the mass media and education shape such a mass society. His point is related to television, but the same could be said of magazines which enjoy a wide audience throughout the country. Thus I hope that by examining a feature shared by these magazines, some general strategies in production of this particular form of popular culture will emerge.

The core of my argument is that these magazines not only provide detail, but also tell their readers what to do and what not to do. The manner in which this is done could be seen as almost patronizing and condescending. Compared to Japanese features, English equivalents may be similarly detailed but do not have the same prescriptive tone.

Take a feature from *JJ* entitled "Hong Kong: It's heaven sent to the girls" (2/93). The article includes photographs of various shops with comments such as "you are likely to regret it if you do not buy them" (*kawa-nai-to kôkaishi-sô*); "one would definitely want to get at least one item here" (*zettai ichi-mai wa te ni ire-tai*); and "you should definitely want to visit this shop if you go to Hong Kong" (*Honkon ni ittara zehi yori-tai*). In comparison, an English *Elle* feature on a Caribbean holiday entitled "Blazing hot, blazing cheap" is full of details of hotels which it recommends, but the commentary is rather different:

> X was opened 17 years ago by French downhill skier René Danrick, who opted for some winter sun after too much snow. Other hip retreats under the tall palms of Las Terrenas include the Italian-run Y... If you're really in for an adventure, you might take a trip to Haiti [where there are] magnificent gingerbread mansions. One of the finest of these is Z ... (12/92)

This is not to say that prescription is unique to Japanese women's magazines. Angela McRobbie comments specifically on the British magazine *Jackie*:

> ... teenage girls are subjected to an explicit attempt to win consent to the dominant order – in terms of femininity, leisure and consumption, i.e. at the level of culture. (1991: 87)

Winship makes a more general point:

> My own characterization of women's magazines has been that they stand as paternalistic friend to readers but encourage a reader-involvement in which the magazine occupies the authoritative position. (1992: 97)

Conversely, sometimes suggestions are also made in Japanese magazines:

> If you want to be chic, light gray or brown are recommended. [*Shikku-ni suru nara awai gurê ya cha ga o-susume.*] (*Non-No* 9/93)

> We suggest co-ordinating clothes for the new era, appropriately for the present day. [*Gendai ni fusawashii shin-jidai no côdineito o teianshi-masu.*] (*25 ans* 10/93)

> We recommend [the bag] to girls who have a lot to carry. [*Nimotsu ôme-na onnanoko ni o-susume.*] (*JJ* 12/94)

This said, audiences are more often told what to look out for:

> Céline motifs ... it is effective to show them off by using a number of them concentrated around the region of your hands. [*Serînu no mochîfu ... te-moto ni kasane-te miseru no ga kôka-teki.*] (*25 ans* 10/93)

The key is to show a simple and fairly large collar. [*Ôki-me no eri sukkiri miseru no ga kagi desu.*] (*JJ* 4/1993)

The loafers which have been popular all this time cannot be overlooked this season either. [*Zutto ninki no rôfâ wa, kon-shîzun mo minogase-nai.*] (*MORE* 10/93)

Japanese magazines know what is right for their audiences and tell them so in no uncertain terms:

It is good to choose those which are 40–50 denier (thickness of yarn). [*40–50 denîru no mono o erabu to yoi.*] (*MORE* 10/93)

It is desirable to have all four basic items. [*Kono kihon no yottsu wa soroe-tai.*] (*With* May/1993)

This is about the best length for the jacket. [*JK no nagasa wa kore-kurai ga besuto.*] (*JJ* 4/93)

You need two types of shoes. [*Hitsuyôna kutsu wa 2 taipu.*] (*Non-No* 9/93)

These magazines even make up their readers' minds for them:

You no longer want anything less than "cheap and good" clothes. [*Mô 'yasukute ii' fuku shika hoshiku-nai.*] (*Non-No* 20/12/95)

We have decided to have your hair done in a bob next time. [*Kondo no kamigata wa bobu ni kimeta.*] (*With* 5/96)

Although statements of this type translate rather nicely into English, in Japanese they may well be regarded as patronizing. Yet the success of the magazines over the years suggests that their readers do not mind such language. My Japanese informants have told me that the tone has never caused them any annoyance or irritation. They all mention as a reason for buying the magazines that they can expect practical and detailed information on fashion and other related matters.

This raises the question as to where such language might come from, and my suggestion, from the resonance of the language, is that it comes from the authoritarian tone used by Japanese teachers in school. This characteristic is even more marked in the expressions which follow, which rely on the use of familiar phrases from the classroom:

The theme of the second lesson on knitwear is how to improve the neckline ... You must graduate from round collars ... [*Nitto lesson dai-2-kai no têma wa, nekkurain no kakuage no hôhôni tsuite, desu ... Raundokarâ wa sotsugyô-shi-te ...*] (*JJ* 12/94)

The thing is to thoroughly master the two ways of dressing, including the perfect mastery of accessories. [*Komono made kanpeki-ni 2-tsu no kikonashi o tetteiteki-ni masutâsuru.*] (*MORE* 10/93)

What is necessary for casual wear is the law of "spend money on what cannot be seen" [*Kajuaru ni hitsuyôna no wa "urawaza-ritchi no hôsoku" datta.*] (*25 ans* 10/93).

[It] neutralizes the degree of "outdoorness" [of the jacket]. [*Autodoa-do wo chûwasa-semasu.*] (*JJ* 12/94)

A laboratory for trying on brown trousers which make you look thinner. [*Chairo no kiyase pantsu shichaku jikkenshitsu.*] (*Non-No* 20/12/95)

The magazines are keen on grading and they sometimes flatter their audience for following what they say by providing the reader with a kind of ranking:

Please enjoy this fashion, which is superior by one rank. [*Wan-ranku ue no o-share o tanoshin-de-kudasai.*] (*MORE* 10/93)

With these 5-stage lessons, you could become an expert, too! [*Kono 5-dankai no ressun de, anata mo kasanegi no tatsujin ni!*] (*Non-No* 20/9/93)

Those who are in the senior grade could give it a finishing touch with a purple scarf. [*Jôkyûsha wa murasaki no sukâfu de kimeru.*] (*25 ans* 10/93)

The thing is to make sure of this year's color co-ordination. If you clear this hurdle, you will be considerably skilled in layering clothes. [*Kotoshi-rashî iro-awase o, shikkari osaeru koto. Koko o kuria-sure-ba, kanari no kasane-gi jôzu ni.*] (*Non-No* 20/9/93)

In *Non-No* and *JJ* expressions reminiscent of school tests are rife:

You get a circle [for a correct answer] for wearing a long knitted jacket or a waistcoat on top. [*Rongu nitto ya besuto no kasane-gi o suru no ga maru.*] (*Non-No* 20/9/93)

A point worth paying attention to! You get a cross [for a wrong answer] for a soft material. [*Yô-chûi pointo! Kuta-tto shita mono wa batsu.*] (*Non-No* 20/9/93)

Items such as trousers can be used to achieve surprisingly good balance, and wearing them scores high marks. [*Pantsu-nado no botomu wa, igai-to baransu yoku tsukae-te, kô-tokuten.*] (*Non-No* 20/9/93)

This suit is only just a borderline pass mark. [*Kono sûtsu wa girigiri gôkaku kennai.*] (*JJ* 4/93)

As *Non-No* and *JJ* cater for the younger segment of the market, including high school students, the language of exams is obviously more familiar – and perhaps more acceptable – to them than to other audiences.

The language of magazines for young women tends to be fairly colloquial, closer to spoken language than is usually the case in a written text, but similar to the language of cram school (*juku*) textbooks, which are meant to reproduce live lectures; many of these prescriptive expressions in women's magazines are strikingly similar to those used in these textbooks. Cram schools for university entrance examinations are extremely common in Japan, and a high proportion of the readership of the magazines would have attended such institutions. In contrast, textbooks for ordinary schools use more the formal style, typical of written language. Here are some examples from cram school textbooks:

> Check each sentence carefully ... [*Ichi-bun zutsu teinei-ni chekku–* ...]
> It can also be applied to others. [*Ōyō mo kiku no desu.*]
> Unexpectedly, many students have overlooked this. [*Igai-to ōku no seito ga minogashi-te imasu.*]
> (from Ogino 1992)

> You make sure that ... [... *to iu tokoro o osaeru*].
> The coming two months are more important. [*Korekara no 2-ka-getsu no hō ga taisetsu.*]
> (from Akiyama 1987)

> Let's pay attention to ... [... *ni chūmokus-himashō*].
> It is probably good to know (it) as one of the techniques. [*1-tsu no tekunikku toshite shitte oku no mo yoi-de-shō.*]
> What you must be careful about is ... [*Koko de chūisu-beki wa* ...]
> (from Tsuchiya 1989)

Of the three magazines which cater for older women, *25 ans* seems to be particularly prescriptive. It frequently uses the expression *beki* (must), which is not commonly used in polite Japanese, nor is it found in the other magazines considered here. However, *25 ans* uses it frequently, as in:

> When it comes to the color, you must decide on an orthodox gray. [*Iro wa seitō-teki gurē ni suru beki.*] (10/93)

> What we must capture next is a country style. [*Watashi-tachi ga tsugi ni kōryaku-su-beki wa kōgai sutairu.*] (10/93)

This tendency of *25 ans* to be even more prescriptive than other magazines may be related to its main objective, which is expressed as "For nurturing discerning eyes and individuality" (Shu 1984). I have argued elsewhere (Tanaka 1990, 1994) that in Japan individuality (*kosei*) is more about being fashionable and sophisticated than about actually "doing one's own thing".

In their attempt to nurture young women readers, these magazines use imperatives and other prescriptive expressions in a way which is unusual in Japanese society. Even in situations where imperatives are commonly used in English, Japanese equivalents are not:

> Whip the cream until it just holds its shape, then fold into the cheese with the caster sugar. (Wright 1985: 65)

> One thinly slices two onions. One chops two rashers of bacon into pieces approximately 1 centimeter long. (*Tamanegi ni-ko wa usu-giri ni shi-masu. Bêkon ni-mai wa yaku 1-senchi-haba ni kiri-masu.*) (Sunô 1988: 47)

Or, again, as in a bilingual computer manual, in which the instructions "Expand the phrase ... Press Return" become:

> One expands the phrase ... One presses the return key. (*Busetsu no nagasa wo nagaku shi-masu ... Return kî wo oshi-masu.*) (Macintosh 1993: 25)

In both the above examples, the Japanese text not only avoids imperatives, it is also characterized by a use of the *masu* (polite) form of the verb. Imperatives are usually confined to family and close friends, or used in the context of a teacher addressing a class. Thus the language used in women's magazines is both authoritarian and intimate:

> Combine it with a sophisticated shape. [*Senrensareta forumu o awase-te.*] (*MORE* 5/94)

> Learn now the understated effect of matching only color or motif. [*Iro ya mochîfu dake soroeru sarigenasa o ima manan-de.*] (*25 ans* 10/93)

> Make sure that the dress you combine [with it] is as good as [it]. [*Awaseru yôfuku mo make-nai gurai ni shi-te.*] (*JJ* 12/94)

> Put a brooch on the coat collar and so on. [*Burôchi wa kôto no eri nado ni tsuke-te.*] (*MORE* 1/96)

This useage contrasts with the language of the advertisements. Hiejima notes that the use of imperatives is frequent in English advertisements, notably seen in verbs such as "buy", "choose", and "get". He shows that the Japanese equivalents are hardly ever in the imperative, though imperative expressions crop up here and there; however they tend to be vague when it comes to what the audience is urged to do, as in:

Those who are walking, stop for a while. [*Aruku hito-tachi yo, tomat-te goran.*] (Matsushita Electrics)

Oh, come and play. [*Ason-de ikina yo.*] (Tokuma Books)

It is September. Please find something good. (*9-gatsu desu. Iimono wo mitsuke-te kudasai.*] (Tokyo Broadcasting Co.) (in Hiejima 1993: 12)

None of these catch phrases directly tell the reader to purchase their product or service in the way their English-language equivalents do.

Japanese women's magazines thus seem to have developed a style which their audience takes to, or at least accepts, just as Fiske (1989) argues that the American tabloid press has. While the latter achieves this "largely through its departures from official (correct) language" and has "a tone of disrespect running through it" (Fiske 1989: 107), Japanese women's magazines manage it by appropriating the language of the classroom and a prescriptive tone.

Repetition and imitation

It is not only the tone of features which links women's magazines to the classroom, but also the frequent use of repetition and imitation. These elements have been described as central to the Japanese learning process, whether it is in learning traditional arts or bringing up young children (see Hendry 1986, 1988; O'Neil 1984).

The repetition found in Japanese women's magazines, in ways which might be regarded as irritating and undesirable by readers of an English magazine, is familiar to Japanese readers, brought up in a tradition of rote learning. A feature entitled "Super models' usual accessories" (*Sûpâmoderu no teiban komono*) (*JJ* 4/93) shows numerous photographs of super models with comments from a fashion critic, analyzing their clothes and accessories. Noting that some of the models wear goods merchandised in the campaign for the film *Malcolm X*, the article points out that "socially-aware super models support '*Malcolm X*'". It then warns the audience "Wear such items only after finding out who '*Malcolm X*' was!" and goes on to explain, concluding by repeating the warning: "Don't go to Roppongi (the Tokyo equivalent of London's Kings Road) wearing a Malcolm X cap unless you understand what it means."

Imitation is another key aspect of the Japanese learning process. For instance in the feature noted above, readers are explicitly encouraged to imitate super models and shown photographs of super models, so as to know what they should aspire to. The article highlights some of the accessories, where they are available and how much they cost. It shows a range of "Malcolm X" goods and tells which is the most popular of all, together with a photograph of a shop where these items can be purchased, plus its address, phone number and opening hours. It may be difficult for the magazines to help readers to look like super models, but they can at least help them to obtain the models' accessories. Indeed, the magazines are keen to draw any lessons from models, the subject including not only beauty, as in:

> Steal the secret of beauty from supermodels. [*Supâ moderu no utsukushisa wo nusume.*] (*With* 5/96)

but also baking:

> Exclusive! Learn how to make Christmas cake from a model. [*Totteoki! Moderu ni narau, kurisumasu kêki.*] (*Non-No* 20/12/95)

Hendry (1986) argues that in bringing up children the Japanese emphasize the importance of showing them good examples and encouraging them to imitate good behavior. What better example can there be for a young woman than a princess? Magazines thus made use of the imperial wedding. *With* carried a special feature entitled "Miss Masako Owada's Noble Fashion: Fully Illustrated" (*Owada Masako-san no kihin aru o-share: Kanzen zukai*) (5/93). The feature notes that the princess-to-be had often been photographed wearing scarves, and suggests achieving individuality (*kosei*) and femininity (*josei-rashisa*) by wearing a scarf the way she does. Photographs of her with a scarf are analyzed, showing what scarves to wear with what jackets and skirts, complete with price and availability. Readers are encouraged to copy the example.

A further element of imitation is provided by advice on how to look intelligent. Princess Masako, a graduate of Harvard and a former student at the universities of Tokyo and Oxford, has justifiably been described as intelligent (*chiteki*). In one feature, a make-up artist is quoted as saying that the princess represents the thesis that polishing the outside alone does not create true beauty, thus paying lip-service to the idea that intelligence may have something to do with an internal quality. However, he goes on to say that she is "intelligent indeed" (*masani chiteki*) because she wears gray eye shadow contrasting with a deep raspberry-pink lipstick, suggesting that intelligence is seen in the choice of her cosmetics, which in turn achieve a true beauty. The comment of a hair-dresser, who looked after the princess' hair for seven years before her marriage, is that her wisdom and intelligence manifest themselves in her hair style.

Japanese advertisements make frequent use of the words "intelligent" (*chiteki*) and "intelligence" (*chisei*) to describe attributes which are not so much to do with mental capacities as with appearance (Tanaka 1990, 1994). Magazines which carry such features reinforce this argument. The terms are really used to describe qualities which are traditionally regarded as desirable in women, such as dress sense and flair with make-up. It may be said that *With* is particularly keen on intelligence, for it claims to be a "... cultural magazine for women who wish to be intelligent and active" (Shu 1984). However, it is certainly not alone in wishing to convey such notions.

Japanese magazines are by no means the only medium depicting self-improvement as achieved purely by changes in clothes and make-up. Douglas Kellner describes the successful film *Pretty Woman* as doing just that:

> ... *Pretty Woman* puts on display the key role of image in the construction of identity in contemporary societies ... The film illustrates the process of self-transformation through fashion, cosmetics, diction, and style, and the extent to which identity is mediated through image and look in contemporary culture ... The message of the film is thus that if you want to become a new you, to transform your identity, to become successful, you need to focus on image, style, and fashion. (1995: 234)

These magazines succeed in turning qualities which are unattainable by the masses (such as those which enable one to become a super model or enter universities such as Tokyo, Harvard and Oxford) into something relatively easily achievable by any young woman. Moreover the magazines turn these qualities into something that is saleable to their audience. The masses need a little bit of help, which the magazines are only too willing to provide, and which they, the readers, are apparently only too happy to receive.

The lessons of recession

With their prescriptive language and emphasis on repetition and imitation, it is clear that the overall purpose of articles in women's magazines is to instruct. A further example of this tendency is a spate of articles teaching young women how to cope with the recent unexpected down-turn in the Japanese economy. Having survived a decade or two in a competitive market, the magazines are resilient. *An An* ran a series of features on "money studies" (*o-kane kenkyû shirîzu*) at the beginning of 1993. Part 3, entitled "How 10,000 yen can be spent!" (*1-man-en wa konna ni tsuka-eru!*) (29/1/93), starts off with ideas on how to save 10,000 yen (about £65 or US$115 in 1993, £55 or US$95 in 1996) and how to make the sum last longer. However, this is only the beginning. It goes on to show how to spend the money you have thus saved: on clothes, tableware, beauty care, presents, eating out and so on. Another feature is "Only 10,000 yen for all this" (*Kore-dake ka-tte-mo 1-man-yen*). In this way, the magazine manages to make even this difficult period in the country's economic life a selling point.

Other magazines do the same, with varying degrees of subtlety: for instance, this passage from a feature entitled "My choice of suits: under different conditions" (*Jôken-betsu: Watashi no sûtsu erabi*):

> What is most striking this autumn are the prices [of suits]. Compared to last year, every brand has lowered its prices by at least 20%. Even though the prices are lower, the quality of the suits has not declined at all, so it is absolutely right to buy them this year. You would definitely find clever suits which have all three attributes, namely, high quality, reasonable (price), and very much in line with this year's fashion! (*MORE* 10/93)

With, which (as noted above) aims to cater for "women who wish to be intelligent and active", carried a feature entitled "Tell us in detail about the 'economic recession' which is much discussed at the office, too!" ("*Kaisha de mo wadai no 'keizai fukyô' no koto, kuwashiku oshie-te!*"); this is advertised as "Not to be missed!" (*Minogase-masen!*). It explains basic terminology, such as "interest rates" and "general election", making one wonder whether the readers, who allegedly aspire to be intelligent, even read a newspaper. The next edition of *With* carried an article, " 'I am stingy!': Reports from proud readers" (*Watashi wa kechi-da!: Jiman repôto*), in which their letters explain how they save money.

Since the economic bubble has burst, *JJ* has also introduced a new way of using the term *nan-chatte*, which has come to mean something like "it's only a joke", by putting it in front of a brand name, as in "*nan-chatte Gucci*" and "*nan-chatte Chanel*", meaning products which look like a real Gucci or Chanel. Mihoko Yamada in *Shûkan Asahi* (*Weekly Asahi* 1/11/93) comments on the expression, quoting a member of *JJ*'s editorial staff saying that their audience stand in contrast with those of CREA, which is full of current news. Yamada adds that it is kinder to *JJ*'s readers to tell them how to overcome the current difficulties in such a cheerful manner, rather than explain how the difficulties have come about in the first place.

The strong educative elements in women's magazines confirms the tendency observed in other forms of popular culture in Japan. Harvey claims that one of the reasons for the unprecedented success of the NHK morning serialized television novel, *Oshin*, was its "educative anti-war position" (1995: 84). He goes on to suggest that *Oshin* might be described as an alternative national textbook which inculcates a post-war anti-militarist ideology.

Brian Powell (1995) argues that the producers of drama create an educational atmosphere and foster in their audiences an attitude of watching enthusiastically. Powell suggests that perhaps being taught is considered pleasurable in Japan.

Conclusion

The thread that appears to run through the features published in the magazines discussed here is the way in which they stand in for authority figures vis-a-vis their readers: giving lessons to their readers, mimicking the language of Japanese educational institutions and encouraging the imitation and repetition which are important elements in learning both at home and at school. To judge from the language used by the magazines, they treat their readers as pupils who aspire to achieve standards defined by the editors. Considering the popularity of these magazines, there appears to be no shortage of pupils who have failed to outgrow their school days. It is just possible that the prescriptive tone common to these women's magazines should not be taken literally, and that readers interpret it as being "tongue-in-cheek", but there is little evidence to support this view.

In reaching such a conclusion, I might be accused of falling into the trap of accepting the myth about Japanese women which the Western media have been accused of propagating (cf. Moon 1992: 206). More specifically, I could be accused of going along with the tendency to treat women as the weak, passive, and subordinate party, as opposed to the powerful, manipulative, and dominant publishing industry. Yet, as Dominic Strinati notes:

> ... the view of women as passive consumers manipulated into desiring commodities and the luxuries of consumption by the culture industries has begun to be challenged by feminist theory and research. Within the context of the emergence of what has been termed "cultural populism", it has been argued that this notion of the passive consumer undervalues the active role they play, the way their appreciation and interpretation of cultural consumption may diverge from that intended by the culture industries, as well as the fact that consumption cannot simply be understood as a process of subordination. (1995: 217)

In short, the relationship between the publishing industry, advertisers and women readers is complex, and Strinati cites Stacy when she concludes that:

... consumption does not simply represent "the power of hegemonic forces in the definition of woman's role as consumer", but rather "is the site of negotiated meanings, of resistance of appropriation as well as of subjection and exploitation" ... (1995: 218)

It is important to keep in mind here the strength of young Japanese women as consumers. The Hakuhodo Institute of Life & Living (1987) has shown how rising disposable income has made Japanese women powerful and how it is women who are the force behind major changes in society. Iwao (1993) has shown how women in Japan have continued to gain greater control, not only in the home, which has been regarded as their traditional domain, but also outside it.

While these caveats are all worthy of attention, it remains the case that these powerful consumers seem to be highly insecure in some respects. Perhaps this is because most Japanese high schools impose upon their pupils a school uniform and detailed and stringent rules concerning hair styles and accessories, such as bags and shoes. When young Japanese women leave school, it is often said that they have little idea as to what to wear. It is little wonder they crave authority figures to instruct them as to how they should cope with this unsettling new world of choice. Further research might concentrate both on the roots of this insecurity and on the multiple ways in which feature writers attempt to maintain the loyalty of their target audience through the use of a tone of authority.

Notes

1   However, Shimanaka concludes that their apparent belief in feminism was not unqualified, adding that all the founders and editors of the magazines were men, including Yûsaku Shimanaka, his own grandfather, who founded *Fujin Kôron*. He was an eminent feminist, but is remembered by his wife and daughter as a "typical Japanese male", who ruled over them as the head of household.

2   *Shuppan nekan 1987 (Publishing Yearbook 1987)* claims that since 1986 Japan has gone into "magazine-low era" (*zat-tei jidai*), but this is only in relation to the earlier boom, for the relative strength of magazine publishing has been maintained. According to *Shuppan nenkan 1992*, in 1991 more than 4.6 billion magazines were published, compared to over 1.4 billion books; and the publishing market's total turnover (books and magazines) was worth more than three trillion yen.

3   This new trend, according to *Asahi Shimbun*, is partly due to pressure on space in bookshops and in homes. The small size of the paperbacks appeals to people in the capital whose housing situation is tight. Moreover their light-heartedness (*tegarusa*) make the paperbacks suitable for reading on the commuter train; they are also like magazines in that they tend to address topical issues (such as the economic recession) and

practical matters (such as how to cope with changes in information technology). Senior editors are said to decide on which books to publish each month, as if they were editing a magazine.

4   The increased interest in magazines in Japan is by no means an isolated phenomenon. In his study of British women's magazines, Braithwaite notes vibrant activity in women's magazines in the 1980s (1995), when over fifty new titles were launched or re-launched.

5   It is surely no coincidence that since the publication of his book the novelist Yasuo Tanaka appears constantly in the type of magazine addressed here. He writes essays on contemporary lifestyle (cf. Kayama 1991; Baba 1993), gives interviews, and chairs discussions. Perhaps he has become not only an interpreter of the 1980s style of consumption, but also a representative of such a lifestyle.

6   Apart from *An An*, the magazines are A4 format, all bigger than their European equivalents, such as *Elle* and *Vogue*. With many color pages and illustrations, the average number of pages per issue is roughly between 280 and 500, compared to the British equivalent of 230 to 280.

7   Kawai (1987) does not explore the ramifications of foreign-sounding titles, whereas Shimanaka (n.d.) claims that their use reflects the fact that Japanese people have ceased to be aware of the distinction between what is Japanese and what is foreign. But he later points out that the use of the title *Hanako* suggests a change in this trend towards a greater awareness of things Japanese.

8   Compared with their British equivalents, these figures are not particularly high. McCracken (1993) notes that advertising in British women's magazines is generally between 40 and 50% of the total content. She singles out *Vogue* as having the largest advertising content, at between 39 and 61%.

9   Half of the magazines studied here have been associated with a type of "subcultural group" described by Bestor:

> Throughout the last several decades, popular fads and fashions pursued by urban Japanese youth have been the basis for informally identified subcultural groups (generally known as *zoku* or tribes), distinguished by their tastes in clothing, music, pastimes, hangouts, and demeanor. Contemporary *zoku* include the *kuristaruzoku* (crystal tribe), the *takenokozoku* (bamboo tribe), and the *bôsôzoku* (speed tribe) (1989: 15).

The *An-Non zoku*, the *JJ gal*, *Olive shôjo* (girl) and *Hanako zoku* are all directly related to women's magazines, and should be added to this list (Kayama 1991; see also Standish, Chapter 3 in this book).

10   An argument against homogeneity also has been put forward by Skov and Moeran (1995). They stress that Japanese companies are producing ever more diversified goods for an increasingly segmented market. Moreover, they argue that magazines have played a crucial role in developing this market segmentation, as in the field of cosmetics. There are undoubtedly subtle differences in the approaches taken by different publishers.

In fact, according to Inoue and Ebara (1995), Shuppan Kagaku Kenkyûjo (Publication Science Research Institute) categorizes women's magazines into fourteen genres, and the six magazines considered here are divided into three close but distinctive genres: the "young fashion magazines", such as *An An*, *Non-No* and *JJ*; the "office ladies" fashion magazines, which include *MORE* and *With*; and the "high society magazines" represented by *25 ans*.

References

Akiyama, H. 1987 *Sûgaku kôgi no jikkyô chûkei* (*Live from Mathematics Lectures*) Tokyo: Gogaku Shunjû Sha.

Baba, Y. 1993 "*Koramu bunshô dokuhon* (How to write Columns)" in *Omoide no teiban awâ* edited by A. Izumi. Tokyo: Kadokawa Shôten, pp. 210–21.

Bestor, T. 1989 "Lifestyles and popular Culture in urban Japan" in Powers and Kato (eds): pp. 1–37.

Bowring, R. and Kornicki, P. (eds) 1993 *The Cambridge Encyclopedia of Japan*. Cambridge: Cambridge University Press.

Braithwaite, B. 1995 *Women's Magazines: The first 300 years*. London: Peter Owen.

Chambers, I. 1986 *Popular Culture: the Metropolitan Experience*. London: Routledge.

Fields, G. 1983 *From Bonsai to Levi's*. New York: Macmillan.

——1989 *Gucci on the Ginza: Japan's new consumer generation*. Tokyo: Kodansha International.

Fiske, J. 1989 *Understanding Popular Culture*. London: Routledge.

Hakuhodo Institute of Life & Living 1987 *Jiryû wa joryû: Madamada kawaru Nihon no onna* (*The Trend of the Times is Women's Trend: Ever-Changing Japanese Women*). Tokyo: Nihon Keizai Shinbunsha.

Harvey, P. 1995 "Interpreting *Ôshin* – war, history and women in modern Japan" in *Women, Media and Consumption in Japan* edited by L. Skov and B. Moeran. Richmond, Surrey: Curzon.

Hendry, J. 1986 *Becoming Japanese: the world of the pre-school child*. Manchester: Manchester University Press.

——1988 *Understanding Japanese Society*. London: Routledge.

Hiejima, I. 1993 *Kôkoku no kotoba: Nichi-ei-go no hikaku to taishô* (*The Language of Advertising: comparison and contrast between Japanese and English*). Tokyo: Gakubunsha.

Inoue, T. and Joesi Zasshi Kenyûkai (eds) 1989 *Josei zasshi wo kaidoku-suru: COMPAREPOLITAN-Nichi, Bei, Mekishiko Hikaku Kenkyû* (*Deciphering women's magazines: COMPAREPOLITAN-Japan, U.S., Mexico comparative studies*). Tokyo: Kakiuchi Shuppan.

——and Ebara Y. 1995 *Josei Dêta Buku dai-2-han: Sei, karada kara seiji sanka made* (*Women's Data Book, 2nd edition: From Sex and Body to Political Participation*). Tokyo: Yuhikaku.

Iwao, S. 1993 *The Japanese Woman: Traditional Image and Changing Reality*. Oxford: MacMillan International.

Kawai, R. 1987 "*Shuppan: Shoseki to zasshi* (Publishing: Books and Magazines)" in Yamamoto and Fujitake (eds): pp. 146–55.

Kayama, R. 1991 "*Oriibu shôjo no yokubô no arika*" (Where the desires of *Olive* girls are) in *Shôjo zasshi ron* (*Debate on Girls' Magazines*) edited by E. Ootsuka. Tokyo: Tokyo Shoseki, pp. 103–24.

Kellner, D. 1995 *Media Culture*. London: Routledge.

Kindai Josei Bunka-shi Kenkyû-kai (eds) 1989 *Fujin zasshi no yoake* (*The Dawn of Women's Magazines*). Tokyo: Ozora-sha.

Kiyota, Y. 1987 "*Shuppan: Gaikan*" (Publishing: An overview) in Yamamoto and Fujitake (eds): pp. 136–45.

Koide T. 1992 *Gendai shuppan sangyô ron: Kyôsô to kyôchô no kôzô* (*Debate on Contemporary Publishing Industry: The Structure of Competition and Co-operation*), Tokyo: Nihon Editor School Publications.

Lakoff R. 1973 "The logic of politeness: or, minding your Ps and Qs", in *Proceedings of the Ninth Regional Meeting of the Chicago Linguistics Society*, pp. 292–305.

Leech, G. W. 1996 *English in Advertising: A linguistic study of advertising in Great Britain*. London: Longman.

Macintosh Japanese Input Method Guide 1993 Cupertino, CA: Apple Computer.

Masubuchi S. 1994 *Kawaii shôkôgun (The Cute Syndrome)*. Tokyo: Nihon Hôsô Shuppan Kyôkai.

Matsubara J. 1988 *Kurowasân shôkôgun (Croissant Syndrome)*. Tokyo: Bungeishunjû.

McCracken, Ellen 1993 *Decoding Women's Magazines: from* Mademoiselle *to* MS. London: Macmillan.

McRobbie, A. 1991 *Feminism and Youth Culture*. Basingstoke: MacMillan.

Moon, O. 1992 "Confucianism and gender segregation in Japan and Korea" in *Ideology and Practice in Modern Japan* edited by R. Goodman and K. Refsing. London: Routledge, pp. 196–209.

Nihon Jôhô Kyôiku Kenkyû-kai (Japanese Association of Information and Education) (ed.) 1993 *Heisei 5-nen Nihon no hakusho: Waga-kuni no genjô to kadai (1993 Japanese White Paper: Our Country's Current Situation and Its Problems)*. Tokyo: Seibun-sha.

Ogino A. 1992 *Ogino Ayako no Chô-kiso Kokugo Juku: Madonna Kobun (Ayako Ogino's Super-Basic Japanese Cram School: Madonna Classical Japanese)*, Tokyo: Gakken.

O'Neil, P. 1984 "Organization and authority in the traditional arts" in *Modern Asian Studies*, vol. 18(4): 631–45.

Powell, B. 1995 "Theatre-going as homework: an aspect of Modern Japanese Theatre" in *Japanese Civilization in the Modern World XI: Amusement* edited by T. Umesada et al. Osaka: National Museum of Ethnology.

Powers, R. and Kato, H. (eds) 1989 *Handbook of Japanese Popular Culture*. Westport, Conn: Greenwood Press.

Reinoruzu-Akiba, K. 1989 *Josei zasshi no kotoba* (The language of women's magazines) in Inoue et al. (eds).

Reischauer, R. 1985 *The Japanese*. Tokyo: Kodansha International.

Shimanaka, Y. n.d. "Transitions in Japanese women's magazines." Unpublished paper presented at the FIPP congress held in London, July 1989.

Shu, R. (ed.) 1984 *Zasshi shinbun sô katarogu 1984-ban (Total Catalogue of Magazines and Newspapers 1984 Edition)*. Tokyo: Media Research Centre.

Shuppan nenkan 1980–93 (Publishing Year Book 1980–93). Tokyo: Shuppannyûsu-sha.

Skov, L. and B. Moeran (eds) 1995 *Women, Media and Consumption*. Richmond, Surrey: Curzon Press.

Strinati, D. 1995 *An Introduction to Popular Culture*. London: Routledge.

Sunô K. 1988 *Non-No kantan okazu hyakka (Non-No's Encyclopedia of Easy Dishes)* Tokyo: Shûeisha.

Tanaka, K. 1990 "'Intelligent elegance': Women in Japanese advertising" in *Unwrapping Japan: Society and Culture in Anthropological Perspective* edited by E. Ben-Ari et al. Manchester: Manchester University Press, pp. 78–96.

——1994 *Advertising Language: A Pragmatic Approach to Advertisements in Britain and Japan*. London: Routledge.

——n.d. "Popular culture in Japanese Men's Magazines." Paper presented at the Japan Anthropology Workshop meeting held in Melbourne, Australia, July 1997.

Tanaka Y. 1981 *Nantonaku kurisutaru* (*Somewhat Crystal*), Tokyo: Kawade Shobô Shinsha.

Tasker, P. 1987 *Inside Japan: Wealth, work and power in the new Japanese empire.* London: Penguin Books.

Tsuchiya H. 1989 *Tsuchiya no kobun: hai-gurêdo hen* (*Tsuchiya's Classical Japanese: High-Grade Edition*) Tokyo: Yamato Shobô.

Van Zoonen, L. 1991 "Feminist perspectives on the media" in *Mass Media and Society* edited by J. Curran and M. Gurevitch. London: Edward Arnold.

Winship, J. 1992 "The impossibility of *Best*: Enterprise Meets Domesticity in the Practical Women's Magazines of the 1989's" in *Come on Down?: Popular Media Culture in Post-war Britain* edited by Dominic Strinati and Stephen Wagg. London: Routledge, pp. 82–115.

Wright, J. 1985 *Just Desserts.* London: Treasure Press.

Yamamoto A. and Fujitake A. (eds) 1987 *Zusetsu Nihon no masu-komyunikêshon* (*Mass Communication in Japan: Illustrated*) (2nd edition). Tokyo: Nihon Hôsô Shuppan Kyôkai.

CHAPTER 7

Nonchan's Dream
NHK morning serialized television novels[1]

PAUL A. S. HARVEY

Introduction

Contemplating a society through the window of its artistic productions is an activity fraught with peril: there will always be distortion, for art is necessarily a selective representation of society and its multiple ideologies. This is as true of sixteenth-century England viewed through the glass of Shakespeare, as it is of the United States distorted in the mirror of *Dallas*, or more recently, in the soap opera parody *Twin Peaks*. Morning serialized television novels (*Asa no renzoku terebi shôsetsu*, hereafter "morning dramas" or *asadora*) are no exception to this. However, for various reasons connected with the genre, production methods, the nature of its audience (in large part women), and NHK's own agenda, this form of television drama is a revealing instance of the contradictory ideologies that go into making modern Japan.

In a nutshell, the dramas proclaim an ideology of "social progress" with regard to the status of women: promoting the ideal of women working outside the home, but at the same time holding up for emulation traditional values such as filial loyalty and self-sacrifice. A complex negotiation can be seen to be taking place between this rhetoric of progress and the stipulations of Japanese tradition. This does not mean, however, that the progressive appeal of the dramas constitutes a mere front for conservative notions relating to women; rather, the "family values" whereby the heroine is expected to marry and raise children in a conventional manner are a form of wrapping that allows the more progressive elements to gain social currency.[2]

We can explain the ideological work done by the *asadora* in terms that relate to two recent discussions on women and traditional Confucian values. Okypyo Moon (1992) discusses the differing impact that Confucian ethics have had on the status of Korean and Japanese women.

She concludes that Korean women have internalized to a greater degree
the Confucian values which subordinate women to the men in the
household than have Japanese women, and she suggests that, from a
Korean perspective, Japanese women exist in a far more permissive
society. According to Moon, the economic development of Japan has
contributed to an unambiguous rise in the status of women precisely
because Confucianism was less deeply rooted; conversely, in Korea
economic development has led, in part, to a loss of status for women.
Above all, Western notions of the "Japanese woman" have hindered any
understanding of differences between these two "oriental" women:

> ... in the study of gender relations, there has been another very powerful
> hindrance to the understanding of the reality of Japanese women: that is, the
> stereotypical image-making about Japanese women by western media as frail,
> submissive and mysterious beings. (Moon 1992: 206)

In contrast, Jan van Bremen (1993) discusses the social influence of
popular educational texts which hold up the followers of an influential
Chinese neo-Confucian philosopher named Wang Yang-ming as exemp-
lary models for the Japanese. These texts are directly analogous to
morning dramas, for I would argue that they do similar work. Both are
imbued with an ethic of self-improvement: "Wang Yang-ming's teachings
instruct a follower to act instantly and spontaneously to repair dis-
parities between ideals and reality, right and wrong, good and bad" (van
Bremen 1992: 136). *Asadora* heroines are cast in this mold, for they are
figures who remake themselves and society in accord with their vision.

There is also another and larger context to the fervent self-
improvement of the women in these dramas, and that is how these
women's roles can be taken as a metaphor for the regeneration and
development of post-war Japan. The conflict with traditional values that
these morning dramas celebrate occurs, in effect is *allowed*, precisely
because the rise in women's status is part of the rhetoric of national self-
improvement and development.

This chapter is divided into four sections: the first will describe the
genre of *asadora*; the second will discuss its popularity; the third will look
briefly at the plot of one very successful morning drama, *Nonchan's
Dream* (*Nonchan no yume*); and the final section will draw together the
themes of the aspirations of modern Japanese women as mediated in
asadora and the ethic of nation-building (*kunizukuri*) which imbues
these morning dramas.

Genre

The first *asadora* was screened over thirty years ago in 1961 (Doiharu
1993: 11). It was developed as a televisual response to the popularity of

post-war radio soap opera, and as a televised version of the novels serialized in Japanese newspapers. A relic of these roots is the continued existence of a narrator who sets the scene and fills in gaps in the story. Like radio soap operas in the UK (for example, *The Archers*), these television dramas are screened daily for about fifteen minutes. It is a morning program screened at 8.15 am, which is repeated at 12.45 pm. Unlike radio soap operas, *asadora* usually last for a period of six months, beginning in April and running through to the autumn; and then another series runs from autumn to spring. There are usually about 160 episodes, and about thirty-six hours of air time are consumed.

While *asadora* constitutes its own genre, it can be said to be part of the Japanese television genre known as "home drama" (*hômu dorama*) as well. Home dramas are situation dramas centered on the homes and families of "ordinary" people. This contrasts with British or Australian soap operas which are often community-based (for example, *Coronation Street, Crossroads, Neighbours, EastEnders*), and with the better-known American soaps which are family-centered, but which focus on the social elites (*Dallas, Dynasty*). Niyekawa quotes an official of Fuji Television, who comments:

> The most popular television fare is "home drama", a form of soap opera without the "sexploitative aspects" of its American counterpart ... The Japanese serials are "rooted in the Japanese character". The constant is less comedy than a home setting. There are hilarious moments but it is mostly serious. They are family-oriented and watched by everyone from grandmother to little children. They present stories of actual family life and allow parents to use some of the materials as examples to children. (Niyekawa 1984: 62)

Asadora is not, however, a soap opera, but shares some of the characteristics of a soap: a cast of individuals with whom the viewer becomes very familiar over six months; a realistic narrative in which a recognizable social environment is the arena of action; and, on the part of the audience, an interactive dialog which in turn influences the content and direction of the drama. This last is reflected in ratings, other media interest, readers' columns and questionnaires.[3] Unlike soap operas, however – and this is an important difference – the time limit of six months means that morning dramas are, from the outset, aiming at some form of closure. This gives the dramas an urgency which soap operas lack. It also means that NHK has a degree of flexibility with regard to the popularity of the program: if one particular drama proves unpopular, then the corporation can cut its losses and plan for the next season. NHK is not committed in the way that, say, the BBC was committed to *Eldorado* in July of 1992. It means that *asadora* is extremely sensitive to social change: in the constant campaign to maintain decent ratings, and at the same time to meet its own agenda, NHK is obliged to ally the program with matters of current popularity and even with population change.

Although not all *asadora* over the past thirty years have based themselves on the family unit (*Romansu* (1984) would be an example), the family is fundamental to the structure and plot of morning dramas. This is true also of other areas of Japanese popular culture: the films of Yamada Yôji all define their leading characters by reference to the family.[4] *Asadora* do the same; the leading character, nearly always a young woman, is defined by her relationship with her family. The comparison with Yamada's film series, *Otoko wa tsurai* (*It's tough being a man*), is instructive: the long-running serial (more than forty-five films since 1969) is a meditation on the trials of Tora, who finds it impossible to get married and start his own family. He is consequently adrift in society and this is symbolized by his job as a pedler. In every episode he is welcomed home by his sister and uncle (he and his sister are adopted), but is forced to leave again by the need to "become a man": to start his own family. The interest of the drama lies in how he will fail this time. Generally all the films have ended with Tora failing in romance and deciding to leave home once again. *It's tough being a man* is the inverse of *asadora*, being the tale of repeated failures, and like morning dramas, it has been hugely popular.

But if Tora is a tragic figure, forever doomed to fail and attract our sympathy with his failure, the heroines of *asadora* are comic heroines, comic in the sense that they are able, through their own efforts, to transform a hostile environment.[5] In a way similar to Tora, one of the hardships with which the heroine is burdened is that her own family background is often one that has been disrupted by ill-fortune. A large number of heroines lack one or both parents: a father who has died a few years before the events of the drama; or a mother who has died in the girl's youth. The second burden which the heroine carries is that she has a dream, and the dream involves contributing to society not simply as a wife or mother, but in an "untraditional way". The pursuit of the dream takes various forms, but essentially it involves a consideration of what it means for a female to enter a male world; and this involves reflecting on the meaning of marriage and family for a woman who has such a dream. The interest of the drama lies in how and whether she will manage to achieve her dream and, at the same time, repair the past by starting her own family: a family on her own terms, since it must accommodate her dream. In other words, these dramas are future-oriented. They are concerned with a compromise between traditional structures such as marriage and the social innovation of women taking jobs with creative responsibilities. The drama *Eenyobo* (1993) deals with precisely this theme: it is the story of a recently married woman doctor who enters a rural community in northern Kyoto prefecture.

The male world which confronts the heroine takes various forms: in recent years the theme of sport has been common, as in *Yôidon* (1982), which is about a girl who becomes an athlete; or *Wakko no kinmedaru* (*Wakko's Gold Medal*) (1989) which concerns a girl who plays volleyball at the time of the 1964 Tokyo Olympics when the Japanese women's team took the gold. Other themes have included: the first woman pilot, a woman photographer in the 1920s, a woman hotelier in the Meiji period (1868–1912); the first woman newsreader on television, a woman who founds her own magazine in the post-war years, or simply the story of an ordinary woman succeeding in a less glamorous vocation but against similar opposition. Hashida Sugako has written two very popular dramas of this nature, *Oshin* (1983) and *Onna wa dokyô* (*Women are brave*) (1992). Although both were successful, it was *Oshin* which went on to be aired in over forty different countries throughout the world.

There have been a handful of dramas which have had male leading characters (seven out of fifty), but they have been less successful: they certainly do not fit the popular conception of what constitutes *asadora*. Also, the genre itself changed in the early 1990s, concentrating, for example, on the relationship between mothers and daughters, or elder and younger sisters, or on divorce.[6] This is notable in the dramas which have been produced by Kanazawa Kôji, such as *Kyô futari* (1990) and *Hirari* (1992), but even these take as their base the relationship between women and work.

The heroine of each drama is cast after an exhaustive process of selection, and is an unknown: the *asadora* role for which she is chosen is her television debut. The individual is chosen not only for her ability to match the particular character in the drama, but equally importantly for her ability to convey the appropriate emotional tone. Just as with many other facets of Japanese life, mood must fit the occasion, and *asadora* – being *morning* drama – must be lively and uplifting.[7] The word used most frequently to describe this tone is "light" (*akarui*). Fujita Tomoko, who played the title part in *Nonchan no yume*, was praised for her ability to convey this tone: she was "cheerful and full of vitality" (*akaruku baitaritî ga aru*). In *Nonchan no yume* this was visually represented by the frequent shots of a clear blue sky. In short, the idea behind these programs is to bring sunshine into the home for a short period in the early morning. This was evident in *Karin* (1993), where the title sequence for each episode was shown against the sky; and in *Piano* (1994) where the title sequence was shot from a helicopter flying over central Osaka. In a sense these dramas are a window into the rural and local landscapes that are not visible from the windows of the high rise flats in Tokyo or Osaka, where access to the sunlight is something charged for in the rent.

The plot of these programs is of the same order: a woman overcomes obstacles and achieves success. The dramas are utopian, showing the world as it ought to be, not as it is. *Asadora* are not, however, just a form of escapist drama offering the female viewer an upbeat start to the day. This might be the case if the program were produced by a private television station whose concern would be simply to maintain ratings in order to attract sponsors. NHK has a completely different agenda, and while the success of the drama is undoubtedly measured by its ratings, the content of the drama is not determined by purely commercial factors. This can be seen in the promotional stance NHK takes with regard to the question of women and work. This particular stance became especially visible after *Oshin*, though it had been an important component for some years. With *Oshin*, the writer, Hashida Sugako, and the producer, Okamoto Yukiko, both women,[8] teamed up to produce the most successful *asadora* in the last twenty years. At the front of the guide written for the drama, Hashida stresses that she had written *Oshin* for the mothers of Japan, and the guide contains a chart detailing women's contributions to the recent history of Japan, paralleled with the life story of the character Oshin, who was born in 1901 (NHK 1983: 186–91).

Okamoto was the driving force behind this emphasis, and in her *Hanegoma* (1986), a story about a woman's struggle to leave her family and become a journalist in the Meiji period, this was delineated even more clearly. In the series guide there is a picture of Saitô Yuki who plays the leading character, Rin, and written against it the words: "Wouldn't it be good to learn something from Rin?" (*Rin kara nanika wo manande iketara ii nâ*) (NHK 1986a: 27). At the end of the guide, as if to underline the emphasis, a chronological list of heroines with regard to women and work is also included.

NHK is sensitive to the accusation that it acts as a mouthpiece for government policy, and it is true that in the 1980s, with an ever-increasing demand for labor, the government was encouraging women to join the workforce. NHK's sensitivity is indicated by an interview given by Hashida some six weeks into the screening of *Oshin*: "I didn't write *Oshin* in order to be praised by the Minister of Education" (*Asahi Shimbun* 1983: 22). But it would be fair to say that this progressive stance is part of the very genre of *asadora* as it developed through the 1970s, and without it one might expect there to be a fall in its popularity. This point was made by Ono Tsutomo in his analysis of the radio drama, *Kimi no na wa* (*What is your name?*);[9] he argues that "because the drama treated private troubles with their social implications, it conveyed a progressive tone to the audience" (1973: 161). In the 1950s, *Kimi no na wa* was an exquisitely modern drama, dealing with recognizably "modern" topics such as divorce. Yet when NHK tried to re-create its success by turning it into an *asadora*, ratings plummeted: one reason being that the drama had changed from being contemporary and progressive with regard to women, to being purely historical. *Asadora*, when set in the recent past, must always be oriented towards the present. The dramas present an ethic of progress and self-improvement whereby the past is literally left behind. This progressive tone and *future-oriented* stance is intrinsic even to historical morning dramas.

Returning to *Oshin*, there is one other reason why Hashida's story of Oshin's trials and tribulations as she grew from being a young girl to maturity and old age might have been praised by the Minister of Education: this is because *asadora* have a definite educational content with regard to Japan and Japanese culture. Education is, of course, part of NHK's mandate as a national broadcasting corporation and with *asadora* the educational content is delivered in two ways. The first is the way in which the individual stories are historically contextualized: as mentioned above, each drama highlights a period in Japan's recent history; and as the story progresses, historical events are introduced to give the drama its own particular flavor. Thus, when viewing *Oshin* one is led from the beginning of the century up to the 1960s, and, along the way, witnessing the century's upheavals and how they impinge on Oshin. In other dramas the time-frame may be much shorter: *Mâchan* (1979) focussed on the twenty years before the Second World War. The second way in which educational content is delivered is that each drama is set in a different area of Japan, and is therefore used to promote that area. This is a rationale that NHK pursues across a range of programs.[10]

NHK must be very careful that its patronage is evenly distributed. Since the ratings of *asadora* are so high, this means that the attention of a large part of the nation is focussed on one particular area, which can sometimes lead to significant economic regeneration. In the case of *Oshin*, a tourist industry sprang up in the town of Sakata within two months of the drama's inception. *Hirari* (1992), set in Ryôgoku in Tokyo, famous for sumo,[11] increased tourism to the area; in the drama guide there is even a map of the area around Ryôgoku station. Two questions put to Shigemori Takako, the writer of *Wakko no kinmedaru* (1989), at the beginning of the production process of that drama were: "When do you want to set the drama? And where do you want to set the drama?" (NHK 1989b: 4). The answers to these questions are not decided by the writer alone: she joins a committee and the period, location and story are decided in discussion. The writer will then produce the dialog, often with the help of a dialect expert from the region in question.

The dramas seek to promote aspects perceived as traditionally Japanese. There are two reasons for this: the first, again, is educational, but it is also gender-specific. Since women carry most of the responsibility for socializing children, it is appropriate that traditional knowledge be passed to them. This process can also be seen in the content of the dramas. For example, in *Miotsukushi* (1985), set in Chôshi in Chiba Prefecture, the making of soy sauce was one of the drama's main themes. Much emphasis was placed on the trouble and ritualistic procedures undergone to achieve the perfect soy sauce. The same occurred in *Kyô Futari*, where much value was placed on the traditional method of making Kyoto pickles. Men may often carry out traditions, but it is women who retain the knowledge.[12] In *asadora*, of course, the women are given the knowledge, but they also become the practitioners of the rituals. This is the other reason that tradition is so important in *asadora*; by choosing a traditional locale within which to place the heroine, the dramas again highlight the main theme: the struggle of a woman to overcome traditional restraints, in a sense to re-write tradition, and to succeed in her chosen role.

This last was specifically picked up by the *Asahi Shimbun* with regard to *Miotsukushi*. The leading character, Kaoru, succeeds "by going beyond traditional customs" (*furui shikitari wo norikoenagara*), but having gone beyond, Kaoru then returns to the making of soy sauce and becomes a guardian of tradition. Hirari, heroine of the eponymous drama, has a dream of entering the world of sumo; she succeeds, but not, however, as a wrestler: she becomes an adviser on nutrition. This dialog between a woman's role in society and "tradition" is a constant theme.

We have, therefore, a potent mix in *asadora*: women confronting tradition and transforming society against the background of a particular period and locale. In discussion with informants at NHK, they suggested that entertainment might form 70–80 per cent of a drama's content, and education some 20–30 per cent. In other words, entertainment consumes more than twice as much of the resources and air time that go into making such a program.

Clearly NHK has the formula right: over the past ten years ratings have been more or less maintained – although they have not achieved the astonishing levels of the 1960s – despite changes in the population structure and despite the fact that the number of working women has increased throughout the 1980s, thus diminishing the potential audience.

Before we go on to look at *Nonchan no yume*, and the way in which it relates to the demands of the genre, it would be well to consider entertainment as an important aspect of these dramas, for it is as entertainment, not for education, that these dramas are watched: What, then, are the bases of *asadora*'s popularity?

Popularity

Within the broad and varying range of modern Japanese popular culture, *asadora* is notable for its huge audience. The ratings have been consistently the highest of all television programs in Japan since the inception of broadcasting. *Nonchan no yume* peaked at 50 per cent for the Tokyo region towards the end of its screening; and this rating does not include the peak lunch-time broadcast which would add a further 20 per cent: a total peak rating of 70 per cent, a figure which, converted into numbers, would be higher than the population of the UK. Although *Nonchan* was not particularly noted for its great popularity, this peak figure indicates the potentially enormous contact the genre has with Japanese society. Bruce Stronach (1989: 148) gives the viewing figure of 62.5 per cent for one week's viewing of *Oshin* in February in 1984: this is nearly double the rating for any other program shown at the time. An average figure over the last ten years of *asadora* for both the Tokyo and Osaka regions would be something more like 31 per cent: this figure is a realistic average for the whole nation, although it may be far too conservative for the more popular dramas.[13]

The potentially formative influence of this genre is also very important. In its first installments in 1961, it was screened at 8.40 am, this was later revised to 8.15 am since the aim was to provide entertainment for women at home after her children and husband had left the house. *Asadora* was to be a drama which the housewife could watch while she sipped a cup of tea before, or even while, she did her housework. From the start *asadora* was designed as a genre that spoke to the Japanese woman on her own terms, meeting her interests and, as already discussed, providing role models. The genre was and is framed by social realities, the most important of which has been the very existence of a large pool of women who sit at home and watch television. In the early years the drama was much more conservative, and from the mid-1970s became consistently more progressive in its theme of women and work. The interactive relationship with its audience might be grounds enough for claiming the importance of *asadora*, but there is a further aspect which we must consider: if one discusses the programs with anyone under the age of forty, one discovers that they have watched *asadora* at some stage in their childhood. In the summer of 1983, for instance, *Oshin* was re-run in the early evening, specifically to build on its popularity with children under the age of eight. There have been very few weekdays in the last thirty-five years when *asadora* have not been aired; they are part of the fabric of Japanese life.

The key to popularity clearly lies in the structure of the drama, which is firmly based on the idealized Japanese family. The importance of the family is attested to by various critics. Egami Teruhiko (1968: 155) discusses *asadora* as a type of home drama and suggests that at the back of the viewer's mind there is an ideal family against which the televised family is measured. This is a useful way to consider *asadora*. The matter of abiding interest must lie in the way the ideal family accommodates, or fails to accommodate, the leading character's dream: if the woman is successful in work and family, this brings about a re-writing of the ideal. In her useful survey of early *asadora*, Muramatsu Yasuko (1979: 8) comments on the way the audience for *Ohanahan* (1966) was tied into the story by the protracted courtship of the leading character. The ratings for this program peaked at 54 per cent for the Tokyo region and never dropped below 36 per cent (Muramatsu 1979: 6–7). Satô Tadao suggests that *asadora* bring together a desire for good morals (*junpu bizoku*) and a desire for freedom (1978: 62–3). Clearly the latter is vital: equally important is the desire to see the leading character succeed against all odds in re-establishing the family. It is in this respect that van Bremen's suggestions discussed above are most valuable: the desire to re-establish the family is, of course, a moral element, a particularly Confucian emphasis.[14] It is the same desire that was central to the *Otoko wa tsurai yo* series. And it explains why it is necessary for the protagonists to be disadvantaged, though by no means are all so positioned, by having only one parent. The heroines are engaged in a quest of self-creation, looking at the same time for a surrogate parent to whom to give filial piety, and the surrogate parent who authorizes the mold-breaking activity of these heroines, as we shall see in the final section of this chapter, is the nation itself.

In discussion with the writer of *Nonchan no yume*, Sato Shigeko,[15] she suggested that the popularity of a given *asadora* depended on the way the writer maintained interest in the leading characters' romances. In her case she did this by skilfully deferring Nonchan's marriage until the very end, and by presenting the two rivals alternatively to the viewers. This technique was used again to similar effect in *Hirari*.

Another intrinsic part of the genre, which is certainly an important factor in its popularity, is the Tokyo region/Osaka region (Kantô/Kansai) rivalry. There is a large gap between the regional ratings and various reasons for this. First of all it should be remembered that the *asadora* are situated in different locations, so interest in a drama is heightened for provincial viewers if it is located in their region. Thus, if the drama is located in Tokyo, as was two-thirds of *Nonchan*, popularity in Osaka is less strong. To date the dramas have been located all over Japan.[16] Also, the population of Tokyo is composed largely of relative newcomers who have left the provinces in the last two generations: by locating the drama in the provinces an impact will also be made in Tokyo viewing figures. Since the majority of Japanese live in Osaka and Tokyo, the dramas are most frequently set in or near these two cities.

Another reason for the popularity differential between the two regions is that the dramas which end up in Tokyo are part of an *asadora* sub-genre known as "going/coming to the capital" (*jôkyô*). As the term indicates, these dramas start in the provinces and finish in the capital. By adopting this plot structure the dramas mirror the post-war history of Japan, when young women and men moved in their millions to Tokyo in pursuit of education and work. For those in the Osaka region, because of their strong regional loyalty, this migration is a difficult one with which to sympathize. For those in Osaka, the centre of Japan is, of course, Osaka. Thus, for the dramas set in the Kansai region, and which have an authentic regional feel to them, the overall ratings are fairly close. Indeed, there has been something of a trend from the 1980s into the 1990s for the ratings between the two regions to draw together: this is due to NHK's attempt to appeal to both areas.

In Tokyo, there is less regional loyalty, but there is a sense of rivalry with Kansai: this is due to the Kansai monopoly on the cultural traditions of Japan. This rivalry is exploited fully in *asadora*: it is a common pattern for the heroine to arrive in the big city and interest in the drama is maintained by the contrast between provincial behavior, often better mannered, which uses more polite (often older) forms of language, with the more direct forms used in Tokyo. The girl from the provinces tends to trust everybody and is easily deceived: this was the case with *Nonchan*. The reverse also has been exploited: in *Kyô futari*, the heroine arrives in Kyoto from Tokyo to find her lost daughter. Here the heroine has big-city sophistication, but must learn the value of tradition. So too in *Onna wa dokyô*, where the heroine has been left an orphan at the beginning of the drama and joins a new family in Osaka who treat her unkindly.

There are also folkloric elements which structure the popularity of *asadora* and which form continuities with earlier forms of theater and performance.[17] Describing these continuities would take another chapter, but suffice it to say that one of the key elements in the popularity of *asadora* is that of bullying/persecution (*ijime*), a staple of Japanese folklore. Bullying is the experience the heroine undergoes when she leaves the security of her own family and enters a new one, either as a bride, an adopted child, or as a worker if she joins a group of people. The interest in the drama lies in how the heroine will put up with and overcome unfriendly treatment. The author of *Oshin*, Hashida, is well known for these sort of dramas.

Asadora might be seen as a transmuted form of the Cinderella story, substituting the "prince" with the goal of work and marriage together, or, if we extend the analogy, the goal of a prosperous nation.[18] The focus in the dramas on the persecution undergone by the women highlights the difficulty of achieving this dream: the fact that this plot technique still has a strong emotional appeal corroborates Hendry's (1981) contention that marriage in Japan is still understood to be a typically non-nuclear institution, with the bride seen to be entering a household of two or more generations, though in actual practice couples often set up households on their own.

A final comment on popularity must consider the way that NHK deliberately ties *asadora* to matters of current interest: this could be seen with *Kokoro wa itsumo ramune iro* (1984) which was based on the life of a stand-up comedian. During the 1980s there was a vogue for the art of comic repartee (*manzai*). More recently, a group popular amongst teen-aged girls, *Dorîmuzu kamu turû*, sang the theme song of *Hirari*, while the plot of the program tied into the extraordinary sumo boom which began in 1990.[19] For *Nonchan no yume*, the title graphics were drawn by Watase Seizo, a well-known comic illustrator again popular amongst teen-aged girls. The reason for NHK pitching *asadora* in this way is that there is a huge loyal audience over the age of fifty, but younger viewers are felt to be more fickle. NHK is trying to stave off the genre's being typecast as an older person's morning entertainment.

The way these various elements – current interests, regional divisions and the ideals of young women – are incorporated is looked at more closely through the lens of *Nonchan no yume* which is described in the next section. The concept of a "dream", part of the program's title, is an important one, which ties all the dramas to a nationalistic dream of prosperity and regeneration. The skilful manipulation of this potent concept accounts in no small part for the success of *asadora*.

Nonchan no yume

Nonchan no yume begins with the gathering of the inhabitants of Aki in the town schoolyard in order to listen to the emperor announce the need to accept defeat on the 15th of August 1945. While the Yûki family hears this news, the daughter of the family, assisted by Nobuko (called Nonchan, an endearment), is giving birth. The beginning of the drama is a symbolic enactment of the fact that on that day one era ended and a new stage in Japan's history began.

The location of the drama is initially the small town of Aki in Kôchi Prefecture, part of Shikoku Island. Nobuko is there, having come from Tokyo with her mother and sister to her uncle's house in order to escape the air-raids and because there is more to eat in the countryside. Her father, who had been an English teacher, died just before they left Tokyo in 1943. The drama emphasizes Nobuko's carefree personality and her energy. She is the perfect embodiment of the essential recurring heroines of *asadora*: the young woman who refuses to give up no matter how hard the going gets.

The love interest of the drama is provided by two suitors: Hasumi Shôi who was a sub-lieutenant and Nobuko's instructor in naval drill; and Takeno Hiroshi, a villager and, thus, a "traditional" man. Takeno becomes the sounding board against which Nobuko expresses her dream. Near the beginning of the series he ridicules Nonchan's desire to work (episode 21); as the drama progresses, however, Takeno becomes instrumental in promoting Nonchan's career. It is due to his influence that she joins the Tokyo magazine where eventually she becomes chief editor. Hasumi, with whom Nobuko had fallen in love before the start of the drama, is acted as a more mysterious individual who goes to the bad. It takes her the length of the series to realize that it is in fact Takeno whom she really loves.

In the village an arranged meeting (*omiai*) is organized for Takeno and Nobuko; she goes along, not realizing that an *omiai* in that area is not simply a formal introduction, but a firm commitment to marriage. In love with Hasumi, Nobuko causes a scene during the *omiai*, pouring tea over Takeno's mother and ripping her kimono. The introduction of the traditional marriage procedures at the start of the drama forms the background against which Nonchan's comparatively radical desire to work, and to put work before marriage, must be understood; in the late 1990s this is much less of a radical choice to make, but this is a development of the last decade. Thus Nonchan's decision to work is historicized in this drama, making her desire more acceptable since it is cast as a reaction to older rural forms of marriage.

The main theme emerges early in the drama and is encapsulated in the phrase: "Girls be ambitious!" This is a re-working of the words uttered in 1877 in Sapporo by the well-known American educator William Clark: "Boys be ambitious!" The re-worked phrase is one which Nonchan's father used to repeat to his daughters. This is characteristic of the kind of re-casting that takes place in these dramas. A male-oriented catchphrase is re-worked into a female mode. The same occurs with the title *Onna wa dokyô* (*Women are brave*), which is taken from the proverb "men are brave, women are sweet" (*otoko wa dokyô, onna wa aikyô*). The words "girls be ambitious" occur frequently in the early parts of *Nonchan no yume*.

Nobuko asserts her belief that a new era has begun: "Now it is up to us women: our battles are just about to begin and I would like to publish a magazine to help women" (publicity material, NHK 1988a: 2–3).

Nonchan's pursuit and realization of this dream leads her to publish a rudimentary newsletter in Aki, from that to sending an example to a Tokyo magazine, then going to Tokyo, joining the company and, after many setbacks, becoming the chief editor of the company in charge of the magazine which is called, appropriately enough: *Dream*. It is a story of success. Takeno likewise has a dream which is mentioned two or three times: he dreams of linking the island of Shikoku to the mainland by a bridge.

The main action takes place in the immediate post-war years and concludes with the marriage of Nobuko and Takeno in 1951. The relationship between these two provides a great deal of interest in the drama: when will Nobuko finally admit that she has fallen in love with Takeno, who has been in love with her from the beginning? She refuses to get married because she puts her magazine work first. The drama is a re-writing of Japanese history, with an emphasis on the contribution of women to Japan's post-war reconstruction. This re-working of history is a common feature of *asadora* and is analogous to the re-phrasing of "boys be ambitious!"

Thus, in *Nonchan no yume* the post-war aspirations of Japanese women with regard to work and the family are re-written as a realizable dream. The dream is implicit in most *asadora*; in *Nonchan* it is explicitly part of the mechanics of the drama. Following van Bremen's analysis of neo-Confucian philosophy, I see a link between the achieving of this dream and neo-Confucian homiletics; for although the *asadora* heroine is clearly not re-making herself and the world around her out of altruistic motives, her self-generated and self-fulfilling dream is nevertheless unambiguously presented as a moral good. Those women who lack a dream, although often characterized in a sympathetic way, are lesser beings. And those who oppose the achievement of the dream are characterized negatively, a role often – but by no means exclusively – filled by the heroine's father.

Dream-building and nation-building

In terms of the embracing context of the drama, the notion of dream has the widest of connotations, and this was most perfectly illustrated by *Nonchan no yume*. As mentioned above, the unit of the family, which the heroine challenges and re-defines by her desire to work, may be extrapolated to the entire community formed by the nation.[20] This context is made clear when we consider the rationale for deciding on the particular period within which to set the drama. The writer of *Wakko no kinmedaru*, Shigemori Takako, gave as her reason for setting the drama in the years between 1955–65 as: "It was the period that built the present Japan" (NHK 1989b: 4). This is why the dramas can be said to be future-oriented: they are imbued with the ethic of national growth. History is considered only in so far as it explains the present. This is why all *asadora* are set within living memory: they are a meditation on the modern identity of Japan *through the vehicle of woman*. If we consider the heroine Oshin, this becomes very clear. Her life history parallels the modern history of Japan; and her final affluence, achieved through the super-market business, is a transparent metaphor. Oshin *is* Japan. Even her name, which is written in the Japanese phonetic alphabet, is open to a wide range of interpretations: the o is a diminutive; "shin" has a variety of meanings ranging from "endurance", "spirit", "truth", "god", "belief" to "new". Oshin stood for the aspirations held by her generation and the next.[21] This must be another reason why *Oshin* was so popular in the 1980s, the heroine's personal aspirations also standing for this national dream of regeneration.

With *Nonchan no yume*, this weighty penumbra was even more apparent. The series was aired to coincide with the completion of the Seto Bridge: the first fixed link between the main island, Honshu, and Shikoku, as well as the final linkage of all four main islands (since Hokkaido and Kyushu already had been connected to Honshu). With the completion of the Seto Bridge, it is now theoretically possible to walk between all four of the main islands of Japan. This bridge was built according to a "Japanese" design, the shape of its pillars modeled on the silhouette of the drum used in noh drama, and using Japanese technology. Television commentary on the bridge compared it to the Golden Gate Bridge in San Francisco, the symbol of another nation's progress. The importance of the bridge was also noted in the drama guide to *Nonchan no yume*: "the long-cherished dream of the opening of the Seto Bridge has come to pass" (1988a: 136). In a sense, the completion of the bridge represented the completion of an era of post-war reconstruction: the interlinking of the main islands and a new age of national confidence.

The drama's very first shot underlines this connection: the camera swoops down to frame a statue of Sakamoto Ryôma (1836–67) which stands sentinel above Kôchi bay. Sakamoto is a national hero, revered for his participation in the Meiji Restoration (1868), and is considered one of the most talented of the far-sighted individuals who set Japan on the road to modernization. His statue inevitably recalls an earlier time of reconstruction, an earlier *period.* The beginning of the drama thus asks us to consider periodicity. Following the shot of Sakamoto the camera moves to the castle; the narrator informs us that this was the only building left standing when Kôchi was bombed in the 1940s; then the camera cuts to the bustle of the modern city: the audience is forced to think on the contrast. Then, back into the drama, the narrator informs us that the time is 15 August 1945, while Nobuko appears on her bicycle bringing the midwife; the birth of Misao's baby follows. Everything underscores the fact that we are again at a historical turning-point: a new age such as was ushered in by Sakamoto and his contemporaries. This is stressed by Nobuko herself when she expresses her desire to do something to help women: "It is because it is a new age." Women were granted new freedoms in the 1947 constitution: her dream is the realization of those freedoms.

And so in 1988 the audience who followed Nonchan's story as she moved from Kôchi Prefecture to Tokyo, overcoming the obstacles that came in her way, were left hanging on Saturday mornings to ensure that they returned to their television sets on Monday to see how she managed the latest stumbling block. As the drama progressed the Japanese could not have known that it was indeed the end of another era: the emperor was dying and 1989 was to be the first year of the new emperor's reign (Heisei). The long Shôwa period, which began in 1926 and during which Japan had been reduced to ashes and then had risen like a phoenix, had come to an end.

Notes

1 I am indebted to Mr Shôji Tôru (producer of *Nonchan no yume*) for many discussions and kindnesses; to Mr Kanazawa Kôji (producer of *Kyô futari* and *Hirari*), Ms Sato Shigeko (scriptwriter of *Nonchan no yume*), Mr Tsuji Banri (editor of *Dorama*), and Mr Takada Hidekazu of Video Research KK. I would like to dedicate this piece to Ms Kubo Hide of Kyoto, who has discussed these dramas with me on many occasions, and who has been a well-loved teacher of young women in Japan since the 1920s. All translations from the Japanese in this article are my own. An earlier version of the paper was given at the Seventh Japanese Anthropology Workshop meeting in Banff, Canada in 1993. I am indebted to Professors Joy Hendry and Arthur Stockwin for opportunities to give presentations at Oxford Brookes University and the Nissan Institute at Oxford University in early 1994.
2 For a discussion of wrapping, see Hendry 1993: 8–26 and compare with Niyekawa 1984: 62.
3 See, for example, the magazine *Sutera* (*Stera*) 1993: 16–17, in which the propriety of the separation of the characters Yukiko and Yoichi in the drama *Hirari* is evaluated. The majority of people polled believed that Yukiko was being over-indulgent (*zeitaku sugiru*) in leaving her husband.
4 Among the best-known of Yamada's films are: the series *It's tough being a man* (*Otoko wa tsurai yo*), *Hometown* (*Furusato*), *Family* (*Kazoku*) and *Son* (*Musuko*).
5 The use of Western dramatic terminology is not out of place. Shakespeare was an influence suggested by Kanazawa Kôji (private communication, 1991) and this is attested to in the program *Hirari* (1992). In this *asadora*,

Hirari's grandfather spends his spare time reading Shakespeare in English and the drama ends with his plan to spend a year in England studying Shakespeare; while her other grandfather is a traditional Tokyo (*Edo*) man, the leader of the local firemen's chorus (a customary and prestigious position dating back to the Tokugawa period). The producer, Kanazawa, along with the scriptwriter, Uchidate, is making a comment about the cultural blending of modern Japan.

6   This tendency was pioneered by *Seishun Kazoku* (A Family in the Springtime of Life) (1989) written by Izawa Man, one of Japan's leading scriptwriters. See Toriyama (1986) for general information on Japanese television drama.

7   See, for example, *Asahi Shimbun* 1979: 13, where the critic remarks approvingly of the "nimble tempo" (*keikai na tempo*) in *Mâchan*; see also *Asahi Shimbun* (1986 back page), where the critic praises the heroine in terms of "being light-hearted and unsophisticated" (*soboku na akarusa*), and because "it is appropriate that the heroine be serious and single-minded" (*jimi de hitamuki na taipu ga fusawashii*) in *Miyako no kaze*.

8   Particularly in the last fifteen years, the majority of the writers of *asadora* have been women.

9   A radio serial broadcast every Thursday at 8.30 pm and famous for emptying women's bath-houses on account of its popularity.

10   Martinez (1992) describes a part of this process in her article on NHK's filming of the making of *noshi awabi* (dried abalone) in Kuzaki ward, Toba City, Mie Prefecture.

11   See Yamaguchi, Chapter 1.

12   See Hendry (1986: 94) for an astute comment on this with regard to wedding ceremonies: men take the official seat, but the women advise from the kitchen.

13   I am indebted to Video Research K.K. for all ratings figures.

14   See Hendry (1981: 13–31) for a discussion of this in relation to marriage. See also Smith (1983) and Befu (1981).

15   This discussion took place on 8 March 1993. Sato has written a wide range of scripts from historical dramas (*jidaigekei*) to modern dramas (*gendaigekei*). She is well known for the upbeat nature of her work in contrast to the work of Hashida Sugako.

16   See Muramatsu (1979: 23) for a map showing the various locations of the dramas.

17   I am indebted to Brian Powell for pointing out continuities between kabuki, *shingeki* (Western-style drama) and *asadora*.

18   A Japanese version of Cinderella, *Ochikubo*, is still performed; a production at the Minamiza Kabuki Theater in Kyoto in March of 1994 played to full houses.

19   Again, see Yamaguchi, Chapter 1.

20   The nexus of serial drama/women/nation is a potent one in popular serial dramas throughout Asia (see Abu-Lughod 1993 and Mankekar 1993).

21   See Harvey (1995) for a further discussion of the complex ideological packaging that constitutes *Oshin*.

References

Abu-Lughod, Lila 1993 "Finding a Place for Islam: Egyptian Television Serials and the National Interest" in *Public Culture* 5(3): 493–513.

Asahi Shimbun 2 April 1979 (morning edition): p. 13.
——19 March 1983 (morning edition): p. 22.
——6 October 1986 (morning edition): back page.
Befu Harumi 1981[1971] *Japan, an Anthropological Introduction.* Tokyo: Charles Tuttle.
Doiharu Sakuro 23 March 1993 "*Terebi Shôsetsu no koto*" (About serialized television drama) in *Yomiuri Shimbun,* (evening edition) page 11.
Egami Teruhiko 1968 *Terebi to bungei* (*Television and art*). Tokyo: Nansosha.
Harvey, Paul A. S. 1995 "Interpreting Oshin: War, History and Women in Modern Japan" in *Women, Media and Consumption in Japan* edited by Lise Skov and Brian Moeran. London: Curzon.
Hendry, Joy 1986[1981] *Marriage in Changing Japan.* Tokyo: Charles Tuttle.
——1993 *Wrapping Culture: Politeness, Presentation and Power in Japan and Other Societies.* Oxford: Clarendon.
Kato Hidetoshi 1973[1959] *Japanese Popular Culture: Studies in Mass Communication and Cultural Change.* Westport, Conn.: Greenwood Press.
Mankekar, Purnima 1993 "National Texts and Gendered Lives: an Ethnography of Television Viewers in a North Indian City" in *American Ethnologist* 20(3): 543–63.
Martinez, D. P. 1992 "NHK comes to Kuzaki: Ideology, Mythology and Documentary Film-making" in *Ideology and Practice in Modern Japan* edited by R. J. Goodman and Kirsten Refsing. London: Routledge.
Moon, Okypyo 1993 "Confucianism and Gender Segregation in Japan and Korea" in *Ideology and Practice in Modern Japan* edited by R. J. Goodman and Kirsten Refsing. London: Routledge.
Muramatsu Yasuko 1979 *Terebi dorama no josei gaku* (*Women's Studies and Television Drama*). Tokyo: Ontaimu Shuppan.
NHK *NHK Dorama gaido: Asa no renzoku terebi shôsetsu* (Guide to the dramas, published to coincide with the first episode of each drama)
——1983 *Oshin.* Tokyo: Nihon Hôsô Shuppan Kyokai.
——1984a *Romansu.* Tokyo: Nihon Hôsô Shuppan Kyokai.
——1984b *Kokoro wa istumo ramune iro.* Tokyo: Nihon Hôsô Shuppan Kyokai.
——1985a *Miotsukushi.* Tokyo: Nihon Hôsô Shuppan Kyokai.
——1985b *Ichiban daiko.* Tokyo: Nihon Hôsô Shuppan Kyokai.
——1986a *Hanegoma.* Tokyo: Nihon Hôsô Shuppan Kyokai.
——1986b *Miyako no kaze.* Tokyo: Nihon Hôsô Shuppan Kyokai.
——1987a *Chotchan.* Tokyo: Nihon Hôsô Shuppan Kyokai.
——1987b *Hassai sensei.* Tokyo: Nihon Hôsô Shuppan Kyokai.
——1988a *Nonchan no yume.* Tokyo: Nihon Hôsô Shuppan Kyokai.
——1988b *Junchan no ôenka.* Tokyo: Nihon Hôsô Shuppan Kyokai.
——1989a *Seishun kazoku.* Tokyo: Nihon Hôsô Shuppan Kyokai.
——1989b *Wakko no kinmedaru.* Tokyo: Nihon Hôsô Shuppan Kyokai.
——1990 *Kyô, futari.* Tokyo: Bunka Shuppan Kyoku.
——1991 *Kimi no na wa.* Tokyo: Nihon Hôsô Shuppan Kyokai.
——1992a *Onna wa dokyô.* Tokyo: Nihon Hôsô Shuppan Kyokai.
——1992b *Hirari.* Tokyo: Nihon Hôsô Shuppan Kyokai.
——1993 *Eenyôbo* Tokyo: Nihon Hôsô Shuppan Kyokai.
Niyekawa, Agnes M. 1984 "Analysis of Conflict in a Television Home Drama" in *Conflict in Japan* edited by Ellis Krauss et al. Honolulu: University of Hawaii Press.
Ono Tsutomu 1973[1959] "An Analysis of *Kimi no na wa*" (*What is your Name?*) in *Japanese Popular Culture* edited by Hidetoshi Kato. Westport, Conn.: Greenwood Press.

Powers, R. G. and Kato Hidetoshi (eds) 1989 *Handbook of Japanese Popular Culture: Studies in mass communication.* Westport, Conn.: Greenwood Press.

Satô Tadao 1978 *Kazoku no yomigaeri no tame ni: homu dorama ron (To bring the Family back to Life: Studies in Television Family Dramas).* Tokyo: Chikushobo.

Smith, R. J. 1983 *Japanese Society, Tradition, Self and Social Order.* Cambridge: Cambridge University Press.

Sutera (Stera) 12 March 1993.

Stronach, Bruce 1989 "Japanese Television" in *Handbook of Japanese Popular Culture* edited by R. G. Powers and Kato Hidetoshi. Westport, Conn.: Greenwood Press.

Toriyama Hiromu 1986 *Nihon terebi dorama-shi (History of Japanese Television Drama).* Tokyo: Eijinsha.

van Bremen, Jan 1993 "A beacon for the twenty-first century" in *Ideology and Practice in Modern Japan* edited by R. J. Goodman and Kirsten Refsing. London: Routledge.

PART IV

Shifting Boundaries

CHAPTER 8

Media Stories of Bliss and Mixed Blessings

HALLDÓR STEFÁNSSON

Introduction

Mutually feeding off each other and into each other, television and the popular press in post-war Japan have been the major agents for the cultural production of popular idols for mass consumption. In the corpus of dramas that are continuously being diffused through the mass media of modern Japanese society, these idols – somewhat like gods in polytheistic mythologies – while transcending ordinary existence also grow out of it and sustain that existence. While the production of these idols by the mass media mirrors a distorted version of social reality, it also plays a key role in creating new social realities.

Thus during the months of December 1992 and January 1993, the mass media in Japan became quasi-obsessed with the love stories of two young couples who suddenly rose to outshine all others in the glittering sky of Japanese celebrities. These were the stories of two "princes" and their "Cinderellas" who, as if by magic, had materialized out of a million possible candidates to become future "princesses". In this chapter, I argue that this pair of media fairytales contain none other than variations on the same classical theme appearing and re-appearing in multiple forms throughout the cultural history of Japan. This theme concerns the art of mastering the "outside" (Origuchi 1965; Yoshida 1981; Komatsu 1985, 1989).

As tradition would have it in Japanese culture, "meditating the blessings and warding off the curses" of the world beyond the local horizon was invariably a male prerogative (Stefánsson 1994). Recently, as the media stories described in this chapter suggest, many of the roles associated with representing and mediating the Other within different classes and professions throughout Japanese society have been undergoing a gender reversal. If Japanese urban women are being progressively "liberated" from their confinement within the household, a tendency to subject them to a new form of marginalization seems to be emerging. Increasingly now Japanese women find attributed to them a role of representing the ambiguous qualities associated with the outside.[1] Given this framework, this chapter will proceed to depict the *leitmotiv*, the characters, and the moods in the two narratives such as they appeared in a highly popularized form in the mass media, with some elaboration on the events' social and cultural significance.

The main characters

One of the fairytale princes was eternally "real". He represented what the Japanese people like to think of and cherish as their particular elite – that show-window of carefully arranged hybrid cultural flowering; those dazzling adornments from the archaic native past; the individuals who demonstrate a perfect mastery of all the paraphernalia of the finest Western arts: the imperial family. The prince was small in stature, but he was blessed with sophistication and an exquisite education.

The other prince was the ephemerally "imagined" common man, the media's favorite son and a manifestation of the public's own local tastes, desires, and pulsations. He had been elevated through the mass media to a symbolic throne. If this prince had the "exterior" of a giant, it later turned out his "interior" was of much smaller proportions.

These characterizations relate to the engagement stories of the imperial Crown Prince, Naruhito (33) heir to the Chrysanthemum throne, and of Takanohana (20), the young and rising super-star of sumo wrestling. The latter was assigned the princely mission of regaining the crown and highest honors of the sport after humiliating losses to the greater weight of foreign kinetic powers, that is to say from the over-sized and the over-weight Hawaiian wrestlers,[2] newly arrived on the scene. The true prince represented the age-old, somewhat effeminate sophistication of aristocratic values, a mastery of all the "soft arts" – words and sounds; the other prince had come to represent all the idealized qualities of masculinity in Japan, a mastery of all the "rough arts" – discipline, perseverance and physical prowess.

Then, by happy coincidence, in a season otherwise plagued by the continued depressing news of the deepening recession, these two key representative agents of the high/low and feminine/masculine strands of Japanese culture announced their plans for marriage. The entire mass media responded, rushing forth as if it had struck gold. In fact there were many reasons for the media's disproportionate carnival-like interest in the love-lives of these national celebrities. The press had long been frustrated by their agreement to refrain from reporting anything on the subject of the Crown Prince's (or, rather, his entourage's) quest for a bride.

Whatever role such media asceticism may have played in inflating the news when it finally broke, the nature of the female partners in both these "romances of the century" accounted for much of the fabulous success of the stories. Like their "princes", who represented such different aspects within the traditional domains of Japanese culture and society, the two young women, who were presented with great pomp as the brides-to-be, could hardly have been more unalike. And yet they shared one essential feature: qualities that made them both outstanding and, as such, ideal personifications of exotic other worlds.

Owada Masako, twenty-nine years old and a diplomat, "materialized" as the chosen super-woman after a search of more than seven years for a suitable spouse for the Crown Prince of Japan. The Imperial Household Agency reportedly investigated the family history and other attributes of about two hundred candidates. Perhaps no coincidence, Owada was the daughter of the highest ranking diplomat in the Japanese foreign service. She had spent half of her life here and there around the globe, as a member of her father's entourage in the various diplomatic assignments of his career. Thus she had received most of her schooling abroad: secondary education in Boston, and tertiary education at Harvard, Tokyo University and Oxford. If the cultural measurements of Masako could be taken, quantitatively as well as qualitatively, she might appear to be only "half-Japanese". Yet, due to her elitist up-bringing, she came up with the highest possible official qualification for dealing professionally with the Other.

The other female partner in this pair of Cinderella-like marriages between the "inside" and "outside" of Japan was Miyazawa Rie, a twenty-year-old actress and fashion model who is biologically "half", as the Japanese call the offspring of Japanese and foreign marriage partners. Rie's mother is Japanese and her father is Dutch. Though born and raised in Japan, Rie was, by the very condition of her family background, always "naturally" associated with the outside. Before her engagement to "the prince of sumo" she was already a rising starlet in the entertainment and popular magazine world in Japan.

In 1992, a wellknown Japanese photographer decided to put out a collection of nude photographs of Rie, and publish them as a book. The model being "half", he thought it most appropriate to portray her nudity against a foreign, exotic background. The artist and his model took themselves off to Santa Fe, New Mexico, where the delicate foreign-but-yet-oh-so-truly-Japanese beauty of Rie's physical features were intensified, cast against the rustic and desolate roughness of the American south-west. The "half-ness" of Rie's beauty was also marked

and enhanced by dressing her in an exotic, artistic gown. Kishin
Shinoyama's book instantly became a best-seller, causing the twin spot-
lights of the Japanese media and its related world of entertainment to
become permanently fixed on Rie. Rie Miyazawa rose from the dust
phoenix-like to become a super-star.

These were the two women the media had promised would serve as
the female protagonists in what everybody seemed to agree were tales of
the ideal *fin de siècle* romance, made in Japan. Both women, designated
to become modern incarnations of the traditional Janus-faced outsider,
the *marebito*[3] – albeit in different ways – seemed to call to mind the
invigorating, enlightening qualities of the outside world. One, with her
intellectual creativity and cosmopolitan wisdom of how to relate to the
heterogeneous Other, was at ease with the multicultural world of the
east coast of America; the other was still untamed, fertile and vigorous,
full of sexual energy which she exuded as she posed in the world of
pioneers of the Wild West.

The events

The coverage of this "miraculous" birth and growth of idealized
romance kept running for many weeks. It was relentlessly broadcast by
every radio and television station throughout the country, filled millions
of copies of all sorts of illustrated publications from hard-core tabloids
to intellectual journals with detailed, worked-over accounts, quoting
and feeding on each other, in an endlessly expanding, tautological
circle.[4] The four different actors of this soap opera, each leading his or
her professional life at what seemed light-years removed from the other,
were constantly being spied upon by armies of reporters. These latter
snatched up and exposed whatever insignificant gossip, rumor, or
general misinformation they could sniff out concerning their "heroes
and heroines of love". When the actors themselves appeared, it was
through carefully staged episodes, played out on the paramount stage
of public life in post-modern Japan: the luxury hotel.

The high temples of Japanese consumer society are modestly named
"hotels". In fact, most major Japanese hotels are institutions serving as
the privileged loci for many of the culturally and socially designated
events in the public and private lives of people from all walks of life.
They provide the elaborate backdrop before which extraordinary events
are carried out and publicly endorsed. In Japanese society they stand for
luxury, designed to give surplus value to weddings (never funerals),
major birthday parties, common celebrations, lovers' rendezvous[5] and,
last but not least, the pronouncement of important public statements at
press conferences.

It was natural therefore that the two almost-simultaneous explosions of media mid-winter interest in the love stories of these celebrities took place during press conferences held at famous luxury hotels (the New Otani, Hotel Pacific, Imperial Hotel, Ambassadeur, etc.). The announcements of the engagement, of the wedding day, and, in the case of the unfortunate Rie–Taka couple, the separately held press meetings for the announcement of their break-up, were all delivered at hotels. Each time, in the best of Japanese modern traditions, between two and four hundred journalists assembled to interview the celebrities. The events consisted in squeezing out statements about main actors' feelings, as well as collecting direct quotations from supposedly private conversations held prior to the public announcements.

At a perfectly staged press meeting, skilfully melting millions of hearts and causing twice as many eyes to water throughout the nation, the soft-spoken imperial prince revealed before the television cameras the simple words which finally, after months of persistent courtship, won him Masako's hand in marriage: "I will do my utmost to protect you for the rest of my life."

On the other hand, the hapless Prince of Sumo seriously outraged the larger part of the Japanese population when stuttering, pouting and sobbing before the cameras, he repeated the abrupt way in which he had announced to Rie, the "half" idol and sex symbol, his sudden decision to break off their engagement: "My love for you has vanished."

Deconstructing these two widely publicized attempts at *kokusaika* (internationalization Japanese-style) – one successful and the other unsuccessful – can provide us with insights into some of the changes that have recently been remodeling Japanese society and culture. Many of these changes have uprooted and transformed so-called traditional sex roles and the division of labor between the sexes inside Japan. They have also radically altered how men and women are in different ways expected to relate to, internalize and represent the world outside Japan.

Inside and outside

The tendency to associate the widely-used classificatory concepts of *uchi* (inside) and *soto* (outside) in Japan with female and male domains respectively is wellknown.[6] Yet, interestingly, the gendered qualification in this form of Japanese classification does not turn out to be rigidly fixed (see Kondo 1990; Bachnik and Quinn 1994). Here one is reminded of the traditional sexual ambiguity of the outsider god, Ebisu, in Japanese popular religion (Namihira 1978; Yoshida 1981; Stefánsson 1994). Ebisu, a uniquely hermaphrodite entity in the imagery of Japanese folk religion, has long constituted one of the major representations of the *soto* in Japanese popular culture. In general, the ambiguity of the *soto* naturally suggests its use as a "wild card", a privileged domain for representing incongruities born out of the social and cultural upheavals in recent years in Japan. Thus, a whole variety of "new" female behavior, oblivious to the proper order of things in the relations between the sexes, or to their "destiny" to become housewives and mothers, has come to be regarded as outlandish. Interestingly, however, this association with the *soto* seems more often than not to make modern Japanese women appear all the more desirable to the male insiders who become their partners.

In Japanese society itself the most elevated ranks of what can be seen to be a privileged aspect of the outside have always been occupied by the imperial family itself. Even within the imperial domain a reversal in the sexual division of labor that formerly applied seems to have taken place in post-war Japan.[7] During the Meiji era the emperor had been dressed up to look like the paramount awe-inspiring (*kowai*) patriarch, who stared eagle-eyed out of his photograph, which was always hung high on the walls of most people's homes; thus the emperor watched over his nation (Fujitani 1992). If neither the Taishô Emperor, nor the Shôwa Emperor (in spite of the latter's long reign) inspired such awe, at least their reigns were still perceived as being of a patriarchal nature.

The post-war period brought about a systematic dissolution of the institutions on which the patriarchal society had rested. The whole of society, from the grass-roots up to the highest echelons of the ruling class, was now to be re-fashioned on the Anglo-American model of democracy. Instead of the emperor's portrait sternly watching over the nation, Japan has become the nation that gets an occasional peek, through the modern forms of the mass media, at the imperial family performing the hygienic formalities of its official duties.

First and foremost, the emperor now appears as a cute (*kawaii*), effeminate figure, spending most of his time and energy pursuing esthetic and intellectual frivolities, as well as acting out cosmopolitan etiquette. The roles played by the present Heisei Emperor and his son, Crown Prince Naruhito, have gradually reduced them to mere decorative symbols. They appear disempowered even within life at court, their domestic sphere. Moreover, the reformed imperial household has recently been introducing a tradition stipulating that its emperors should marry clear-headed, modern women from outside aristocratic circles; women who are capable of dealing with the more mundane aspects of royal life. This has given rise to what appears to the public to be a succession of increasingly empowered women at court (Michiko, Masako ...). These women have been engaged in energetically introducing long-repressed (subversive) female concerns at the very foundation of the paramount institution of patriarchy in the country. In fact this apparent reversal in the balance of power between the sexes within the imperial domain is but a reflection of what has otherwise been happening throughout society in Japan during the post-war period.

The Meiji authorities took it as their mission to educate the whole of the Japanese population to make it obey Confucian ethics. According to these, all should submit to patriarchal figures in a hierarchy of power relations that placed women at or even below the bottom of society. Compliance became the cardinal virtue. In the domestic sphere, the master (*kachô*) of the household (*ie*) had absolute authority.

The Japanese defeat at the end of World War II and the American occupation not only introduced democratic ways of ruling and organizing the country, but provoked changes in the worldview and ethics of the population as well. The imperial institution was allowed to survive, but it did so merely as a living ghost for nearly half a century, until the death of Emperor Hirohito, the last patriarchal emperor. With the arrival of his son Akihito on the throne, the reformed institution was ripe to impose itself, once again, as an idealized model for life in society.

For this purpose the royal family had to be convincingly "resurrected" by the mass media. It had to be shown to incarnate in a crystal-pure form some of the "new" core values that had taken root and developed among the common people during the post-war years; foremost among these was the equality of the sexes in the domestic sphere. Even if the *kachô* now seem to have gone the way of the dinosaurs, women speaking politely to strangers often refer to their husbands as "my master" (*uchi no shujin*). In reality, however, the manifold changes that have transformed Japanese society and culture post-war have made Japanese women the absolute controllers of everything relating to the domestic sphere of life in the country. Family finances, children's education, consumption, community affairs, all these practical aspects of life are now, for the most part, run and dominated by housewives in Japan (Iwao 1992).

From early childhood Crown Prince Naruhito was raised to master two sets of disparate qualities: one identified with the ways of Japanese tradition and the other with the mores and manners of a cosmopolitan elite (cf. Sugiyama-Lebra 1992). During the 1980s when "internationalization" (*kokusaika*) became an official ideology and a fashionable trend in Japanese society (Stefánsson 1994), Naruhito emerged as a role model for many broad-minded, middle-class Japanese youths. Having been initiated in the most exclusive circles of the foreign Other, Oxford, and being at the same time so carefully enshrouded in the mystique of imperial tradition (that is, being at the same time more foreign and more Japanese than the rest of his countrymen) turned Naruhito into a beloved princely mediator. Naturally his bride, Owada Masako, turned out to be the perfect match, since she herself was a sort of neat "half": she had one foot in the Japanese inside world, with her high-bourgeois family background, and the other in the outside with her first-hand experience in diplomacy and her familiarity with foreign cultures. Naruhito and Masako were the perfect ingredients for the making of a successful "all-Japanese international marriage".

Rie, the newly produced sex symbol, seen to be "international" in Japan, seemed taken aback at the meeting at the New Otani Hotel in late January, when she was told by her fiancé that their "story" was over and that he did not love her any more. Having recovered from the first shock she, in turn, reserved a hall at the Pacific Hotel and called a press conference. A talented and professional actress – unlike her uncouth, stuttering partner – she won her audience by playing her role appropriately and producing the right dramatic impact. With a most sincere and hurt expression but no tears, Rie looked straight into the hundreds of flashing cameras and, without a blink, artistically delivered the lines which were then repeatedly televised throughout 27 January 1993:

> We will not become the most important partners in each other's life. I don't think it matters in the affairs of the heart to ask, when it doesn't work, whose fault it is. Anyway, I have no intention of becoming the heroine of some sort of tragic love story.

Taka's entourage reacted to Rie's performance by hastily calling a press conference the same evening, this time at his father's sumo stable, the Fujishima-*beya*. A mass media battalion of four hundred journalists was present. For several reasons it turned into something rather rare in Japan: a media fiasco. Wrestlers are quite accustomed to the press, but mainly within the highly conventional frame of the world of sumo where they are not expected to wax eloquent. Within the confines of the sumo world, for example, in interviews following an outstanding performance, the wrestler is merely expected to grunt and to breathe heavily into the microphone. When asked to explain his sudden falling out of love with Rie, all Taka could manage was: "I told her: 'I don't love you any more'."

This would have been insensitive enough, thrown in the face of the ex-loved one, but bluntly aired at a press conference, his speech instantly turned the star of sumo into a crashing meteorite, at least as far as the female population was concerned. Things were all the more awkward for their timing: this event occurred the very day Taka had been officially promoted to the title of *Ozeki*, the second highest rank in sumo, and had taken on his father's name, Takanohana. Normally, this would have been a day of most intense, joyful celebrations, and in Japan one is not allowed to neglect norms. Thus, in one day the hapless wrestler was rushed back and forth between heaven and hell.

Omnivorous and insatiable as is the press, this could not be the end of the story. Every day brought follow-ups and endless speculation as to what and why things had gone wrong between these two stars whom everyone had been led to believe were born to shine together. The reasons the investigators of the tabloid press suggested for the failure of the common people's "international marriage of the century" were revealing.

It was suggested that the young couple had probably been too hasty in announcing their engagement, that they had omitted to test the ground with their entourage, and forgotten to find out what others felt about their marriage. The young and carefree celebrities were simply said to have started dating each other, thinking they looked splendid as "the beauty and the beast", as a "half" outlandish sex symbol and an astoundingly handsome Japanese *rikishi*.

Somewhat pathetically, the only blame that was openly cast on Rie was that, despite her promise to withdraw from the world of entertainment and retire definitely to the "inside" – a condition for marrying her sumo star – she continued appearing in commercials and flying off to lend her image to US politics, attending President Bill Clinton's inauguration party. In fact, as she later revealed, that was a false claim since she had made it clear she would give up her career before getting married.

Some interpreters thought it more fatal for the outcome of the story that the stars' families or – more importantly – their mothers, did not seem to get along together. It was suggested that Rie's mother got drunk and started boasting to her future in-laws of her daughter's exploits as a sex symbol, that is to say, enumerating the famous men who had manifested their desire for her. Of course sumo wrestlers are well known for their association with the floating world (Japan's demi-monde), but when it comes to marriage, their expectations are conservative and future brides are expected to be virgins. Rie's mother inadvertently, while she thought she was just confirming the qualities that had assured her daughter a super-star's place in the world of entertainment, was in fact trampling on the conservative moral code of the world of sumo. Rie's plans for the future were jeopardized as she dropped out of the picture.

In one final hypothesis, the failure of this love story to evolve into a proper marriage was squarely blamed on the National Sumo Association. As rumor had it, its leaders had found the union an unbecoming one for someone who was heir to one of the most prestigious stables in

the whole of the sumo world. In their judgement marriage with someone who was only half Japanese was a most inappropriate match for a
savior: a young man intended to retrieve sumo from the hands of the
foreigners who had lately come to invade and dominate it.

As it turned out, the small but truly imperial prince with the big heart,
acting pretty much of his own accord, went out and struggled to win his
female *marebito*-turned-princess. By doing so, he gained a "liberator"
who gave him privileged access to the "real world". On the other hand,
the self-indulgent giant prince of sumo, by spontaneously falling for the
star of another solar system, lacked the necessary courage to head off
opposition, and retreated, tail between his legs, into his familiar and
closed world of sumo. But is this not being a bit too harsh on Taka? He
had, in fact, nowhere to go. As a "prince" he was non-existent outside
the world of sumo. He could flirt with the outside, but by no means was
he allowed to marry into it! If there was any domain within Japanese
society and culture that did not aspire to "internationalization", that was
definitely not in a *kokusai* mood, that did not desire an invigorating
marriage to the outside, that desperately felt the need to generate
power from within its own ranks and abhorred the idea of any more
ijin,[8] male or female, it was the world of sumo.

Conclusion

Japan has a long history of inventing dualistic cultural idioms for recon-
ciling incongruities arising in the inevitable encounters between the
inside and the outside, the local and the alien, tradition and modernity
(*honji-suijaku*, *wakon-kansai*, *wakon-yôsai* and so on). Such idioms have
been employed throughout much of the known history of Japan,
doubtless helping to sustain a distinct identity. Throughout Japanese
cultural history, boundaries between the collective "inside" and the surrounding world have been maintained by inventing, re-inventing and
instituting various cultural processes to drive and to regulate accultur-
ation: to permit a "complex adoption and final acceptance of, and a
profound alienation from outward alien form as necessary for the
expression of otherwise ineffable Japanese meaning" (Pollack 1986: 58).

In this chapter I have used a set of representative media stories to
demonstrate what seems to be the recent tendency in Japan, a tendency
to re-cast the onerous, but important, taks of domesticating the ever-
growing influence from the outside world through a gendered division
of labor. Important historical changes during the post-war era have
affected many aspects of the relations between the sexes, in the private
as well as in the public domain. In retrospect, great efforts have been
made towards promoting social equality between the sexes. Provisions

in the new post-war constitution, the progressive rise in the numbers of women attaining higher education, and the passing of an equal employment opportunity law are all undeniable signs of such a process.

In practice, however, apart from the extraordinary times of the recent, but short-lived, economic carnival commonly known as the "bubble years", only modest progress has been made towards integrating women into the permanent workforce in Japan on an equal basis. Outstandingly, though, women have been recruited in greater numbers than men to serve in numerous professions which have prospered as a result of the campaign of internationalization which has been officially promoted. Thus women are beginning to dominate in jobs such as television announcers, journalists, language teachers, tour guides, interpreters, public relations consultants, diplomats, etc. If the idealized male role now consists of being the guardian of the inside, incarnating the real essence of Japaneseness, the one the more ambitious among Japanese women seem to have made their own is the art of mastering alien forms. As such, women are liable to be ascribed all the ambiguities of the pair familiar from the deity Ebisu-*ijin*.

Kokusaika or "internationalization Japanese-style" has been a part of the political and educational agenda in Japan now for more than a decade. Furthermore, it has seeped into and filtered down through society where it has found multiple imaginative expressions in popular culture. In this most fertile ground, where the seeds of *kokusaika* have fallen, rival meanings are contested, changes in mood are legend, ambiguity abounds. Just as Captain James Cook could be "in and out of season" in Hawaii – first celebrated as the god Lono, then slain upon his untimely, latter appearance (Sahlins 1985: 120–35) – the media stories related above show that circumstances in different settings of social life in Japan guide the often diametrically opposed and fickle reactions that people demonstrate in their encounters with the outside and its embodiments.

Notes

1   See the editor's introduction for an argument on how women are both "outsiders" and yet must become "insiders" in Japanese society.
2   Here I am referring to the two best known among the foreign stars of sumo, Konishiki and Akebono. The former is of Samoan descent, born and raised on Hawaii, but has recently become a Japanese national. The second is of mixed native Hawaiian and Caucasian-American descent, and American by nationality.
3   A name for the ambiguous "stranger" in Japanese folklore. The *marebito* were the privileged possessors of mystical powers, to be adored, pacified, or prayed to for such practical purposes as driving out evil spirits or turning away any of the myriad forms of human suffering.

4   The mass media material studied for the writing of this article consisted of a broad sample of newspaper articles; numerous variety shows on television (such as the *Waido Shô*); and popular magazines, such as *Shukan Asahi, Asahi Geino, Mainichi Gurafu,* and so on.

5   Some of the famous as well as infamous "love hotels" are now being turned into "boutique hotels". These innovative businesses are cashing in on the idea that the "mood for love" can be noticeably enhanced when warmed up with designer-label luxury gifts (*burando seihin*, lit. "brand products").

6   On this see Smith 1987.

7   See Chapter 1.

8   Another term for "stranger" in Japanese.

References

Bachnik, J. and Quinn, C. J. (eds) 1994 *Situated Meaning, Inside and Outside in Japanese Self, Society and Language.* Princeton: Princeton University Press.

Fujitani T. 1992 "Electronic Pageantry and Japan's 'Symbolic Emperor'" in *Journal of Asian Studies* vol. 15(4): 824–51.

Iwao Sumiko 1992 *The Japanese Woman: Traditional image and changing reality.* New York: The Free Press.

Komatsu K. 1985 *Ijinron (Essay on the Stranger).* Tokyo: Seidosha.

——1989 *Akureiron (A Study of Evil Spirits).* Tokyo: Seidosha.

Kondo, D. 1990 *Crafting Selves: Power, gender and discourses of identity in a Japanese workplace.* Chicago: University of Chicago Press.

Namihira E. 1978 "*Suishitai wo Ebisu toshite matsuru shinkô: Sono imi to kaishaku*" (The Belief Behind Worshipping a Corpse as a Manifestation of Ebisu: Its meaning and interpretation) in *Minzokugaku Kenkyû* vol. 1(42): 334–55.

Origuchi, S. 1975–76 *Origuchi Shinobu Zenshû (Collected works of Origuchi Shinobu)* vols. I, II, VII. Tokyo: Chûôkôronsha.

Pollack, David 1986 *The Fracture of Meaning: Japan's Synthesis of China from the Eighth through the Eighteenth Centuries.* Princeton: Princeton University Press.

Sahlins, M. 1985 *Islands of History.* Chicago: University of Chicago Press.

Smith, R. 1987 "Gender Inequality in Contemporary Japan" in *Journal of Japanese Studies* vol. 13(1).

Stefánsson, H. 1994 "The 'outside' and the 'outsider' in Japan: the gender of the *kokusaika*" in *Bulletin of the Cultural and the Natural Sciences in Osaka Gakuin University,* no. 29.

Sugiyama-Lebra, Takie 1992 *Above the Clouds: Status culture of the modern Japanese.* Berkeley: University of California Press.

Yoshida T. 1981 "The Stranger as God: the Place of the Outsider in Japanese Folk Religion" in *Ethnology* vol. 20(2): 87–99.

CHAPTER 9

The Cult of Oguricap
Or, how women changed the social value of Japanese horse-racing

NAGASHIMA NOBUHIRO

Introduction

This chapter is mainly concerned with a race horse named Oguricap and, as a complement, with a jockey named Take Yutake.[1] Their story begins in the early 1980s when the social status of horse-racing in Japan began to change and improve. This was brought about mainly by the efforts of the Japan Racing Association (JRA);[2] coupled with the fortuitous appearances of two successive triple crown horses, Mr CB (1983) and Simbori Rudolf (1984) on the courses. But the really drastic change began in the year 1988 when there emerged two great popular heroes: Oguricap, the horse known as the gray monster, and Take Yutaka, the brilliant, handsome young jockey. Women of all ages were fascinated with these new heroes and they not only created a new atmosphere at race courses, which had been dominated by rather melancholy-looking men, but they also transformed this socially unacceptable form of gambling into an enjoyable, if not fully respectable, form of leisure.

The phenomena focussed around the horse – beginning with the sudden increased enthusiasm for him[3] – I shall term "the cult of Oguricap", for three reasons. First, the extent to which he was, and still is after retirement, admired is really extravagant (as will be shown below) and this alone accords with a dictionary definition of a "cult". Second, he has been surrounded by myth and deified as it were by his followers, and the process of the formation of followers is comparable to that of a new religion. Third, the stud where he now lives as a stallion has become a sort of shrine where endless pilgrims visit; this can also be likened to religious worship. I shall call the fanatical following of the jockey "the cult of Take Yutaka", since it has certain parallels with the above, though to a lesser degree.

Negative attitudes towards racing and race-goers in the recent past

Until recently in Japan horse-racing had been one of several unpopular
events which were regarded more as a form of mere gambling than as
sport.[4] Ordinary citizens have tended to look down on race-goers and
have been known to cast suspicious or scornful looks on the latter as they
made their way to a local race-course. It was socially dangerous to talk
about horse-racing in public, especially in one's office over lunch or a
cup of coffee, because its negative aspects and suspected bad influence
were taken for granted among those who had never been to the races
themselves. Bank employees and high-ranking civil servants could lose
their jobs if found to be horse-racing fans. Thus, race-lovers could be
said to be heavily discriminated against. These attitudes, however, were
diametrically opposed to those in early modern times, when horse-racing
was considered one of the most prestigious sports and was under the
patronage of the Emperor Meiji.

Modern racing in Japan has been a "tradition" since before Meiji
(1868–1912) when it was introduced by British diplomats, on the beach
at Yokohama in 1861. The Edo government took an interest in this,
helped the foreigners to build a race course, and soon Japanese samurai
joined as the first jockeys. During the previous period, Edo (1615–1868),
gambling by ordinary citizens, amongst whom there existed the deeply-
rooted notion that any form of gambling was abominable, had been
totally prohibited.[5] There did exist a small sector of the population to
whose gambling the authorities turned a blind eye and these people were
usually called *asobinin* (play people).[6]

The Meiji government, which overthrew the Edo government in 1868,
inherited the criminal code under which any form of gambling was
illegal. On the other hand, it realized that it was natural for British
residents to bet on horses and they were allowed to do so, at first privately
and then in an organized way. Selected passages from an early Meiji
novel illustrate the prestigious nature of the sport at this time:

> It was on the 28th of April, 1886, the second day of the spring meeting held at
> the Shinobazu-no-ike area, honoured by the presence of His Majesty the
> Emperor Meiji ... Not only nobles and gentlemen but also many others from
> remote areas were hurrying either in coaches or rickshaws to Ueno Park,
> where the race course was temporarily set up ... The crowd was so numerous
> that the ground could not be seen ... At the fence of the higher stand were
> spread deep-purple curtains. Noble ladies, young and old, were dressed so
> colorfully that they looked as though hundreds of beautiful flowers were in
> competition ... (Sudo 1887, cited in Kida 1966: 168–9)

Indeed this was just like a miniature Royal Ascot and was attended by
hundreds of women and noble ladies. The latter had jointly contributed

to the winner's prize. The government also made horse-racing the occasion for social intercourse between upper-class Japanese and foreign elites. The official justification for holding meets was given as a military one: to improve the quality of Japanese horses for cavalries.

In 1888 the Japanese Racing Club, which was run by foreigners, started to sell printed betting slips at one dollar each. In due course, several horse-racing clubs run by Japanese were formed, the Ikegami club petitioned the government for permission to sell betting slips and this was officially granted in 1905. The price of a bet to win was fixed at ten yen, much too expensive for ordinary citizens. Yet on the day of the first Ikegami meeting, officials were astonished not only at the sheer number of people attending, which was large, but also at the atmosphere, which was predominantly that of gamblers. Many *yakuza*-type newcomers were excited at this semi-legalized gambling. Even upper-class gentlemen were there to taste the hitherto-prohibited fruit. What had been a place of elegant social intercourse with an international flavour was thus changed into one of a *tekkaba* (lit. "the place of red hot iron"; an allusion to a gambler's den). The "fever" for this type of new gambling grew as time passed and criticism of it also became more heated. Newspapers such as the Osaka *Asahi* noted:

> Even gentlemen wearing silk hats and frock coats ... army officers, bank and company executives, the head of a hospital, (in so far as they bet on the horses) are no more than *bakuchiuchi* (illegal gamblers). (13 September 1908)

Gambling became a national issue and the government had to prohibit the sale of betting slips. When betting was re-introduced fifteen years later, the scene at any race course had become entirely different, filled mainly with punters, although a small number of committed aristocrats, business tycoons and politicians remained fans. The glorious days of horse-racing had gone and it became almost a forbidden thing for ordinary citizens.

From this period on until recently, race-goers were mostly men, who were either compulsive gamblers connected somehow with the darker side of Japanese society, or a small number of ordinary citizens concealing their own identity in order to enjoy the thrills of both horse-racing and the unpopular adventure of betting. Together they created a culture of twisted manliness, not unlike that developed by the *yakuza*. From their point of view, there could be no room for women and children at a race course.

This is the socio-historical background against which the two cults emerged. I will first describe their main features, then the role played by women in these cults. I will make special reference to the stuffed

Oguricap toys and, finally, I shall also consider the extent to which horse-racing today can be regarded as a form of popular culture.

The horse and jockey

Oguricap, a gray two-year-old out of Silver Shark by Dancing Cap, started his racing at Kasamatsu, one of the Chihô (regional) courses in May 1987. He lost his first race, being placed second, but then won eight races in a row. The rumor that a gray monster (*ashige no kaibutsu*) had appeared reached race fans all over Japan. Expectations that he might run at Chûô (Central) race courses grew and Mr Oguri, his owner, sold Oguricap so that he was finally transferred to JRA courses in January of 1988, after winning ten races out of twelve.

By this time, Oguricap was being compared to Haiseiko, the legendary race-horse of the 1970s, who had also moved from Chihô to Chûô after a brilliant record on the former courses. Haiseiko had won six races in a row on Chihô courses and on Chûô courses went on to win four successive Group races,[7] including the Satsuki-Shô which is equivalent to the British 2,000 Guineas. A so-called Haiseiko boom spread like fever throughout Japan, temporarily arousing positive interest in racing from the general public for the first time since 1908. Haiseiko could be seen as Oguricap's forerunner, in that the former can be credited with the honor of heralding the present popularity of horse-racing in Japan. Haiseiko's defeat at the Derby in 1973 produced nationwide lamentation.

Fifteen years later Oguricap fulfilled all expectations that he would repeat the feats of Haiseiko. By the middle of July he had won three Group 3 (G3) and two Group 2 (G2) races in a row. It was his tragic misfortune that he was not entered in the "classic" races for three-year-olds, for both his owner and trainer did not dream that he had such a brilliant career before him.

Oguricap's first four races in Chûô were all run on western courses (Osaka, Kyoto and Nagoya), and his first appearance in Tokyo was for the New Zealand Trophy (G3) in June. I was there for the event, and I remember that as soon as I entered the gate that day, I felt that something was different about the atmosphere. Looking around, I perceived that there were more women there than I had ever seen before, and that there were also more young men. This was an early stage in the cult of Oguricap.

At the paddock, I heard the call "Oguri-*chan*".[8] Also, I heard sighs and grumbles from old fans along the lines of: "Hasn't the world changed?" "These people don't know anything about horse-racing." Or: "What are these *gaki* (kids) doing in this sacred adult space?"

An easy win in this race fueled the Oguri-fever, which spread at his next outing in early October for the Group 2 race, Mainichi Oukan. He also won this easily and at the following Emperor's Prize (Tennô Shô), a G1 race, fans treated him as if he were a defending champion rather than a three-year-old challenger up against a field of tougher older horses, headed by another gray, Tamamo Cross.[9] Indeed the two grays dominated the field, finishing first and second, but the winner was Tamamo Cross. Oguricap's strong, late run never seemed dangerous, although it was deeply satisfying to those who had come only to watch him. This first defeat was graciously accepted by Oguricap's fans, since Tamamo Cross was in his prime at the age of four, and the duel was to be talked about for many years.

The next November came the Japan Cup, the only international race held in this closed society. Here again Oguricap fought bravely against a combined invasion force of British, French and American horses, as well as against top-ranked Japanese horses. He finished third behind Pay the Butler (USA) and Tamamo Cross in a very close finish.

Then came the Arima Kinen (G1) race on the last Sunday of the year. This race has the feel of a festival in which the sound of *Jingle Bells* and Beethoven's Ninth Symphony mix with the noises of end-of-the-year sales. If we can call the atmosphere of the Derby "Apollonion", that of Arima is surely "Dionysian", carnival-like. The main runners for this race are determined by the votes of fans, who thus directly participate in this race, making for great excitement.

The jockey riding Oguricap this time was Okabe Yukio, the number one jockey of the day. The race became another, and final, duel between Oguricap and Tamamo Cross. Oguricap won by half a length. The followers of Oguricap swelled enormously with this victory and his cult was firmly established. But, unfortunately, Oguricap was found to be injured and had to be laid off for nine months after this race. Tamamo Cross then retired with the title of "Horse of the Year" and Oguricap was named "best three-year-old".

Meanwhile, Take Yutaka, who had obtained his jockey's license only in March of 1987 at the age of 18, proved himself a very promising rider from the start. It was a great feat for him, as a novice, to have won the November Kikuka Shô (a G1 race, equivalent to the St Leger) and the Ouka Shô (again, G1) in April of the next year. He also won many races, breaking various records. As a son of the famous ex-jockey and trainer, Take Kunihiko, this novice was actually seen as a "thoroughbred" and his wins proved that he richly deserved the metaphor and he was soon nicknamed *tensai* (genius).

Again, Take Yutaka was following in the footsteps of a precursor, the jockey Mickey (Matsunaga Mikio), a handsome novice who had attracted the attention of many young women, just like a pop star. Super-star jockeys were a new phenomenon in the racing world. Now the advent of Yutaka accelerated this trend. For the first time in the history of Japanese horse-racing, the front parts of both the paddock and the rail were occupied by women who did not seem to know much about racing. Indeed little did they care how a race was run, as long as they could watch Yutaka. In due course older women also became interested in this much-talked about "prince" and in racing itself.

In this way, two different, but mutually influencing cults, that of Oguricap and Take Yutake, were formed throughout 1988–89. The horse and man were fated to meet.

The final stretch

Oguricap came back in September 1989 for the All Comers Race (G3), and his win over lesser rivals was greeted with loud cheers. Next he won the Mainichi Oukan (G2) in a very close finish. Then came the Tennô Shô (G1), where he had to face top horses, especially Super Creek ridden by Take Yutaka. Again he fought in his typically gallant way, but was narrowly defeated by Super Creek. At the Japan Cup, the field was seemingly dominated by European and American horses, but the winner was Hollicks, an Australian, and Oguricap ran a very close second – both marking a record time of 2 minutes 22.2 seconds for 2,400 metres, more than two seconds faster than the previous year's time. Perhaps this exhausted him: Oguricap finished fifth in the Arima Kinen, and then had to again take a rest.

He reappeared in May 1990 in the Yasuda Kinen (G1), ridden for the first time by Take Yutaka, but he looked like a different horse: feeble and tired. Nevertheless, Oguricap won this race brilliantly. "I said so," his delighted followers cried out. Next he lost the Takarazuka Kinen (G1) in June. Although placed second, it was a complete defeat which left him trailing behind the winner. His followers started to recall the scandal of the previous year, when his then-owner was expelled from the Owners' Association after he was found guilty of tax evasion, and Oguricap was sold to his third owner at an alleged 300 million yen. Rumors said that in order to recover the amount of money he had paid, Oguricap's owner wanted him to run as many times as possible – irrespective of his physical condition. "Otherwise," cried his fans, most of whom were men, "the strongest horse in our time could not have been defeated in such a miserable way."

Nonetheless, Oguricap challenged in the Tennô Shô in October 1990. It was clear that he was not fully recovered and when I myself saw him at the paddock, I thought it inhuman to make him run on that day, he

looked so weak. The result was as feared by many: sixth place behind
Yaenomuteki; but the distance by which he lost was less than four
lengths, a heartening defeat. I saw many girls burst into tears, crying:
"Oguri-*chan*, Oguri-*chan*".

Against a storm of protests, he was again entered for the Japan Cup
and it turned out to be his worst race, coming eleventh in a field of
fifteen. His retirement was thought to be imminent, but to everybody's
surprise it was announced that he would run in that year's Arima Kinen.
Eventually he was under starter's orders, ridden by Take Yutaka. For this
race, the Nakayama race course was filled with thunderous cries and
sixteen horses cut through the roar. Oguricap was just behind the early
leaders until the last corner when Yutaka urged him to the front. "Too
early", thought many, but the jockey fought it out to the finish and won.
"Oguri! Oguri! Oguri!" The three cheers lasted more than ten minutes.
There was a standing ovation. Tears ran down the faces of both men and
women; it was at this moment that Oguricap, the gray monster, became
a living legend.

Recently, in my university staff room, I was asked by a woman who is a
professor in education whether I had a photograph of Oguricap. "Yes
indeed, but why?" I asked.

"I like him," was the response.
"Since when?"
"I saw the Arima Kinen on television and was much moved."

By this she meant his last Arima race. I have found that many women
became followers of Oguricap after his final run. Many of them appear
never to have seen Oguricap racing in the flesh or at all.

Oguricap as talisman

One type of commercial goods which contributed enormously towards
making Oguricap known among the wider population and which
expanded his cult was the *nuigurumi*, or stuffed toy. A version of this toy
was first sold in the autumn of 1989 and it proved an instant success. Its
size varied, the smallest being about 20 centimetres and sold for 2,000
yen. The biggest toy cost 40,000 yen. The face of the toy was covered with
nice-looking cloth and on its back there was another cloth with Oguricap's racing number. It was very cute and also felt nice to touch. Its
popularity far exceeded the manufacturer's expectations, and those who
wanted to buy them had to wait many weeks. It became a fashion to place
small Oguricap toys in the back of cars where they could be seen from
the outside. Although women were the main buyers, men also joined
the craze.

I have interviewed three women who are experts in the field, asking each of them how they interpreted the sudden participation of women in horse-racing and the role played by the Oguricap *nuigurumi* in this phenomenon. Their thoughts on the subject were quite complex and revealed more about inner states than about sociological processes. With apologies to them, I present some of their ideas here in a simplified version.

Ms Komaki Shun, who has been writing articles about both horse-racing and riding, stressed the healing effects of Oguricap and of his *nuigurumi*. She described the initial stage of the cult as a fashion into which young women plunged blindly without any sense of guilt. They had a desire to belong to something and Oguricap, who seemed always to them to shine with glory, offered them an identity. Through this identification, they were less lonely, they were "healed" of loneliness. Then the production of his *nuigurumi* made it possible for each of them to possess their own personal Oguricap, thus fragmenting the one living Oguricap into many private Oguri-*chan*. A young woman could fondle her own toy, thinking that hers was entirely different from anyone else's. She might talk to it, wishing that it might carry her message to Oguricap and that he would then also understand her. Ms Komaki added that each woman developed her own way of playing with the *nuigurumi*, thus further confirming that she was different from other women.

Ms Takahashi Naoko, who has published three books on her observations of horses, races and on her own betting records, is one of the most popular writers in this genre, focussed upon the narcissism of women which, she believed, was promoted by Oguricap and his *nuigurumi*. Each woman who loved Oguricap felt that he was her own possession, and was sure that the way she watched Oguricap at a race or in the paddock was different from anyone else. That she could love him in such a unique way was very satisfactory to her ego, and this made her realize that after all she loved herself best. Having established empathy with him, she could talk about many things in relation to him. For young women, Oguricap's successful and tragedy-filled career, especially his last triumph, was the basis for a variety of fairy tales, all of which played on the theme of getting not what one expects, but what one wants: Love is rewarded. In regard to the *nuigurumi*, it produced a sense of closeness and could be given trust as it could never betray its owner. A young woman might take her toy to a race course, or she might play with it or even "train" it at home as a kind of sympathetic magic worked in order to win a coming race.

Some men also seem to have benefited from owning a *nuigurumi*. Ms Takahashi told me of the case of a 38-year-old businessman. The man was poor when young, but succeeded in business and drove a Mercedes as proof of his success.

This man bought a huge *nuigurumi* of Oguricap at the cost of 40,000 yen because he saw in Oguricap the very image of himself. Ms Takahashi also made the interesting observation that women in their early twenties were obsessive about their *nuigurumi*, but in their early thirties they might thoughtfully reflect on the relationship between Oguricap and themselves: perhaps this may be based on her own experience. She added that most women did not keep their *nuigurumi* for ever, but would throw it away after a time.

Ms Nase Moemi, who has published a cartoon book (*manga*) on Oguricap, created the heroine Keiko. Keiko is the friend of a racing journalist, known for his predictions, who gathers his information by observing the horses in training. The journalist always carefully studies the condition of Oguricap, and his final pronouncements are not always favorable to the horse, while Keiko insists on selecting him as the winner of each race. In the cartoon, she is often ridiculed by her friend who suggests that any forecast should be based on reason and not sentiment, but Keiko does not listen to him. It is with feelings of surprise as well as indignation and happiness that she observes her friend choosing Oguricap as his favorite for the last Arima Kinen race. Rational to the end, he explains to her that in spite of generally unfavorable reports about Oguricap's current condition, he has found signs of recovery in the horse's last gallop on the training course. The journalist is right, of course, and on their way home from the Nakayama race, Keiko feels closer to her friend than ever before, and she pats the *nuigurumi* she has been holding throughout the race. Her friend notices the toy for the first time and remarks that it looks cute and unexpectedly meek. "Yes, of course," says Keiko, "he has always been meek."

The author of this story, Ms Nase, claims that Oguricap had a special aura, which distinguished him from all other horses. He was like a human, having to trust other human beings from birth. When he was in a bad way, he would not eat. That is like a human, she says. His reactions were very quick and he understood what he was being asked to do. She also suggested that the attractiveness of Oguricap's career was summed up in the story of his last win. This is what heroes do: win against all odds.

All three women stressed different points, all of which seem plausible and insightful, but there is one feature common to their respective accounts: the psychological element. The fact that none of them is an expert in this field is immaterial for two reasons. One is that the psychological factor is one of the important components of the cult of Oguricap and such shrewd observers as these three women could not miss what went on in the mind of those of the same sex. The other is that to narrate aspects of popular culture psychologically is itself a constituent element of popular culture.

The two cults compared

There are more differences and contrasting features than similarities between the cult of Oguricap and that of Take Yutaka. These are mainly based upon the differences in followers, including gender, which in turn reflect differences between Oguricap and Take Yutaka.

Oguricap's pedigree was unremarkable: he had no famous kin. So he was first typed as a second-class racer, registered to a Chihô course and not entered for the classic races. In contrast, Yutaka was born and bred as an elite member both of the racing world and as a JRA jockey who rode at Chûô courses. In physical appearance, Oguricap was cute and even funny, with a gray-spotted face, but could not be said to be beautiful. Yutaka, on the other hand, was the tallest among Japanese jockeys, smart and handsome, with a charming, so said the women, smile. He spoke softly and, except for the occasional sharp comment, he talked cautiously and diplomatically about others and his skill.

To sum up, the accepted image of Oguricap was that of a talented "boy" born in a poor family, destined to be the lowest of the low (*shitazumi*, literally: the lowest layer of goods in a packing box), who through his own wits and efforts successfully climbed up the social ladder without losing his early charm. That of Yutaka was of a born thoroughbred who achieved even more than was expected of him. The contrast was of under-dog versus elite, or puritanism versus epicureanism.

Gender factors were very noticeable in the two cults from the very beginning. In the early 1980s the percentage of women fans was probably less than 10 per cent. At present it is estimated as being between 20 and 25 per cent of all fans. From the brief accounts of women followers of these two cults given above, it seems necessary to underline only three points here.

First, most of them did not share with men the sense of guilt in joining in horse-racing, because it was not, for them, a form of gambling (to which, as I have noted, there is a deeply cultivated aversion in Japanese society) but a new form of entertainment and fashion. Betting was not their main concern and this supported their sense of innocence. Girls I talked to at the Tokyo race course said: "What is wrong with horse-racing? It is no different from going to a disco or concert;" or "We are poor and don't bet much. Maybe 100 yen to win on Oguri."

Second, a real love for Oguricap – not unlike their love for the opposite sex – began to grow in many women. At this stage every such woman wanted to be as different as possible from the others; and each developed her own way of loving the horse. She might also learn to love herself as was suggested by my three interviewees. It does not seem that the same happened with the fans of Yutaka, whose passion faded away as both they and the jockey grew older.

Third, new followers are continuing to emerge even after Oguricap's retirement. Pilgrimages to his stud farm are continually increasing. We can therefore safely assume that the cult is consolidated and will last for a considerable time.

Male followers of Oguricap differ in several ways from women. Many of them seem to regard Oguricap as a representation of themselves, because their social backgrounds are as obscure as his. In such cases, the basis for a shared identity is the sense of being an under-dog. For these men, the success of Oguricap often signifies any one or all of the following possibilities: he may symbolize their already-abandoned dreams, as well as a hope that they might still emulate him; and a very satisfactory revenge against the dominant elites. To some, Oguricap represents their own success, which has been achieved through hard effort; and in this case an element of narcissism is even more apparent than in the case of some young women.

Even some young men from more elite strata of society joined the cult, perhaps because they also felt frustrated by the seemingly eternal yoke of the age–seniority system in the big organizations for which they work. Thus, Oguricap's conquests over established horses might be seen to stand for what they vainly hope will happen in their own lives.

A man might say that he loved Oguricap, but the nature of this love seems different from that of a woman's affection for the horse: it seems to lack the elements which might make it like the emotion one feels towards the opposite sex. Also, at the periphery of the cult, more objective followers exist, especially among intellectuals such as journalists. These people simply admire his performances as having been of high quality.

There are of course anti-Oguricap male factions comprising those who think the fever was caused by the cheap sensationalism of sports journalism. They tend to be very cool about his final win, pointing to the very slow time and the weak opposition in the race. After all, these are the very men who have long been race-goers and have a strong sense of anti-establishment feeling. They could not stand the almost unopposed glory given to Oguricap.

On reflection, it can be said that most of the descriptions given above are also true of the followers of the horse Haiseiko, who reached fame fifteen years before Oguricap, one large difference seemingly being that of scale: Oguricap reached a wider audience. In this, however, we can see a real difference: his audience included women, Haiseiko's did not.

In comparison with Take Yutaka, I know of men of different generations who respected, praised and admired Yutaka on various occasions,
but have seldom met any who were fanatical fans of his. In general these
fans are cooler, more technically-minded or betting-obsessed men. On
the other hand, I have observed many impassioned Yutaka-haters among
men, and it is true that he was the most heckled jockey in Kanto. That he
belonged to the Kansai block might partly account for this anti-Yutaka
feeling in Kantô, but a more reasonable explanation might be that he
was too remote for ordinary men to have empathy with. He was a symbol
of an elite, who – like other dominant elites of Japan – earn envy, jealousy
and hatred, but not love. It seemed difficult even for young men to admit
that they might be Yutaka fans, for it might attract either the contempt or
enmity of other men.

Even in the initial stage contrasts between the horse and jockey were
obvious. The cult of Oguricap included a far wider population, incor-
porating a revival of the Haiseiko cult for men, and the utterly new
experience of being attracted to a human-like horse for women. Some
followers dropped out as they were ashamed of being among such
mindless admirers, but this has not undermined the cult. Yutaka en-
chanted many young girls, but he also provoked hatred among men
on a hitherto unknown scale, and thus revealed a deeply rooted
ambivalence implicit in any hero cult in Japanese society. Yutaka secured
the top rank among jockeys, closely followed by Okabe Yukio, and he is
now more respected than admired. This is the main difference between
them: Oguricap is loved and Yutaka is respected.

Women members of both cults, immune to the conventional negative
image of horse-racing, began unknowingly to neutralize the sport. They
have succeeded in this to such an extent that main bastions of the mass
media such as *Asahi* newspaper, which had led the denigration of the
sport and never seriously reported racing, had to abandon its policy and
gradually increase its coverage of horse-racing.

Conclusion

The social and moral values imposed upon horse-racing have slowly
changed from being mostly negative to almost permissible, though not
yet fully positive. There are various factors which have brought this
about, but I take the participation of young women as the most
influential one. As already noted, they were mostly ignorant of the
aversion to racing felt by older generations; and the fact that the
majority of them did not think of racing in terms of gambling helped
greatly in their pursuit of this new pleasure. They could easily say that
horse-racing was more than gambling, which had been said thousands

of times in vain by men affiliated to the racing scene, and somehow succeed in persuading many conservatives that this was so. There remain, however, many more conservatives who still regard it as mere gambling and who insist that it is a bad example to the young. The notion of pedagogic influence is always a key concept when any form of popular culture is discussed or condemned and the enticing of young children away from their studies is an objection often raised, even when patently ridiculous.

Not all men who are racing fans have welcomed the changes which include the presence of young women at race courses, not because women took the initiative in coming, but because they feel nostalgia for the good old "bad" days. The very unpopularity which had surrounded race-goers was, from their point of view, thrilling and gave the satisfaction of rebellion against the dominant system. The more they were condemned, the more they felt they were different from ordinary, square, status-minded bores: that they were outlaws, rubbing shoulders with those true desperados, the *yakuza*. These men now talk with regret about the excitement which in the past grew out of the heated atmosphere created by "real" gamblers. Even some young men long for this lost past. It can be said that under the surface of most Japanese popular culture there is an element of danger[10] that is often associated with the counterculture of the *yakuza*, a sort of recklessness and rudeness most often seen in the behavior of fans. In this respect, simply being part of the audience can be seen as a sort of release from the straitjacket of everyday life. The admission of women into this world has changed it irrevocably.

Notes

1   This chapter is based on both unintended and intended fieldwork, conducted mostly at the Tokyo race course intermittently over the last six years. By unintended fieldwork, I mean what I have seen, heard and been told while at the course as an ordinary race-goer; I have no written record of this. In short, my memory is my only source and, in a sense, this chapter is partly a folktale narrated by me in the guise of a native elder.

  By intended fieldwork, I mean interviews which I have conducted, separately, with the ladies Komaki Shun, Takahashi Naoko and Nase Moemi. I thank them all for their help and insightful remarks. I am also grateful to Mr. Sato Yoichiro and Mr. Takahashi Genichiro for their critical comments.

2   The JRA used to be known as Chûô Keibakai. In fact, there are two different horse-racing organizations in Japan. One is the JRA, still referred to as Chûô (the Central), which has ten race courses distributed from Hokkaido to Kyûshû; it is a special association, supervised by the Ministry of

Agriculture and Fishing and, in 1992, it made more than three billion yen from bets. The other racing association is the Nihon Racing Association, or NRA, and any race course belonging to this is called *Chihô* meaning "regional" or "local", implying marginality and inferiority.

3   In Japan, animals do not take personal pronouns; however here I use the personal pronouns "he", "his" and "him" for Oguricap not in order to follow English language conventions, but to show how human Oguricap's followers felt him to be.

4   In Japan, a betting license is given to four kinds of racing: horse, motor-boat, motorcycle and bicycle. These are organized either by special foundations or by local governments. Any other type of betting is illegal; although private betting on golf and other contests flourishes.

5   It is to be noted that the custom of placing small bets does not appear to have been part of Japanese culture before this, although gambling with cash or with precious goods had been prominent during the Heian era (794–1185).

6   *Asobinin* are the precursors of the modern *yakuza* (gangsters or Japanese mafia).

7   Following the Western system, the big races in Japan are classified as G (standing for Group in the UK and Australasia, and Grade in the USA) races which are sub-divided into G1, G2, G3, in order of importance.

8   "*Chan*" is a term of endearment, replacing the more formal *san* or *sama*, often used for children, or between close friends.

9   The reason why gray horses attract affection, notably from women, is enigmatic, but relevant may be the fact that their faces are said to look rather "funny" and that there are so few gray horses. Ms Takahashi Naoko is the champion of those who advocate the charms of gray horses.

10   For other examples of this, see the chapters by Standish, Gill, Napier, Yamaguchi, and Kelly.

References

Nagashima Nobuhiro 1988 *Keiba no jinruigaku* (*The Anthropology of Horseracing*). Tokyo: Iwanami Shôten.

——1991 "Interview with Take Yutake" in *Views*, vol. 1(1). Tokyo: Kodansha.

Nase Moemi 1991 *Oguricap ni nijûmaru* (*Oguricap is my nap*). Tokyo: Konomisou Kikaku.

Needham, Rodney 1971 *Rethinking Kinship and Marriage*. London: Tavistock Publications.

Sudo Nansui (1887) 1966 "*Ryoku sa tan*" in Kida Junichiro's *Nihon no Gamburâ* (*Japan's Gamblers*). Tokyo: Togensha.

Takahashi Naoko 1991 *Keiba no kuni no Alice* (*Alice in the World of Horse-Racing*). Tokyo: Chikuma Shobo.

——1992 *Asige no Anne* (*Anne the Gray*). Tokyo: Chikuma Shobo.

——1993 *Paddoku no Cinderella* (*The Cinderella of the Paddock*). Tokyo: Chikuma Shobo.

CHAPTER 10

Soccer Shinhatsubai
What are Japanese consumers making of the J. League?

JONATHAN WATTS

Introduction

The subject of this chapter is the consumption of soccer (football) in
Japan, the nature of which has changed completely as a result of the
establishment of the Japanese Professional Football League, known as
the J. League, in May 1993.[1] How and why this came about are
considered by putting soccer in a historical perspective, comparing it
with other Japanese sports and examining the marketing techniques
used in its promotion. In particular the *shinhatsubai* strategy (the launch
of a new product) is considered in detail. On a broader level, the
J. League is used to consider Miller's (1987) theories about the way in
which cultural development and consumption are interrelated.

I chose this subject because during the three years I first lived in Japan
(1990–93), the biggest and certainly the most noticeable development
that took place was the establishment of the Japanese Professional
Football League. More than the ousting of the Liberal Democrat Party
(LDP), more even than the imperial wedding, the most talked-about
subject among my acquaintances was the start of the new soccer league.
Now I accept that this may have been a reflection of the sort of company
I keep, but there was also a historical perspective: it had taken over a
century for soccer to be transformed in this way. The wait for the LDP to
be ousted was a mere forty-six years, and the crown prince's search for a
bride had lasted just under a decade.

It was fascinating, coming from the country with the world's oldest
football league, watching a new one being born on the other side of
the world. In Britain, association football is an institution. In Japan it
was the latest fashion. I was curious to see what people would make
of it.

Trying to understand what people make of soccer in Japan and how they go about it is the aim of this chapter. Using Daniel Miller's theory of consumption (1987), I consider the questions by emphasizing the role of the consumer. In this context "consumer" means anyone who spends time, money or effort (physical or mental) on the game. Soccer itself is presented as an industry. The best way I could understand the advent of the J. League was as the launch of a new product, which the Japanese call *shinhatsubai*.

The approach outlined here follows what seems to be a tradition in Japanese studies: looking at sport as anything but sport. For example, sumo is viewed as a religious ritual (Cuyler 1979), baseball players as "samurai" (Whiting 1977) and the High School Tournament at Koshien transformed into, "the cult of youthful purity" (Buruma 1984). This may be because theoretical work on the anthropology of sport is still relatively new (certainly in the UK). It may also reflect a feeling that sport is a tabloid subject, unworthy of academic attention. Whatever the reasons, in writing this chapter there was only distantly related secondary material to choose from. Wagner's (1991) excellent collection of data on sport in Asia and Africa was the single exception.

Miller, consumption, *shinhatsubai* and soccer

The theory upon which my approach is based is derived from Miller's *Material Culture and Mass Consumption* (1987). In simplest terms, this considers what people make of things; the ways in which consumers are able to re-appropriate products for themselves. For Miller, this is the positive potential of consumption as a means of asserting and re-forming identity. He suggests that changing economic conditions in post-industrial societies have increased the range and possibilities of consumer behavior. In a broader sense, Miller uses Hegel's dialectic to present culture as a state of becoming: not fixed, but ceaselessly undergoing change.

In post-industrial society Miller observes the birth of the consumer at the commanding heights of the political economy and one such economy is Japan's. The post-war era of export drives, high saving rates, hard work and self-sacrifice is being succeeded by one where the economy relies upon sustained or growing domestic consumer demand; it is now important for Japanese business that its population work less and spend more (Muto 1989). Thus values are changing. A survey by the government in June 1994 revealed that only four per cent of Japanese give priority to their job (Tass 1994). In contrast 42 per cent said their families were most important. Leisure hours and personal consumption were also increasing (Muto 1989: 45–60). Then the recession saw a boom in the sales of discount stores, suggesting that consumers had become more independent in their buying habits and not as easily influenced by the media as had been thought previously.

Following Miller's work we need to consider how the process of cultural development is mirrored in Japanese industry by the constant updating of goods. These new updated and re-packaged goods are marketed under the label *shinhatsubai*, a term which corresponds to the English "New Improved, Now on Sale". In this word, we find the character for "new" (*shin*) followed by a character with a dynamic meaning: "discharge, start, leave" (*hatsu*); the last character means "sell" (*bai*). The expression conveys a sense of a new movement of goods to the market place (Henshall 1988).

The idea of new movement also encapsulates a process of transformation. *Shinhatsubai* are usually released alongside a company's existing brands in order to extend the range of goods on offer; for example, a new flavor of instant noodles. At other times the goods are launched as the cutting edge of technology; a more compact compact disc or a faster computer printer. However, sometimes the only major difference is in the name; beer companies are forever bringing out new brands, often with no discernible difference in taste from those of existing lagers. The new name is used to directly target a specific market, as in the cases of "Autumn Beer", "Winters Tale Beer", "Tigers Beer" (for the Hanshin Baseball Club), and of course "J. League Beer". The list goes on and on. This kind of campaigning has been successful in attracting new consumers, in particular women (Muto 1991: 121). Successful *shinhatsubai* are able to establish themselves alongside the original market leaders, but many others disappear a short time after they are launched.

Compared to the Fordist aim of "One product to fit all", *shinhatsubai* represent a greater sensitivity towards the diverse and changing needs of the consumer. They increase the range of goods available and update them with a greater frequency. They also represent a new way in which culture is continually re-inventing itself, as new goods which become established are in effect sublated into a new cultural identity. In the following section I argue that soccer has undergone a *shinhatsubai* transformation in the launching of the J. League: a re-invention and re-marketing of the old product to meet changing market conditions.

An ethnographic sketch: match atmosphere before and after the J. League

In the summer of 1991 I attended my first football match in Japan. The match between Brazil's Vasco da Gama and that year's English FA Cup winners, Tottenham Hotspur, was held at the Universiad Stadium, slightly to the north of Kobe city. The ground had been built for the world student athletic games. It did not have much atmosphere: the pitch was awful, full of puddles, and the enormous terraces were less than a third full. The only crowd activity was the occasional half-hearted Mexican wave initiated by a handful of foreigners in the main stand. The few thousand who had come to watch the match did so quietly. The game was dull; the crowd was boring. It seemed to me that they had not managed to cross the barrier between spectators and supporters. One reason was the lack of local interest in a match involving two foreign teams. However Ray Clemence, the Tottenham coach at the time, recalls that even for the game against the national team in Tokyo a week later, "the support was very sedated".[2] When I asked why he thought the spectators were so passive he replied, "It is what you would expect really, considering the national character."

Less than two years later, I returned to the Universiad Stadium for the J. League All Star match (also known as the Coca-Cola Cup) on 17 July 1993. It was an overwhelming experience. The ground was filled to capacity and it seemed as if every one of the 42,790 spectators owned either a flag or a t-shirt. Because it was an All Star game, East versus West Japan, each of the J. League's ten teams[3] was represented both on the pitch and on the terraces, bathing the stadium with color. The predominant color was the green of Japan's most popular club, Verdy Kawasaki, most of whose supporters seemed to be teenage girls. The blue of the local Gamba Osaka team and the red of the first stage winners, Kashima Antlers, were also well represented. In addition there were pockets where the supporters of the other seven clubs were concentrated. There were no physical barriers separating the fans; it was possible to walk from one end of the ground to the other and nowhere on the way was there any hint of violence. However, the noise was cacophonic thanks to drums, cheer horns[4] and the competing chants of the rival supporters. The overall rhythm definitely showed a South American influence and some groups of fans were even dancing a samba. The match itself had not even started, but this was some of the best football entertainment I had ever witnessed. Ray Clemence would certainly have been amazed.

What had happened to the "sedate national character"? J. League soccer seems to represent an antithesis of "traditional Japanese culture". In the first place it is a foreign game. In 1993, the presence of players such as Littbarski, Arcindo, Santos and Moneru on the pitch was a reminder of the large number of overseas players in the J. League.[5] Moreover the game appeared to represent a number of non-Japanese values. In contrast to the unchanging expressions of the sumo *rikishi* (wrestlers) after winning or losing a bout, soccer players in Japan, like soccer players the world over, expressed their emotions at winning or losing in emphatic fashion. Similarly, in the 1993 game described above, teammates rushed to hug Kazuyoshi Miura (Kazu) after he scored the first goal; a remarkable display in a country where greetings are made without physical contact. In soccer, individual skill was given at least equal importance as teamwork. A typical magazine article which demonstrated this advised aspiring young soccer enthusiasts to try to enter Teikyo High School because it has the best reputation for producing *koseitekina* (individualistic) players (Verdy Yearbook 1994: 47).

Hisashi Kato, former Shimizu S. Pulse defender and chairman of the J. League technical committee, has explained it in these terms: "We are the first professional athletes [in Japan] permitted to display our personalities" (*Newsweek*, 13 June 1994). Self-expression was not restricted to the playingfield either, but manifested itself in fashion off it. The most notable example was Verdy's Kitahama whose flowing locks have become his trademark. In the two high schools where I was teaching at the time,[6] baseball club members had uniform *bôsô* haircuts (crew cuts). In contrast the hair of soccer club members was not only longer, it was also more likely to be dyed. In the 1993 High School Soccer Tournament one player who appeared in the final was a *yankî* (the Japanese equivalent of a punk). This would have been unthinkable in the baseball tournament at Koshien, no matter how good the player was.

The extreme example of a soccer player who stands out as an individual is Kazuyoshi Miura (Kazu). Widely regarded as one of Japan's most talented players, he learnt his skills in Brazil where he went to school. He shows little respect for authority and shocked many when he congratulated the imperial couple on their wedding using ordinary Japanese rather than the formalized language that is meant to be used when referring to the imperial family.[7] Contrary to the much-quoted Japanese saying that "a nail which sticks up must be knocked down", Kazu has not suffered too severely from social censure. Far from it: Kazu was made Japanese footballer of the year in the J. League's first season. A year later he was transferred to the Italian club, Genoa, which was a chance to play in the world's top league, the Seri A, and earn a reported two million dollars. In 1977 Whiting observed that no Japanese baseball player had yet left the country to join a foreign team.[8] The reason, he suggested, was that in Japan, baseball was the national sport and for a player to leave the Japanese league would be seen as an unforgivable act of treachery. In contrast, for Kazu to be worth that much money and to play with the best was considered an honor for both him and football in Japan. Although he suffered injury and struggled to break into the first team, he pioneered the way for other Japanese stars, such as baseball's

Hideo Nomo, to try their luck overseas. A new role model had emerged. To put this in perspective it is necessary to consider the historical background of sport in Japan.

Soccer on the margins

This section takes a selective look at the history of sport in Japan. The aims are twofold: first, to demonstrate Stokvis's assertion that changes in sporting activity mirror social change (1989: 37) and to identify certain eras. Secondly, to show that throughout the long history of soccer in Japan it has been on the margins of sporting culture and to consider why this was so.

The earliest known sports in Japan were the pastimes of the aristocracy, such as the record of hunting from the fourth century (Saeki 1989: 55). In addition horse-racing and archery are recorded as having been played since the seventh century.[9] Sports with religious significance also emerged at this time. Sumo was associated in particular with the harvest festival (see Chapter 1). Another sport from this era was *kemari*, which bears a striking resemblance to soccer in that the essence of the game is passing a ball from person to person without letting it hit the ground and without the use of the hands. However the resemblance ends there since *kemari* was played within a sacred space marked at the four corners by saplings representing the seasons (pine, cherry, plum and bamboo) and the game timed with a stick of incense. In the Genroku era it was the sport of noblemen; during Edo it was less popular and played only by a few wealthy tradesmen and today it is played by only a handful of people in just a few temples in Japan. *Kemari* has appealed to different sectors of society throughout its history.

During the Tokugawa Shogunate that stretched into the nineteenth century, Japan was ruled by a warrior class and sporting activity reflected the pursuits of this dominant group. Schools were set up to develop military skills, including horsemanship, *jujitsu* and archery. The training method was repetition of established techniques. This was part of *bushidô*, the "way" (*dô*)[10] of the warrior. Its aim was to attain a disciplined *seishin* ("mind"/"spirit")[11] through loss of self-awareness (*muga*) in the activity undertaken. These training techniques were antecedents for, amongst others, kendô and, much later, jûdô.

With the end of Japan's isolation in the Meiji era, Western sports flooded into Japan and were adopted in the same enthusiastic manner as foreign philosophy, political theory and science. Football was introduced during this period. Commander Douglas of the Royal Navy is recorded as having played the first game in Tokyo in September 1873. In the same period tennis, athletics, baseball and many other activities were adopted. These international sports were spread through the education system by teachers who had learnt them at university.

Nationwide organization and what Stokvis calls "the industrialization of sport" (1989: 43) did not take place until the 1920s. The Japanese Amateur Sports Association was established in 1917, under the control of the Ministry of Education (Monbushô). It provided an umbrella for the individual sports bodies which were set up in the following decade. The Japanese Football Association was established in September 1921. Sports in Japan were being modernized and made to conform to a universally applicable set of regulations. This made commercialism possible and newspapers began to use sport as a means of selling newspapers. A pioneer of this was the *Osaka Asahi Shimbun* which sponsored the Koshien High School Baseball Tournament. A further consequence of this centralization was the politicization of sport, particularly in the 1930s. Baseball was "naturalized" and *kanji* (Chinese character) equivalents were invented to replace its foreign terminology. The term "*yakyûdô*" was even coined, meaning "the way of baseball" to achieve a strong spirit. Football in this period was both centralized and given an international dimension.[12] Yet it was not popularized to anything like the same extent as baseball. We can only speculate as to why baseball was adopted as a central part of Japanese culture while football failed to make much of an impact. One reason was probably a change in international relations in this period. The JFA was established just as the Anglo-Japanese alliance was coming to an end. Tokyo-Washington relations had become far more important; consequently baseball was a more suitable vehicle for cultural exchange. A further reason might be found by remembering the link between sport and religion in Japan noted earlier. Unlike *kemari*, which was played in a sacred (therefore cleansed) place, football may have suffered because it involved playing with the foot. This part of the body, according to Ohnuki-Tierney (1987), is considered polluted in Shintô belief through its association with the unclean floor. Work at this level, such as *tatami*-making was traditionally given to the *burakumin* (the Japanese untouchable class).

Immediately after the war, baseball was viewed as a nationalist sport by (ironically) the US Occupation authorities. One crucial consequence of this was the introduction of soccer into the national curriculum as an alternative. In 1947, the emperor also gave his stamp of approval to the sport and established the annual Emperor's Cup Competition. However baseball was pardoned during the "Reverse Course" and became more popular than ever especially as a symbol of Japanese-American relations (Whiting 1977: 80). Soccer was pushed to the margins.

In the mid-1960s football did enjoy a mini-boom. The Japanese Olympic team reached the quarter finals in Tokyo and four years later won the bronze medal in Mexico. In between, the Japan Soccer League was established in 1965. "Football" had become "soccer". This was done in order to avoid confusion with American football, but it also served to replace a label that may have carried overtones of pollution.

When the Japanese team lost its top players in the 1970s, interest in the sport waned. This was despite an overall growth in the demand for sport in general as Japanese society became more affluent. The 1970s and 1980s saw the opening of golf ranges and tennis clubs throughout Japan. The so-called bubble economy of the late 1980s and early 1990s also saw a huge increase in disposable income in Japan, much of which was fed into sports-related pastimes (Chen 1990: 33). In particular female consumers fueled a series of booms. Baseball attendances rose as more women went to watch matches. Sumo enjoyed a resurgence of interest, particularly in the handsome brothers Takanohana and Wakahanada (see Chapter 8). Newspapers attributed a rise in gambling on horse-racing to the numbers of women who went to watch the good-looking jockeys (see Chapter 9).

Thus sport in Japan had progressed from being the pastime of aristocrats and priests to a form of training for samurai warriors. It was internationalized during Meiji and centralized before the war. Since then it has become increasingly popularized and commercialized. However, football – as a result of Japan's international priorities and (possibly) an unclean image – had never been adopted as a truly Japanese sport. A survey carried out in 1989 showed that just 4 per cent of the population participated in soccer, putting it in 24th place, only narrowly ahead of gate ball (a game similar to croquet). However, an untapped market did exist. Women's soccer had been growing since 1979 and the Japan Soccer League attendance figures rose rapidly in 1990 with the announcement of the J. League timed to coincide with the World Cup finals in Italy. Japan's football authorities decided that the time was right to capitalize on the growing demand for the sport.

The point of production: the *shinhatsubai* process

Winning capital investment was the first requirement of the *shinhatsubai* of soccer. The idea of a new football league had to be sold to public and private institutions which could provide the financial boost needed to rebuild the soccer infrastructure. In 1989 when the JFA went cap in hand to major companies and local authorities, few imagined the J. League would be a financial success; indeed Dentsu, Japan's largest PR firm, predicted it would flop and they pulled out of involvement in the project. Economic dividends were not expected, so the J. League was not initially sold as a good business prospect. However in the so-called bubble economy of the late 1980s there was a large surplus of capital in Japan's economy and companies and local authorities used much of it to promote their image through altruistic investment. The J. League was thus sold to these institutions as a community project. This section will examine how this was achieved.

For Bellah (1970) a characteristic of Japanese society is its "goal orientated dynamism": the establishment of a group objective and the willingness to make individual sacrifices to achieve it. The benefits are twofold: first, the cohesion of a group identity is formed through shared aims; secondly, the successful realization of an objective strengthens the group's position vis-a-vis other groups. We can see in this analysis echoes of Befu's (1980) social exchange model or Nakane's (1971) vertical society. In each case group identity is formed through internal co-operation and external competition. Obviously, sport well fits this "goal orientated" model.

Viewed from a country such as Britain, where hooligans have been associated with football violence for two decades, the idea of utilizing soccer as a means of achieving social harmony seems a contradiction in terms. Nevertheless, that is one of the main reasons why local governments in Japan were keen to invest in the sport. They saw it as a chance to re-forge local identity around a common ambition. By establishing themselves as a "hometown" (*furusato*) for a J. League team, different areas of Japan were able to make use of this social glue.

The need to become a more cohesive society may be seen as a solution to the breakdown in modern urban society of what once was a strong communal identity (Dore 1959; Bestor 1989; Robertson 1991). Both Robertson and Bestor have considered countermeasures employed to re-establish a sense of community in Japanese cities and we can see the adoption of a soccer team in a similar light. One of the rules governing membership of the J. League states that all teams must have a "hometown". A "hometown" is a municipal authority which is not only the site of the prerequisite 15,000 minimum-capacity stadium, but which also provides a financial package of twenty billion yen (approx. £120 million) towards the initial cost of establishing a team, and a billion yen (£6 million) a year for ten years thereafter. It is also obliged to work towards community support for the team (J. League Profile 1994). In adopting a team, the "hometown" hope to provide a focus for a community togetherness. Thus it is working towards the same ends as *furusato zukuri* (or the creation of a village-like identity) (Robertson 1991) or "traditionalism" (Bestor 1989). However, rather than using the nostalgia for an idealized past to achieve these ends, it aims towards a future goal: the championship.

Kashima, a small coastal town in Ibaraki Prefecture, has been held up as the best example of soccer uniting a disparate community (*Japan Quarterly* 1994: 27). Since the arrival of Sumitomo Metal Industries in 1960 into what had previously been a rural farming and fishing community, the town had been split between the old residents and the newcomers. This was typical of the disruption caused by the relocation of industry to suburban or rural areas, described in detail in Smith's ethnography of Kurusu (1978). In a gamble to "unite the disparate community" the prefectural government, five municipalities, Sumitomo Industries and twenty-four other local companies invested 8.4 billion yen (or approximately £50 million) in a new stadium and more than 3 million dollars recruiting a number of Brazilian players, including the 40-year-old super-star Zico. That gamble paid off handsomely; the Kashima Antlers won the first stage of the J. League's championship and Arcindo, their striker, was the top scorer. In the first few years of the J. League each home game earned approximately 15 million yen (£1 million), officials say the local economy has been rejuvenated, attributing major rail and road projects in the area to the influence of the Antlers. As for uniting the community, the supporters' club increased from three members in October 1992 to 3,000 less than a year later, the migration of young people from the town has halted and soccer was even held responsible for the disappearance of *bôsôzoku* (motorcycle gangs) from the city centre (*Japan Quarterly* 1994).

Reading the claims made about Kashima it would seem that the J. League did not just create a soccer boom, it had heralded a soccer miracle. There were no shortage of municipal authorities willing to believe this. Representatives from forty cities and towns have visited Kashima to observe the shining light of the J. League's "hometown" policy. The words of Serizawa Mamoru, an official of Koriyama in Fukushima Prefecture, summed up their attitude: "Becoming a home-town for a soccer team is an ideal way to rejuvenate our community" (*Japan Quarterly* 1994: 33). The Kashima story demonstrates the way in which municipal authorities appropriated soccer for themselves. This originally "foreign" sport has found a very important place in Kashima City's social organization. It was localized and not just for commercial reasons.

The goal of soccer success is also enticing since it is well rewarded in terms of prestige. Levels of participation in sport are seen as an index of a nation's development (Stokvis 1989). This is first because it is seen to indicate the presence of a strong infrastructure; as Stokvis has noted, "The effective propagation of modern sports depends on an efficient transport system and centrally organized education" (Stokvis 1989: 14). Thus to win the bid to stage the World Cup finals represents international recognition of a nation's level of development. The Tokyo Olympics had already impressed on the Japanese people the benefits to be had from such events. As several chapters in this book have noted, the 1964 Olympics were symbolically very important to the Japanese (see especially Harvey).

In addition, increased sporting activity is associated with a more affluent population (Stokvis 1989), since it requires leisure time, health and wealth. It manifests both conspicuous leisure and conspicuous consumption. In this sense the J. League is a kind of national extravagance, a proclamation of the population's consumer power. As such it is an appropriate response to the criticism directed at Japan that its economic strength masks a poor standard of living for its overworked population. Although it has not been claimed as such, the J. League is nationalistic in that it demonstrates the power of Japanese consumption.

"One day we will catch up with the world's best" is one of the slogans of the JFA, echoing what Dore (1973: 203) called the "national catching-up objective" in industry that can be traced back to the Meiji era. The slogan then was *fukoku kyôhei* ("a wealthy country and a strong army"): the two areas where the government concentrated its efforts to catch up with the West and make Japan a world power. *Fukyoku* has remained the objective of Japanese governments, but since the war *kyôhei* has become domestically and internationally unacceptable, leaving vacant one of two spheres of activity in which the nation had achieved internal unity and exerted itself externally. Frustration that national identity was being seen merely in terms of economics has resulted in the growth of *nihonjinron* ("theories of Japaneseness") discourses and the promotion of Japanese cultural exhibitions abroad. However these have a limited reach. Soccer, as a world game, carrying enormous cultural prestige outside the economic sphere, may well have become one of the new goals for Japanese society. As in the Meiji era, the nation has been trying to make up lost ground by learning from the world's leaders. Foreign stars have been imported and their coaching as well as playing responsibilities have been emphasized. Similarly, an elite of aspiring young players are honing their skills by spending a year or two in Brazil, following the stud-marks of Kazuyoshii Miura. The cost of such a soccer education is estimated at two million yen per year (about twelve thousand pounds).

Another parallel with the Meiji effort to catch up with the outside world is the role of national education since Monbushô had been instrumental in propagating the sport since long before the J. League succeeded. According to Bellah's theory, a feature of this goal-orientated dynamism is the single-minded way in which the "objective" takes priority over all else. It is not so surprising, then, that the discovery of a 2,600-year-old Jomon settlement on the site being prepared for the construction of a new soccer stadium in Aomori Prefecture caused heated debate between those looking to the past for a Japanese identity and those looking to the future.

Soccer for consumption

In Japan soccer was sold to institutional investors as a focus for communal identity through shared objectives. As the JFA slogan for the 2002 World Cup bid reads, "Japan Loves Goals", a feeling with which Bellah would identify. Financial capital was thus made available for the *shinhatsubai* of soccer for essentially conservative reasons.

In order to understand the suddenness and scale of the soccer boom in the immediate wake of the J. League's inauguration, we must return to the concept of *shinhatsubai*. Using the example of the beer industry, we observed how brewers constantly launched "new" products, specifically aimed at capturing a certain untapped share of the market through re-packaging and re-marketing. Reference was also made as to how in the electronics industry products are constantly updated and improved, for example, making CD players that much more compact and computer games that much more sophisticated. These processes of re-invention, re-packaging and re-marketing are all aspects of *shinhatsubai* and we can see them at work in the series of transformations of soccer that led to the re-launch of the sport under a new label: The J. League.

The first stage of the process is the reconsideration of the product itself in the light of a changing market environment. This is the point at which we can observe the interaction of producer and consumer, with the former trying to anticipate the needs of the latter in order to ensure sufficient demand for the goods they are planning to make. The JFA employed the services of the Hakuhodo advertising agency to perform this task. Hakuhodo carried out a full market survey, something unprecedented in Japanese sports marketing. From this it was able to give a positive assessment of the J. League's prospects, which gave the JFA a boost in their efforts to lure sponsors into an untried market. The information it garnered about consumer opinion was then utilized at further stages in the process.

From the market research it was evident that winning the young female market would be crucial to the success of the J. League as a commercial venture (*Financial Times*, August 1994). The earlier booms in baseball, sumo and horse-racing had demonstrated the impact this group of consumers could make. The reason was not so much that women in Japan control the family purse strings – generally speaking this does not happen until after marriage – but because of the increasing number of young female employees: the OLs (Office Ladies) who typically live with their parents, leaving the lion's share of their salaries as disposable income.[13] The image of the J. League was produced with this market in mind. Sony Creative Products was given control over the design of logos for the league's member teams and came up with a set of cute cartoon animals. These logos adorn the multitude of ôen guzzu (supporters' merchandise) making items more accessible to teenage girls who might otherwise have difficulty identifying with a sport they are unlikely to have played. Image creation did not stop at the logo: the Hakuhodo executive responsible for soccer explained the company's strategy: "We set out to make soccer like a disco, lots of vivid color, lights, fashion, music" (Financial Times, August 1994).

It was not just the image, but the very existence of guzzu (merchandise) which made soccer more accessible to a wider audience. Material culture, to use Miller's terminology, gave the sport a physical presence it had previously lacked. It allowed soccer, until then mostly limited to a weekly ninety-minute rendezvous at selected sports grounds, to be purchased at department stores and all-night convenience outlets. In addition a number of specialized J. League stores was established.

As argued above, consumer interest in soccer had previously grown during periods when the national team was performing well. Interest in soccer also rose during World Cup finals or Olympics, indicating that a market existed for a quality international product. However until 1993, Japan's amateur/semi-professional domestic soccer was, for the most part, considered an inferior product. The creation of the J. League was an attempt to transform this image. Sponsors pumped money into the sport, adding to its value. In addition new facilities were constructed, creating an impressive new socialized environment for soccer. Some rules were changed to make the game more exciting; for example, all matches ending in a draw, not just cup tie matches as in Europe, go into "sudden death overtime" and if neither team scores during the 30 minutes of overtime, the winner is decided by a penalty shoot-out. Furthermore, the introduction of a number of genuine world-class, albeit past their prime, soccer stars such as Lineker, Zico and Littbarski, also upgraded the game and made it more exciting. J. League teams were professionalized, elevating the status of Japanese players at this level.

A further status leap was achieved through sponsorship. Event sponsorship was used for (according to the Hakuhodo spokesman) the first time in the history of Japanese sports marketing. This meant that companies sponsored particular tournaments (the Nicos Series, the Suntory Series, the Toyota Cup, the Coca-Cola All Star Game) as well as particular teams. It also meant that soccer was being promoted by its sponsors since Coca-Cola, Suntory and the like used the sport in their own marketing campaigns. Soccer was suddenly everywhere: on cans of drink, on credit cards, on beer commercials and so on. The effect was to link the game in the minds of consumers to established high-quality household-name products. This helped to lift the status of soccer.

The transformations outlined above established soccer as a clear alternative to existing mainstream sports. Compared to nine innings of baseball or eighteen holes of golf it is a fast-moving and energetic game. Compared to sumo it is less formalized and restricted. In baseball supporters are expected to follow the team associated with their company. However, in soccer, loyalty was focussed on a person's place of residence by the hometown system. In effect this meant a shift from support based on a place of production (company) to support based on a place of consumption (home). Baseball had become associated with a *saruriman* (white-collar worker) lifestyle. Soccer provided an alternative for the *shinjinrui* (new lifestyle people).

According to Mr Ono, a spokesman for the Hakuhodo agency, the campaign to promote the J. League has had dramatic effect. *Shinhatsubai* transformed the old soccer product. This meant that consumers could approach the sport more comfortably. The *shinhatsubai* process re-created and re-located soccer in Japan, in effect "Japanizing" it, but also offering considerably greater access for individual consumers to appropriate the sport for themselves.

The response of consumers

To what extent then, did this *shinhatsubai* process succeed? Would it generate interest among consumers? And, more importantly, could it outlive the hype to establish itself alongside other market leaders, such as baseball and sumo?

The initial results were spectacular. With the inauguration of the J. League in May 1993, soccer, dormant for over a hundred years in Japan, erupted. The effect was apparent in a number of ways. The media, national newspapers such as the *Mainichi*, the *Yomiuri* or the *Asahi*, began to devote almost as many column inches to soccer as they did to baseball. In 1992 there was less than one hour of soccer shown on television in a week, usually in the early hours of the morning and, not surprisingly, it was hardly watched. However, the World Cup qualifier between Japan and Iraq on 28 October 1993 was the most watched sporting event in Japan. The last gasp equalizer by Iraq, which denied Japan a place in the World Cup finals, reduced even the NHK commentator to a fit of uncontrollable sobbing. Undoubtedly the depth of despair felt by the millions watching the match on television actually marked the high point of the soccer boom to date. The viewing figures for that match were 48 per cent, making it second only to the royal wedding in 1993.

Research by Saeki (1989) has revealed that sport is the most talked-about subject in Japan and soccer seized a share of that chatter, making Kazu, Ramos and Arcindo into household names. The attention being paid to it means that it has become the focus of sports advertising. Whereas a few years ago marketing companies would look first to a golfer or a baseball star to promote a new brand of pot noodles or beer, after the inauguration of the J. League it was football players who earned the most from commercials and endorsements.

The J. League also generated an enormous market of its own. First, attendance figures rocketed; almost every game in the first season was sold out. More than one million people applied for the 60,000 available tickets for the opening match of the league. The demand for tickets was so great that the ability to obtain seats for a big game became a status symbol. Whilst sales for baseball went down 6 per cent, the gate receipts for J. League games earned eleven billion yen (some £220 million) in the first season.

Soccer was not just something to watch or play, it was also something to buy and own, and the market for J. League merchandising was estimated to have been worth over 56 billion yen (£330 million). Team sponsors who had to put up a billion yen (£6 million) per year to fund ground development, higher wage bills and the maintenance of youth teams, estimated that they would earn a dividend within five years. Overall, for advertising, sponsorship, ticket sales and merchandising, the revenue of the J. League was estimated to have been one hundred and forty billion yen (£870 million) in its first year of business, despite the fact that Japan was then going through its worst recession since the oil shocks of the mid-1970s.

People were also investing a great deal more time and energy in the sport than before the establishment of the J. League. Membership in Japan's amateur soccer league rose rapidly and high school junior soccer clubs began to recruit more members than those for baseball. In May 1993, a survey asking junior school boys what they wanted to be when they grew up found that football player was well behind baseball star, astronaut and scholar; in 1994 it was streets ahead of anything else. The list goes on and on. All the statistics confirmed that the soccer industry had arrived and was booming. As the J. League's founding father, Saburo Kawabuchi, stated: "Performance topped our expectations" (*Financial Times*, August 1994).

Riding this wave of enthusiasm, the J. League expanded from ten teams in 1993 to seventeen teams in 1997. In addition, many of the original clubs also constructed larger stadiums, partly to meet the un-satisfied demand in the original season, and partly in a bid to host the World Cup in 2002. The decision in the summer of 1996, by the International Federation of Football Associations (FIFA), to share the tournament between Japan and South Korea came as a huge blow. Coming just as the *shin* (new) element of the *shinhatsubai* was wearing off, it dented the new-found prestige of soccer, causing attendance and viewing figures to plummet. After peaking at 6.1 million fans in 1995, the aggregate annual attendance almost halved the following year to 3.2 million. Television stations also began to lose interest. In 1993, some 41 J. League matches were broadcast live, with average ratings of over 10 per cent. Three years later, ratings had dropped to little over 7 per cent and only 34 games were aired live. Clearly, those who were interested in soccer as a fashion were moving on to a different scene.

Those in the sport have tried to shake off the implications of the fall in interest. Mastunori Fujiguchi, departing secretary of the J. League, was reported as saying: "We're not really concerned. In some ways the temporary fashion of the J. League is being stripped away and that is allowing the core support to come out clearly" (*Daily Yomiuri*, 9 May 1997). He pointed out that soccer remains as popular as baseball among children, adding that the J. League is itself still in its infancy. To show just how far ahead it is looking, the J. League has adopted a "100-year plan", the first stage of which is to slowly build up local support. Officials point out that the smallest crowd at the start of the 1997 season was at JEF United's Ichihara Stadium, which is too far removed from the club's training ground and offices to satisfy the "hometown" ideal.

How, then, to interpret the response of consumers since the start of the J. League? Initially, the *shinhatsubai* process succeeded in generating huge interest. This provided the momentum for further transfor-mations in the sport's infrastructure, such as more teams and bigger stadiums. It also provided the funds and the motivation for an improve-ment in the quality of football: not only because more foreign stars came to Japan, but because domestic players raised their standards as evidenced by Japan's victory over Brazil in the 1996 Olympics and the nation's first appearance in FIFA's top 20 rankings.

Since those early days, interest in soccer has fallen sharply. However, big games continue to draw attendances of over 30,000, enthusiasm among young supporters remains strong and advertisers continue to use football stars to promote their products. Thus, despite the bursting of the soccer bubble, the game continues to maintain a far greater share of the sports market than many commentators had thought possible. Soccer has clearly moved off the sidelines.

Conclusion: the incorporation of soccer into Japanese culture

It is possible to divide the world between those who play baseball and those who play soccer. (Izumi 1989: 40)

The view expressed here by Sei-ichi Izumi typified the pre-J. League perception of football as a foreign sport. Despite the introduction of the game over one hundred and twenty years previously, soccer had never been fully adopted as part of Japanese culture in the way that baseball had. However, in recent times two important developments have been taking place: changes in the world system which led the Japanese government to seek a stronger international identity independent of its relations with the USA; and changes in the structure of Japanese society, such as the shifts from an export-led economy to a consumer economy and from a work-centered identity to a domestic identity for Japanese men. I noted above that the history of Japanese sport supported Stokvis's theory (1989) that sport participation patterns are shaped by such external developments. Thus new developments in sport can be an expected response to the changing socio-economic environment. Taking such a tack has provided an answer to the question as to why the J. League came into existence: in effect it was a sort of "natural selection" process, but this does not explain how the transformation was achieved.

This chapter has attempted to answer the latter question. First posited was Hegel's dialectic as a basis for cultural development through the objectification and then sublation process. Next we saw how this had been applied by Miller to the issue of consumption; the way people are able to appropriate things for themselves. Finally, this chapter looked at this process by examining the way in which the Japanese re-invented and re-located soccer. This was achieved by updating the image of the game to make it more attractive and competitive with world-class teams and, at the same time, by giving the game a material form, moving it from the international to the domestic arena, shifting it from the margins to the mainstream. In terms of marketing this was the "new movement" dynamic of *shinhatsubai* that aimed to give consumers the choice of an updated and more easily available product.

Consumers, at both macro (local authorities, company sponsors, etc.) and micro (individual) levels, have been able to appropriate soccer in a wide variety of ways. Business institutions see soccer as a way of making a profit (that is, the J. League's revenues); public authorities see the

sport as a means of strengthening community spirit by adopting the
J. League's hometown system; and the government appears to see it as
a way of strengthening national identity, through the support of the
Japanese national team and the hosting of the 2002 World Cup finals.
Both the national team and the bid for the World Cup might provide
new objectives for what Bellah (1970) calls Japan's "goal-orientated
society". As football becomes objectified in these ways it begins to seem
less alien.

The ultimate goal of the *shinhatsubai* process is to create a new niche
in the market for a product. To return to the brewing industry for an
example, Suntory Malts has successfully made the transition from
shinhatsubai to established brand. In so doing it altered the pattern of
beer drinking in Japan, introducing both a new generation of young
consumers into the market and providing an alternative to the lager
beers which previously accounted for almost all sales. Suntory Malts
was thus subsumed into the beer market. The JFA is hoping that the
J. League will achieve a similar success by becoming an established
brand. As their spokesman, Mr Kato, said: "Our aim is that the people
of Japan will come to recognize soccer as part of our culture" (pers.
comm.). For this to happen the J. League will have to both transform
and be incorporated into Japanese culture.

It would appear that this synthesis is already well under way. As has
been shown soccer is being Japanized: the rules have been changed to
introduce an element of *shobu* ("showdown"); there is an enormous
emphasis on fair play, amateur players bow to one another before and
after each game, and supporters' chanting is orchestrated by an ap-
pointed leader. Yet the J. League also symbolizes a new Japanese
identity: players and fans are more expressive; the large number of
foreign stars gives the sport an international flavor; team loyalties are
determined by the hometown (the point of consumption) rather than
the company (the point of production); and female consumers are
being encouraged, for economic reasons, to become more involved.

Despite this strong beginning, we cannot say yet whether soccer will
ultimately succeed in carving out a permanent niche in the Japanese
sports market. Already much of the euphoria which greeted the J.
League has faded as the "*shin*" ("newness") of the *shinhatsubai* has worn
off and baseball has fought hard to regain its previously dominant
position. Attendances now, four years on, are well down on the 1993
peak. However, co-hosting the World Cup finals in 2002 with South
Korea should ensure that for the medium term at least, soccer will be
able to maintain a healthy prominence.

Even if it does fall victim to the whims of consumer taste, the J. League
marks a departure from previous sports marketing campaigns. The

shinhatsubai process (through its market surveys, expansion of the means of appropriation and the raising of quality standards) clearly illustrated how the promoters of sport, like the producers of any product, are increasingly aware of the need to consult, provide access for, and strive to satisfy potential consumers. As such, it is a recognition of Miller's (1987) assertion that the consumer is now at the commanding heights of the modern economy.

And should the J. League succeed in establishing itself as a major cultural institution, 1993 will be seen to have heralded a new era in Japanese sport. Adding to May's (1989: 181) description of baseball as "the story of Japan's successful union of Japanese spirit and western technique", and sumo as "the myth of Japan's divine origins", we can perhaps see in soccer a new symbol for the international power of Japanese consumption.

Notes

1   The primary material for this chapter is drawn from newspapers, magazine articles and information provided by Hakuhodo (the marketing agency in charge of promoting the J. League), and the Japanese Football Association (JFA). The brief survey I conducted was half done through face-to-face interviews with Japanese people I knew in London and half by correspondence, through a questionnaire sent to friends in Japan. In addition I have tried to draw on my own experience of soccer in Japan, both before and after the establishment of the J. League, at large matches, in the Sunday League and in the school where I taught. Although I did not know it at the time, it was the fieldwork for this paper. Many thanks to all the interviewees and friends who sent articles from Japan. I appreciate the kind help of Mr Ono at Hakuhodo and Mr Kato at the JFA. Special thanks to Sumiko and Hiroki Okita who helped me become involved in soccer in Japan. I must also thank Ray Clemence, Dr J. Williams, Kayoko Kamimura, Seàchi Saito, Yukari Satio, Kyoko Kamide, Hiroko Kamide, Akira Hayasaka, Miki Yamaguchi, Hiroki Okita, Sumiko Okita, Masahiro Nagayo, "Bobby" Akaishi, Keichi Tanaka, Katsuyuki Deguchi, Yumiko Deguchi and Minoru Kinoshita.

2   From a personal interview with Ray Clemence, former England International goal keeper, now manager of Barnet FC. In 1991 he was responsible for the Tottenham team during the Asahi Tournament in Japan, in which Tottenham and the national sides of Thailand and Japan competed.

3   The J. League began with ten clubs: Gamba Osaka, JEF United Ichihara, Kashima Antlers, Nagoya Grampus Eight, Sanfreece Hiroshima, Shimizu S. Pulse, Urawa Red Diamonds, Verdy Kawasaki, Yokohama Flugels, Yokohama Marinos. In 1998 there are eighteen clubs, and in the long term two leagues are planned.

4   "Cheer horns" have since been prohibited, after complaints from residents living near stadiums.

5 There is a restriction on more than five foreign players on any team and only three of these can play at one time. All together fifty-six foreign players, the majority from Brazil, played in the J. League in its first season. Thus each team used its allotment to the full.
6 Imamiya Koritsu Koko and Izuo Koritsu Koko, both state secondary schools in Osaka.
7 When speaking of matters concerning the imperial family, the convention is to use a particular form of *keigo* (polite language). When interviewed on Japanese television, Kazu used ordinary, rather rude, Japanese. In an interesting reversal, Ramos, the naturalized Brazilian footballer, used the appropriate form.
8 The baseball player Nomo's success with the Los Angeles Dodgers in the 1995 season has set an astonishing precedent, but even this followed Kazu's move.
9 For a brief history of modern horse-racing and betting see Chapter 9.
10 See also Kelly's discussion of *dô* in Chapter 4 of this book.
11 *Seishin* is a difficult word to translate, but it approximates "spirit" or "mind" (cf. Moeran 1989).
12 Japan's first international football match was played in 1927 against the Philippines.
13 A 1991 survey in Tokyo found that although 76 per cent of unmarried women in their 20s lived with their parents, few contributed to the household budget (*Economist*, 22 October 1994, p. 150).

References

Asahi Shimbun 1 August 1994 "Yakyu yori sakka senshu".
——15 August 1994 "Sakka ryugaku kyuzo and Kazu mitai ni naru".
——24 August 1994 "Boom mikoshi ryugaku bizinesu".
Befu, H. 1980 *Japan: An anthropological introduction*. San Francisco: Scranton; London, Toronto: Chandler Publishing.
Bellah, R. 1970 *Tokugawa Religion: the values of pre-industrial Japan*. Boston: Beacon Press.
Bestor, T. 1985 "Tradition and Japanese social organization: institutional development in a Tokyo neighbourhood" in *Ethnography*, vol. xxiv (2).
——1989 *Neighborhood Tokyo*. Stanford: Stanford University Press.
Buruma, I. 1984 *A Japanese Mirror: heroes and villains of Japanese culture*. London: Jonathan Cape.
Chen, D. (1990) *Analyses of Japanese Consumption Patterns, an application of DAP*. Perth: University of Western Australia.
Cuyler, P. 1979 *Sumo: from rite to sport*. New York: Weatherhill.
Dore, R. 1959 *City Life in Japan*. Berkeley: University of California Press.
——1973 *British Factory, Japanese Factory*. Berkeley: University of California Press.
Financial Times 26 July 1994 "In the throes of transformation" and "Imported beers boost market share in Japan".
——30 August 1994 "Soccer scores in Japan" and "Women mean business".
Henshall, K. G. 1988 *A Guide to Remembering Japanese Characters*. Tokyo: Tuttle.
Herald Tribune 7 August 1994 "In Japan soccer is kicking baseball around".
Hokkaido Shimbum 15 July 1994 "*J. Rîgu chosa kara: keizai futan*".

I. D. September 1994 "A view from the Tokyo terraces".

Izumi S. 1989 "Japanese sports" in *Handbook of Japanese Popular Culture* edited by R. Powers and H. Kato. New York: Greenwood Press.

J. League Profile 1994 Rules of Membership.

Japan Quarterly 1994 "Scoring big with soccer". Issue 10–12.

Kawakita Shinpo 11 January 1994 *"J. Rîgu o yoba; Stadium o motomita Yamagata da shomae kasudu kaishi".*

——18 March 1994a *"J. Rîgu no shiyôchini senyô stadium o shomei o soete Yamagata ken ni chinjou".*

——19 July 1994b *"Aomori no Sannouchimaruyama isseki hozon mondai nado o kyôgi".*

Miller, D. 1987 *Material Culture and Mass Consumption.* Oxford: Blackwell.

Moeran, Brian 1989 *Language and Popular Culture.* Manchester: University of Manchester Press.

Muto 1989 *Consumer Society of Japan in Year 2000.*

——1991 *Alcohol Consumption in Japan.*

Nakane, C. 1971 *Japanese Society.* London: Penguin.

Newsweek 13 June 1994 "In a league of its own".

Ohnuki-Tierney, Emiko 1987 *The Monkey as Mirror.* Princeton: Princeton University Press.

Robertson, J. 1991 *Native and Newcomer: Making and Remaking a Japanese City.* Berkeley: University of California Press.

Saeki Toshio 1989 "Sport in Japan" in Wagner (ed.) pp. 49–70.

Smith, R. 1978 *Kurusu: the price of progress in a Japanese village 1951–1975.* Stanford: Stanford University Press.

Stokvis, R. 1989 "The international and national expansion of sports" in Wagner (ed.) pp. 13–24.

Tass News Agency 17 July 1994 "Poll: 4% of Japanese People Priority is Work".

Verdy Yearbook 1994 *Teikyo Pawa, Kosei o tobasu shido.*

Wagner, E. A. (ed.) 1989 *Sport in Asia and Africa.* Greenwood: New York.

Whiting, J. 1977 *The Chrysanthemum and the bat: the game the Japanese play.* Tokyo: Termanent Press.

World News Report 9 October 1993 "Japan adopts its winning strategy to soccer".

Documents

The following documents were kindly provided by the World Cup Japan 2002 Bidding Committee Secretariat (Football Association of Japan) and although not directly referred to in the text were useful in its writing:

J. League: Suntory Series

The Early Days of the Football Association of Japan (JFA)

Pro Jidai no Paionia, Yasuhiko Okudera

Women's Football in Japan

World Cup Japan 2002: Japan loves goals

The Emperor's Cup

1993 – A review of football in Japan

J. League 1994 Profile

Index

Abashiri bangaichi series, 72, 73
Abu-Lughod, L., 149
adolescents, 6, 42–43
  females, 70, 78, 93, 184
  males, 56, 65, 67, 69
advertisers, 10, 15, 114, 127, 188, 192
  advertising, 4, 33, 92, 115–116
age, 7, 8, 50, 77, 116, 178
  adults, 48, 112
  groups, 6, 81, 83–84, 177
  lifecycle 7, 14
  middle, 8, 48, 86,
aidoru, see idols
Akira, 7, 11, 56–73, 107
  characters in, 63, 65, 66–68, 71–72
aku-basho (bad spaces), *see* space
Alien, 102
Allen, R. C., 56, 73
America, *see* USA
Anderson, B., 2, 16
Anderson, J. T., 58, 73
Ang, Ien, 11, 16
animals, 39, 40, 101
  association with color, 39–40, 41
  byakko (mythical tiger), 23
  fox, 22, 46
  genbu (mythical giraffe), 23
  hô (phoenix), 38, 40, 48
  insects, 101
  kirin (fiery horse), 38, 40, 47
  leopard, 39, 43
  ryû (dragon), 38, 40, 43, 46, 48, 52
  seiryû (mythical dragon), 23
  shishi (lion), 38, 40, 48
  suzaku (mythical bird), 23
  tanuki (raccoon), 46

  tenma (sacred horse), 38, 40, 47
  transformations, 45–46
anthropology, 1, 3
  anthropologists, 2, 5, 12–13, 15,
  approaches in, 1, 3–4, 12–13, 28
  of popular culture, 3–5, 11, 13, 15
  participant observation in, 12, 179
  structuralist, 3, 12
appropriation, 4, 10
Archers, The, 135
arts, 3, 82
asadora (asa no renzoku terebi shôsetsu),
  133–149
  audiences, 133, 135, 138–139, 141,
    147–148
  Eenyobo, 136–137
  going/coming to capital genre (*jôkyô*),
    143
  Hanegoma, 138
  Hirari, 137, 142, 148
  Karin, 137
  Kimi no na wa, 138–139
  Kokoro wa itsumo ramune iro, 144
  Kyô futari, 137, 140
  Mâchan, 139
  Miotsukushi, 140
  Ohananhan, 142
  Onna wa dokyô, 137, 145
  Piano, 137
  Romansu, 136
  Wakko no kinmedaru, 137, 146
asobi (play/leisure), 7, 57–58, 83, 182
  asobinin (lit. play people), 168, 180
  contemporary, 75–76, 83
  traditional activities, 22, 75
Atsumi Reiko, 85, 87

audiences, 11, 27, 56, 64, 70, 93, 99, 105, 177
  adolescent males, 56, 65
  karaoke, 79, 81
  magazine, 116, 118–120, 124–127
  of *asadora*, 133, 135, 138–139, 141, 147–148
  pre-school, 37
  ratings, 33
  Western, 70
  women, 105, 133, 177
Auerbach, N., 97, 108

Baba, Y., 129, 130
Bachnik, J., 159, 166
Banana Yoshimoto, 71, 92
bars, 76, 77, 83
Bartholomew Fair, 22
baseball, 12, 54, 82, 182, 183, 185, 186, 187, 192, 194, 195, 196, 198, 200
  see also sports
Baudrillard, J., 6, 16, 65–66, 73
Beauty and the Beast, 102
Befu, H., 149, 150, 189, 200
Bellah, R., 189, 191–192, 198, 200
Ben–Ari, E., 50, 54
Benedict, R., 16
Bernier, B., 28, 29
Bestor, T., 114–115, 129, 130, 189, 200
Bhabha, H., 2, 16
Blade Runner, 57, 62, 66, 68–69, 70, 72
blood, 41–2, 95, 100, 101, 102, 106
  and fire, 41–2
  and vampirism, 97
  menstruation, 97, 107
body, 50
  and mind, 49, 53, 186
bôsôzoku, 6, 8, 185, 190
  as sub-culture, 7, 56–62, 129
  definition of, 70
  see also sub-cultures
boundaries, 3, 8–9, 62
Bourdieu, P., 15, 16
Bowring, R., 113, 130
Braithwaite, B., 129, 130
Britain, 3, 8, 9, 12, 19, 47, 80, 81, 85, 133, 135
  football in, 181, 183–184, 189
  Power Rangers in, 42
Buddhism, 6, 20, 78
  esoteric, 13, 21
  five sins, 52
  temples, 21, 22
  Zen, 12, 48
Bunce, W. K., 45, 53
burakumin (caste), 187

Buruma, I., 12, 16, 53, 54, 182, 200

capitalism, 10, 11, 71
carnival, *see* spectacle
cartoons (animated), 34
  AA, Harimanada, 25
  Anpanman, 50
  Atomu Taishi, 49
  Battle Fever J, 40
  Cutey Honey Flash, 34
  Doraemon, 47
  Dragonball, 49
  Dragonball Z, 70
  Gridman, 37–38
  Jan Pâson, 44–45
  Nihon mukashi-banashi, 46
ceremony, 20, 22–23, 28, 34, 45, 140
  agricultural, 19, 27
  and sumo, 27, 182, 186
  kan'name-sai (first fruit offering), 27
  shihôhai (New Year's), 27
Chamberlain, B. H., 86, 87
Chen, D. 188, 200
children, 2, 5, 12, 38, 43, 44, 48, 52, 59, 141, 143, 169, 180, 196
  as heroes, 49–50
  as technocrats, 38, 47
  boys, 7, 46, 70, 195
  British, 51
  consciousness of color, 41
  exposure to *manga*, 92, 104
  girls, 7, 103
  pre-pubescent girls, 7, 92, 103
  socialization of, 123, 133, 140
  television programs for, 6, 13, 33–51, 103
China, 10, 24, 27, 42
  characters, 60
  culture, 52
  mythology, 49
  philosophy, 53
Chûshingura, 61–62, 68
Cinderella, 144, 155, 157
  Japanese version (*Ochikubo*), 149
class, 1, 3, 8, 14, 15, 57, 71, 111, 155
  blue-collar, 6, 40, 57–59, 71
  bourgeois, 95, 162
  and culture, 3
  middle (white-collar), 5, 6, 7, 8, 14, 40, 58–59, 105, 115, 161, 194
  system, 40
  upper, 169, 177
  see also status
classification, 50–51
Clemence, Ray, 184, 198
Cohen, A., 59, 69, 73

color, 13, 50
  and animals, 23, 38–40
  black, 39–42, 53
  blue, 23, 35, 38–42, 47
  children's consciousness of, 41
  coding, 38–44, 50, 52
  green, 38–41, 43, 48
  orange, 39, 41
  pink, 38–42, 48, 51, 53
  purple, 42, 44–45
  red, 23, 34, 35, 37, 38–43, 44, 48, 51–2,
    53, 63
  silver, 34, 37, 44
  and status, 39–42, 44–45
  white, 23, 34, 39–41, 43, 51–2, 53
  yellow, 23, 35, 38–42, 47, 50, 70
comics (*manga*), 4, 6, 7, 12, 15, 49, 86, 92,
    113
  Akira, 56, 64, 67, 70
  American, 92
  British, 92
  Buddhist, 6
  Devil Hunter Yoko, 92, 108
  narratives, 64
  shôjo, 94, 105, 107
  sumo, 25
  Western audiences of, 93
  and women, 93, 94, 103, 105
  see also cartoons
commodities, 71, 76, 82
  see also consumption, products
community, 137, 189, 198
  imagined, 2, 6, 10
company, 2, 14, 63, 129
  see also men
Confucianism, 24, 52, 133
  ethics, 73, 133–134, 161
  ideals, 10, 134
  neo-, 146
  and society, 67, 69
consumption, 4, 5, 7, 11, 28, 127–128, 129,
    181–182
  consumerism, 9, 111, 115, 127
  consumers, 10–11, 12, 15, 16, 106, 127,
    182, 197
  of culture, 6, 94, 191
  of football, 182, 194
  of goods, 8, 105, 115, 183
  and knowledge, 15
  see also commodities
Cornwall, A., 8, 16
Coronation Street, 135
cosmology, 19, 22–23, 28
  fû–sui (wind and flowing water),
    23, 27
Crossroads, 135

Crown Prince, 26, 29, 156–159, 160,
    161–162, 164
  engagment, 5, 157
  marriage, 25, 26–27, 162
Crown Princess (Owada Masako), 14, 91,
    124, 157–159, 162, 164
  wedding, 25, 124, 181, 195
Croissant shôkôgun, 112
culture, 1, 9, 33, 44, 56, 57, 95, 182
  and knowledge, 66, 162
  definition, 3–4
  elite, 5–6, 28, 98, 169, 177
  global, 3, 5–6, 76
  Japanese, 12, 62, 82, 96, 106, 117, 143,
    157, 161, 184, 197
  material, 3, 5
  national, 2, 14, 96
  postmodern, 8, 11, 20, 125
  rural, 19, 137
  studies, 4, 11
  Western notions of, 5
  see also popular culture
Cuyler, P., 182, 200
cyborgs, *see* robots

Dale, P., 70, 73
Dallas, 133, 135
danger, 7–9, 14, 179
Darth Vader, 37
Davis, W., 45, 54
demons, 45–46, 95–97
deities, 7, 28, 36, 99, 155,
  Ebisu, 159–160, 165
delinquents, 57–58, 70
  sub-culture, 59, 67
DeVos, G., 58, 73
Diana, Princess of Wales, 16
Dickey, S., 11, 16
dô, see way of
dohyô (ring), *see* sumo
Doi Takeo, 84, 87
Doiharu S., 134, 150
domestication, 10–11, 51, 187, 197
Dore, R., 189, 200
Dower, J. W., 53, 54
dream, 144, 146, 147
Dynasty, 135
dystopia, 69, 70, 101, 107

Eastenders, 135
Eastwood, Clint, 9
Edo period (1603–1867), 19, 20, 21–22,
    24
  citizens, 19, 149, 168
  the city (Tokyo), 19
  government, 168

education, 2, 58–59, 139, 143, 164, 186
    content of televison dramas, 139–140
    language of, 117–123
Egami Teruhiko, 142, 150
Eldorado, 135
emperor, 19, 23, 24–26, 28, 160, 187
    and sumo, 25–27
    cosmological role of, 23–24
    emperorship (*tennôsei*), 22, 26–27
    Heisei, 148, 160, 161
    Meiji, 168
    Shôwa, 26, 144, 148, 160, 161
    Taishô, 160
    see also Crown Prince, imperial family
empowerment, 100, 103, 106, 160
enkaigei (party trick), 81, 86
entertainment, 141, 176
    see also asobi
esthetics, 2, 27, 64, 66

family, *see* household
fantasy, 13, 101, 103, 105, 106
    fiction, 6, 100
female, 6, 13, 73, 91–108, 156
    and psychic powers, 93, 95, 98–100,
        106
    association with outside, 159, 164
    colors associated with, 38–41
    construction of, 7, 91, 93, 160
    see also gender, women
Fields, G., 115, 130
film, 15, 25, 93
    analysis, 11, 56
    anime (animated), 92, 102
    Arashi o yobu otoko, 72
    Bibappu haisukûru, 71
    cyberpunk, 56
    Daitôyô sensô to kokusai saiban, 73
    gender specificity of, 70, 91
    haha mono (mother movies), 91
    Hana no Asuka-gumi, 70
    Japan's Longest Day, 63, 73
    Japanese, 9, 24
    jidai–geki, 68
    Jingi naki tatakai, 73
    Kimi wa boku o sukini naru, 67
    Kumo nagaruru hateni, 71
    nagare-mono (drifter), 57, 62–63, 67–68,
        72–73
    newsreels, 25
    Ningen gyorai kaiten, 71
    Ningen gyorai shutsugeki su, 71
    Nodo jiman, 81
    noir, 62
    science fiction/horror, 57, 68, 69
    Sono otoko kyôbôni tsuki, 70

Toei Film 38, 40–41, 49
    war-retro, 60, 68, 73
    yakuza, 62–63, 68, 72–73
Fiske, J., 61, 73, 123, 130
folklore, 4, 13, 45–46, 49–50, 97, 143, 155,
    165, 179
football, 1, 9, 14, 181–200
    American, 188
    FIFA, 196
    and gender, 9, 188
    in Japan, 4, 8–9, 181–200
    World Cup, 188, 190–191, 193, 194–195,
        196, 198
football clubs,
    Genoa (Italy), 185
    original ten in Japan, 198
    Shimizu S. Pulse, 185
    Tottenham Hotspur (UK), 184, 198
    Vasco da Gama (Brazil), 183–184
    Verdy Kawasaki, 184
France, 19, 40
Friedman, J., 93, 108
Freud, S., 106, 108
Fujitani T., 160, 166
fû-sui (wind and flowing water), *see*
    cosmology

gambling, 8, 13, 82, 167–169, 176, 178,
    180, 188, 200
    as national issue, 169
Gellner, E., 1, 16
gender, 3, 6, 7, 13, 50, 60, 70, 140, 156,
    164, 176
    complementarity, 7, 134, 159
    equality of, 161
    and football, 9
    identity, 14, 69, 91, 96
    and *manga*, 94
ghosts, 22, 46
Gillespie, M., 11, 16
Greenfeld, K. T., 70, 71, 73
globalization, 4, 8, 9
    relationship with local, 11, 13, 164
Gluck, C., 10, 16
gods, goddesses, *see* deities
Godzilla (*Gojira*), 7, 9
Gomery, D., 56, 73
Goodman, R., 50, 54
group, the, 15, 80–81, 82, 83, 84, 129

Harootunian, H. D., 85, 87
Hartley, J., 73
Harvey, D., 11, 16, 69, 74
Hebdige, D., 61, 74
Hegel, G. W. F., 182, 197
Heian period (794–1185), 27, 42, 180

Hendry, J., 4, 16, 50, 54, 87, 123–124, 130, 144, 148, 149, 150
heroes, 67, 78
  tragic, 61–62
  see also super-heroes
heterogeneity, 15, 77, 84, 85
Hiejima I., 122, 130
hierarchy, 2, 40, 50, 77, 161
  of civil servants (gogyô), 42, 44
  senpai/kôhai (senior/junior), 86
Higuchi Keiko, 50, 54
hisshô (certain victory), 49, 54
history, 2, 164
Hobsbawm, E., 4, 10, 16
hometown (furusato), 14, 189–190, 192, 198
homogeneity, 2, 15, 57, 70, 76–77, 85, 111, 117, 129
Hori Ichiro, 28, 29
horse–racing, 8, 9, 167–180, 186, 188, 192, 200
  and gender, 9, 167, 169, 179
  in Japan, 168–170
  manga, 12, 175
hotels, 76–77, 158–159, 162, 166
household (ie), 7, 8, 58, 67, 83, 136, 142
  master of (kachô), 161
  women's association with, 14, 97, 134, 144, 155–156
Hume, K., 106, 108
hyperreality, 6, 65–66, 68, 105

Ichikawa Danjûrô, 21, 28
identity, 62, 71, 125, 189
  Bildungsroman (quest for), 102–103, 142
  choice, 93, 106
  class/status, 14, 177
  gendered, 14, 69, 91, 93, 96, 100
  Japanese, 14, 191–192, 197, 198
  new cultural, 183
ideology, 1, 58, 91, 127, 133
  dominant, 2, 10, 15, 62
  patriarchal, 7, 91
idols (aidoru), 27, 78, 85, 155
  see also super-stars
Imamura, A. E., 14, 15, 17
imperial family, 8, 23, 27, 44, 156, 160, 185
  and kabuki, 13, 27
  and sumo, 13, 22–24
  Household Agency, 157, 160
  tradition, 161–162
incorporation (gattai), 45–48
individuality, 81, 86, 121–122
  koseitekina (individualistic), 185
individuals, 34, 69, 84, 86, 185
Inoue J., 129, 130

inside (uchi) 7–9, 14, 159
  as female domain, 7, 159, 163, 164, 165
internationalization (kokusaika), 14, 159, 161, 164–165
  see also Japan
Ippongatana dohyô-iri, 28
Irons, G., 92, 106, 108
Ivy, M., 10, 17, 28, 29
Iwao S., 128, 130, 161, 166
Izumi Kyoka, 106, 108
Izumi S., 197, 200

J. League (Japanese Professional Football League), 181–200
  status of, 193–194
  see also football, hometown
Jackson, R., 106, 108
Jameson, F., 11, 17, 62, 74
Japan, 1, 26, 57
  consumer culture, 94, 158, 182, 191, 197
  contemporary, 1, 4, 96, 133
  feudal, 2, 19, 22, 42
  as international, 8–9, 14, 159, 161, 197–198
  nation-state, 1–6, 15, 76, 91, 160
  postmodern, 4, 8, 20, 69
  post-war, 58, 73, 91, 94, 134, 135, 143, 146–147, 155, 160, 161, 164–165, 182, 191
  post-post-war, 93
  representations of, 1, 2
  rural, 1, 22, 143
  socialization in, 50, 123
  urban, 1, 143, 189
Japan Racing Association (JRA), 167, 170, 179–180
Japanese, 12
  Gothic, 95, 96
  literature, 13, 93
  mythology, 44, 46, 49–50
  recession, 125–127, 128, 156
  society, 1–3, 12, 56–57, 63, 75–76, 84, 91, 105, 117, 136, 155, 161, 189, 197
  traditions, 13, 111, 133, 161
Japanese Sumo Association, 26, 28, 163
Japaneseness, 8, 10, 50
  ideology of (nihonjinron), 1, 133, 191
Jenkins, H., 11, 17
Jong, Erica, 103, 108, 112
Jonson, Ben, 22
jû hachiban (eighteen pieces), see kabuki
jûdô, see sports

kabuki, 6, 20, 21, 28, 52, 149
  and the imperial family, 13, 27
  Ichikawa family and, 21, 28

jû hachiban (eighteen pieces), 21, 28, 80, 86
roppô (stamping), 21
kamaboko, 41, 51
Kamakura, 95, 96
kamikaze, 36, 53, 60
karaoke, 6, 7, 12, 14, 75–87
  as communication, 77, 79
  as global, 76, 78, 86
  as social lubricator, 77, 84
  boxes, 76–77, 82, 83, 85
  dô, 80, 86
  outside Japan, 9, 76, 78, 86
  performance of, 79–84
  technology of, 76, 84
Kato Hidetoshi, 5, 17, 131, 150
kan'name-sai, see ceremony
Kansai, 1, 76, 85, 142–143, 178
Kantô, 1, 142
Kawai R., 110, 114, 115, 129, 130
Kayama R., 129, 130
keigo, see language
Kellner, D., 125, 130
kendô, see sports
keshô-mawashi (decorated apron), *see* sumo
King, Stephen, 100, 108
Kitchin, 67, 70
Kiyota Y., 113–114, 130
Kobe, 85, 184
Koide T., 111, 112, 114, 131
Kokugikan, the, 21, 24
  see also sumo
kokusaika, see internationalization
Komatsu K., 155, 166
Kondo, D., 10, 17, 159, 166
Korea, 10, 13, 24, 76, 196, 198
  women in, 133–134
  wrestling (*silmu*), 19, 22, 28
Kornicki, P., 113, 130
Kôya hijiri, 106
Krauss, E., 11
Kurahashi Yumiko, 106
Kyoto, 1, 23, 85, 95, 96, 116, 137, 140, 170

Lady who Loves Insects, The, 108
language, 117–123
  polite (*keigo*), 4, 117, 185, 200
  prescriptive character in women's
    magazines, 117–123, 125
Lash, S., 71, 74, 93, 108
Leach, E., 51, 54
leisure, *see asobi*
Lent, J., 92, 108
Lévi-Strauss, C., 4, 17, 40
Lindisfarne, N., 8, 16
Linhart, S., 78, 82, 87

literature, 13, 106
Little Mermaid, The, 102
London, 22, 66, 117, 198s
Los Angeles, 62, 66
luck, 34, 40
Lull, J., 16, 17

Mad Max, 43
Madonna, 61
magazines, 15, 114, 137, 145, 146, 198
  An-An, 114, 115–116, 129
  Angle, 112
  Aruru, 112
  Croissant, 112
  Doresu Mêkingu, 110–111
  educative elements in, 117–125, 126–127
  EF, 112
  female readership, 12
  Fujin Gahô, 110
  Fujin Kôron, 110
  Fujin Kurabu, 110, 111, 113
  Fujin seikatsu, 110, 111, 113
  Hai Fasshion, 111
  Hanako, 113
  JJ, 114–116, 118, 126, 129
  Junon, 114
  Katei Gahô, 111
  Madamu, 111
  Misesu, 111
  MORE, 112, 115–116, 129
  Non-No, 114, 115–116, 129
  Orange Page, 113
  Shufu, 110
  Shufu no tomo, 110, 111
  Shufu to seikatsu, 110, 111
  Sôen, 110
  25 ans, 115–116
  With, 115–116, 124, 126, 129
  Western, 112, 115, 117–118, 123, 129
  women's, 110–129
magic, 34, 39, 42, 46
  balls, 49–50
Mai the psychic girl, 92, 94, 98–100, 107
Malcolm X, 123–124
male, 6, 62, 73, 86, 156
  as outsiders, 62–63, 69
  association with inside, 159, 164
  construction of, 7, 67
  kôha (hard type), 67–68
  nanpa (soft type), 67
  quest for identity, 102–103, 197
  status of, 16, 41, 57–58
  see also gender, men
manga, see comics
Mankekar, P., 149, 150
marebito (outsider, stranger), *see* stranger

marriage, 5, 25, 27, 136, 143–144, 145, 158, 192
  as media event, 155–159
  omiai (arranged), 145
martial arts, *see* sports
Marxism, 10, 15
  neo-Marxism, 2, 15
mass culture, *see* popular culture
Matsubara J., 112, 131
Matthew, R., 12, 17
Mauss, M., 4, 17
McCracken, E., 116, 129, 131
McLuhan, Marshall, 9, 17
McRobbie, A., 118, 131
media, 2, 11, 15, 24, 26, 58, 60, 77, 156–158, 166
  Japanese scholars of, 6, 57, 77
  newspapers, 135, 155, 159, 162, 169, 198
  radio, 135
  stories, 155–166
  studies, 4, 11
  Western, 127
Meiji Era (1868–1911), 24, 137, 138, 160, 186, 188, 191
  authorities, 161, 168
  Restoration (1868), 20, 24, 147
men, 2, 7–9, 14, 78, 140
  and leisure, 78, 82, 167
  association with danger, 8, 179
  businessmen (*saruriman*), 2, 8, 76, 83, 194
  young, 5, 7, 8, 14, 75, 170
  see also gender, male
militarism (*kurai tani*), 25, 62, 63, 65–66
Miller, D., 4, 5, 17, 28, 29, 181–183, 193, 197–198, 201
Miyazawa Rie, 26, 157–159, 163
modernization, 19, 164
Moeran, Brian, 10, 12, 15, 17, 129, 131, 200, 201
monsters, 33, 36, 37, 45, 50, 51, 52
  bake-mono (thing that changes), 45
  Barutan Seijin (Baltan Starman), 36
  bogeys (*yôkai*), 43, 45, 48
  King Kong, 36
  Tyrannosaurus Rex, 37, 39
  women as, 43
Moon, O., 127, 131, 133–134, 150
morals, ethics, 12, 83, 142, 146
Morley, D., 16, 17
Mouer, R., 1, 10, 17, 70, 71, 74
Muramatsu Yasuko, 142, 150
music, 5, 27
  see also singers, songs
myths, 2, 11, 20, 44, 46, 92, 167, 198
  about Japanese women, 127, 134

machine-age, 46
  of social and cultural homogeneity, 57, 70
  super-hero, 38, 49

Nakane Chie, 16, 17, 189
Namihira E., 159, 166
Nantonaku kurisutaru, 114–115
narration, 2, 60, 64, 66, 135
  Hollywood forms of, 64, 71
Nase Moemi, 175, 180
nation, 11, 86, 142, 147, 160, 184, 190
  history of, 12, 58, 73, 91, 94, 134, 135, 143, 146–147
  nation-building (*kunizukuri*), 6, 14, 134, 147
  nation-state, 1–2, 10, 13
nationalism, 2, 10–11, 13, 198
Nausicaä, 93, 94, 100–103, 107
  anime version, 102, 107
Needham, R., 28, 29, 180
Neighbours, 135
New York, 66, 117
Newitz, A., 104, 109
NHK (Nihon Hôsô Kaisha), 12, 16, 133, 138–140, 145, 149, 150, 195
Niyekawa A., 135, 148, 150
Noh, 21, 96, 147
Nonchan's Dream (Nonchan no yume), 134, 137, 140, 142–148
nostalgia, 28, 62, 69, 83, 189
novels, 6, 13
numbers, 41, 50, 52–53
  five natural elements (*gogyô*), 52
  four, 41, 52
  gangs of five, 40–42, 52
  six, 42–43

Oba Minako, 93, 109
occult, the, 92–93
Oe Kenzaburo, 92, 109
Ogawa Hiroshi, 78, 86, 87
Oguricap, 167–180
  cult of, 13, 167–180
  male followers of, 173–75, 177
  stuffed toys of (*nuigurumi*), 169–170, 173–175
  women's involvement with, 167, 169–170, 173–75
ohako, see jû hachiban
Ohnuki-Tierney, E., 15, 17, 33, 54, 187, 201
Okakura Kakuzo, 82, 87
OLs (young office ladies), *see* women
Olympics, 193
  1964, 63, 137, 187, 191
  1968, 188
  1996, 196

O'Neil, P., 123, 131
onmyôdô (secret rituals), *see* Taoism
Ono Tsutomo, 138, 150
Origuchi S., 155, 166
Osaka, 1, 77, 85, 137, 138, 141, 142–143, 170
Oshin, 126, 137, 138–139, 141, 144, 147, 149
Other, the, 8, 107, 155, 158, 161, 164
    otherness, 58, 62, 96, 99
    see also stranger
Otoko wa tsurai yo (*It's tough being a man*),
    136, 142, 148
Otsuka Eiji, 100, 109
outside (*soto*), 7–9, 155, 159–160
    and danger, 7–9
    and the male domain, 7–9, 62–63, 69
    and women, 155, 156, 159, 164, 165
outsiders, 24, 62–63, 69
    outsider god Ebisu, 159–160, 165
Owada Masako, *see* Crown Princess
Oxford, 26, 161
    University, 124, 125, 157
ôzeki, *see* sumo

patriarchy, 91, 160–161
Pharr, S., 11, 17
Plath, D., 16, 17, 85, 87
politics, 11, 77
Pollack, David, 164, 166
pollution, 8, 107, 187
popular culture, 1–2, 4, 5, 9–10, 12, 14, 16,
    25, 29, 33, 92, 176
    anthropology of, 3, 11, 13
    ideology and, 2, 91, 179
    images of women in, 91, 98, 102, 106, 127
    Japanese 1–2, 5–6, 11–12, 27, 67, 106,
        136, 141, 160
    myth and, 2–3, 11
    political, 2, 11
    symbolic, 2, 5
Postman Pat, 9
postmodernity, 5, 11, 20, 22, 63, 66, 93
Powell, B., 127, 131, 149
power, 7, 27, 28, 36, 61, 95, 128, 161, 165
    of Japanese consumption, 191, 198
    of popular culture, 92
    problem of, 7, 95, 97, 99
    psychic, 67, 93, 95, 98–100, 103, 106, 107
    superhuman, 93
    telekinetic, 100, 102
Powers, R., 5, 17, 131, 151, 201
prints (*ukiyoe*), 24, 45
producers, 10, 12, 16
products, 15, 33, 129, 173, 193
    burando seihin (brand), 166
    and television series, 33, 104
    see also shinhatsubai

publishing 113–114, 127
purity, 45, 68, 182

Quinn, C. J., 159, 166

radio, 25, 158
Ranger, T., 4, 10, 16
Rangers series, 38–44, 48, 53
    characters in, 38
    color coding of, 38–41
    Dai Renjâ (*Great Rangers*), 38, 43, 47, 50,
        52
    in the USA, 42–43
    Jû Renjâ (*Power Rangers*), 9, 14, 42–43
    Kaku Renjâ (*Hidden Rangers*), 38, 43, 47,
        53
    leaders of, 41, 44
    O Renjâ (*Great Rangers*), 38
reality, 8, 155
Reischauer, R., 117, 131
religion, 4, 10, 20, 45, 167, 187
    Jikôson (new religion), 28
    relationship with sumo, 19, 22–24, 27,
        182, 186
    traditional Japanese, 19, 159
    see also ceremony, cosmology
replicants, *see* robots
representations, 10, 14
resistance, 62, 107, 177
Richie, D., 58
rikishi, *see* sumo wrestlers
ritual, *see* ceremony
Robertson, J., 10, 18, 189, 201
robots, 44–45, 47–48, 50, 62, 68–69, 105
    cyborg women, 104
Rohlen, T., 75, 79, 80, 84, 87
roppô (stamping), *see* kabuki
Rose of Versailles (*Beryûsai no bara*), 92, 106
Rosenberger, N., 10, 18
Ryôgoku, 22, 139

Saeki Toshio, 195, 201
Sahlins, M., 165, 166
Saito Seiji, 42, 54
Sakamoto Ryôma, 147
salaryman (*saruriman*), *see* men
Sailor Moon, 34, 70, 94, 103–104
Samuel, R., 2, 18
samurai, 2, 46, 50, 72, 182, 186
    bushidô (way of), 186
    drama, 6, 11, 133
Sanshirô, 106–107
Satô Ikuya, 57–61, 64–65, 67, 71, 74
Satô Tadao, 142, 150
Schilling, M., 47, 55
Schodt, F., 12, 15, 18, 49, 55, 106

science fiction, 12, 15, 92, 93, 105
Second World War, 15, 24, 26, 49, 53, 60,
    73, 110, 113, 139, 161, 187
  Japan's defeat in, 12, 35, 144, 147
  Occupation (1945–52), 45, 161, 187
self, the, 10, 46, 86, 186
  expression, 78, 185
  self-improvement for women, 134, 142
sensei (master, teacher), 44
sex, sexuality, 44, 53, 76, 94, 106, 107
  words, 75
Sheena, 102
shihôhai (New Year's ritual), see
    ceremony
Shimanaka Y, 110–113, 117, 128, 131
shimenawa (straw rope), 20
shinhatsubai (new product), 181–200
  process, 188–192, 194, 196, 198–199
  see also products
Shintô, 13, 20, 28, 187
  priests, 23, 188
  shamanesses, 96
  shrines, 22, 23
shôjo (young girl), 91–92, 93–96, 98, 100,
    102
  as sub-culture, 94, 129
  manga, 94, 105, 107
Shu R., 121, 131
Silverstone, R., 16, 18
singers, singing, 5, 77, 78, 79, 80–81, 84
  see also songs
Skov, L., 15, 18, 129, 131
Smith, R., 149, 150, 166, 190, 201
soccer, see football
social, the, 69, 77
  construction of, 7, 165
society, 1–2, 3, 100, 133, 161
  gender in, 8, 140, 155, 161
  postmodern, 71, 182
  pre-capitalist, 4
sociology, 4, 15–16
Soeda Yoshiya, 92, 109
songs, 75, 79, 83, 86
  see also singers
Sontag, S., 68, 69, 74
Soseki Natsume, 106, 109
space, 20–22, 27
spectacle, 61, 64
  as carnival, 61, 71, 156, 171
  medatsu koto (being seen), 61–62
spectator, see audiences
spirit (seishin), 48, 186, 200
spirits, 45, 46, 165
  fox, 22, 46
sports, 9, 15, 22, 28, 82, 92, 178, 185, 186
  archery, 186

gate ball, 188
golf, 188, 194
  Japanese, 24, 186–188
jûdô, 25, 53, 186
karate, 53
kendô, 25, 186
sumo as a pre-modern sport, 19, 186
tennis, 82, 188
see also baseball, football, sumo
Star Trek, 11
status, 8, 14, 15, 16, 48, 50, 58, 77, 133, 176
  linked with color, 39–41
  occupational, 58–59, 69
  see also class
Stokvis, R., 186, 187, 190, 201
stranger (marebito), 158, 164, 165
  ijin, 164, 166
Strinati, D., 127, 131
Stronach, B., 141, 151
sub-culture (zoku), 7, 56–59, 94, 129, 179
  An-Non zoku, 116, 129
  dokushin kizoku (unmarried aristocrats)
    as, 59, 67, 71
  Hanako zoku, 129
  JJ gal, 129
  kurisutaru-zoku, 115, 129
  Olive shôjo, 129
  shinjinrui, 194
  takenokozoku, 129
  yankî, 57, 70, 185
Sudo Nansui, 168, 180
Sugimoto, Y., 1, 10, 17, 70, 71, 74
Sugiyama-Lebra, T., 10, 18, 71, 74, 161, 166
sumo, 1, 5, 19–28, 33, 52, 139, 156, 162,
    164, 182, 186, 188, 192, 194, 198
  48-te (ways of winning), 20, 21
  and the imperial family, 13, 22
  and the mass media, 24–25
  as battle, 20, 22
  dohyô–iri (entering the ring), 21, 28
  drums in, 21, 28
  keshô-mawashi (decorated apron), 21
  kokugikan (stadium), 21–22
  popularity, 24–25, 27
  religious symbolism of, 8, 28, 198
  ring (dohyô), 20, 25
  seihi (rituals), 27
  stamping in, 20
  village performances of, 20, 22, 23
sumo wrestlers (rikishi), 20, 22, 23, 25, 28,
    156, 163, 184–185
  Akebono, 26
  Futabayama, 24–25, 28
  Konishiki, 26
  Nayoroiwa, 24
  ôzeki (rank), 24, 162

Wakahanada, 26
Wakanohana, 24
yokozuna, 20, 21, 26, 28
Superman, 34–38, 43
supernatural, 33
Superwoman, 102
super-heroes, 33–51
  Akachanman, 50
  American, 34–38, 46
  Astro boy, 49
  Batman, 46
  Captain America, 35
  Gridman, 37–38, 43, 46–47, 50
  Incredible Hulk, 46
  Issun–bôshi, 49
  Kintaro, 49
  Momotaro, 49–50, 53
  purple, 44–45
  Spiderman, 46
  Superman (Clark Kent), 34–38, 43, 46, 51
  Tom Thumb, 49
  Ultraman, 34–38, 43, 45, 46–47, 50, 54
  Ultraman King, 44
  Ultraman Taro, 36
  Yaiba, 49–50
  see also heroes
super-stars, 158, 172
  rock, 9
  sumo, 27, 156
  see also idols
symbols, 15, 21, 23, 33, 60

Tagawa Tadasu, 78, 87
taishû bunka, *see* popular culture
Takanohana, 26–27, 29, 156–159, 162, 164, 188
Takashi Naoko, 174–175, 180
Take Yutaka, 167, 170–172, 173, 176, 178
  men's like of, 178
  women's idolization of, 172, 177
Tale of the Bamboo Cutter, The, 108
Tanaka Yasuo, 114–115, 129, 132
Taoism, 13, 21
  onmyôdô (secret rituals) in, 21
Tasker, P., 111, 132
Tayama R., 69, 74
technology, 33, 37, 66, 104, 183
  innovations in, 76, 84
Teenage Mutant Ninja Turtles, 43
television, 6, 14, 24, 33, 58, 93, 117, 137, 155, 158–159, 165, 196, 200
  and karaoke, 81
  and sumo, 25, 27
  British, 28, 81
  children's programs, 6, 13, 103

drama, 133, 135–141
  Fuji Television, 49
  home dramas, 6, 9, 12, 14
  TBS TV, 34, 37
  TV Asahi, 38, 45, 49–50
tennôsei (emperorship), *see* emperor
Thomas the Tank Engine, 9
Thompson, P., 2, 18
Thunderbirds, 52, 54
Tobin, J., 10, 11, 18, 51, 55
Tokyo, 1, 22, 24, 62, 72, 78, 115, 138, 139, 141–142, 144–145, 146, 170, 176, 179, 186
  neo-, 63, 66
  University, 124, 125, 157
Tokyo Association of Sumo, 24
Tokugawa era (1625–1867), 81, 149
Toriyama Hiromu, 149, 151
totemism, 23, 40
tradition, 9, 13–14, 58, 62, 96, 98, 140, 164
  invented, 4, 13
  Judeo-Christian, 36
  traditionalism, 189
transformations (*henshin* or *henkei*), 45–48
  bio-, 46–47
  mecha-, 46–47
Treat, J. W., 94, 109
tsukiai, 85, 87
Tulloch, J., 11, 17
Twin Peaks, 133

Ultraman series, 14, 34–38, 43–44
  films, 52
  in the USA, 42, 51
Umehara Takeshi, 28, 29
USA, 9, 19, 34–36, 40, 42, 80, 133, 158
  Japan Security Treaty (*Anpo*), 63
  nationalism, 35

values, 133, 184
  amae, 84
  aristocratic, 156, 161
  filial loyalty, 34, 133, 142
  fraternal solidarity, 34
  gaman (endurance), 48
  harmony, 2, 79
  loyalty, 67–69
  jingi (humanity and justice), 72–73
  makoto (purity of motive), 67–68
  seken, 59
  self-sacrifice, 133
  teamwork, 34
  traditional Japanese, 14, 69, 134, 156
Vampire Club, 106

Vampire Princess Miyu, 92–93, 94–98, 107
vampires, 7, 13, 94–98, 102
    female, 95–97, 106
    Western tradition of, 95, 106
van Bremen, J., 51, 55, 134, 142, 146, 151
van Cleef, Lee, 9
violence, 2, 42, 53, 65–66, 67, 189
vitality (*genki*), 49, 52, 53

Wang Yang-ming, 134
way of (*dō*), 11, 81–82, 86, 200
    bushidō, 186
    karaoke, 75, 80–81
    martial arts, 86
    shodō (calligraphy), 86
    tea, 5, 81
Weiner, M., 1, 18, 70, 74
Whiting, R., 12, 18, 82, 87, 182, 185, 187, 201
Williams, R., 15, 18
Winship, J., 113, 118, 132
women, 2, 7–9, 13, 193
    career, 86, 111, 117, 136, 165
    as consumers, 6, 8, 106, 127–128, 183, 188, 192, 198
    disposable income of, 7, 111
    flying, 91, 103, 112

as holders of tradition, 14, 98, 138, 140
and horse-racing, 9, 167–180
housewives, 6, 8, 14, 91, 111, 116, 160
images of, 91, 104
as marginal, 7, 14, 97, 156
as mediators, 7, 14
as monsters (*yōkai*), 43
as mothers, 7, 8, 14, 38, 91, 98, 105, 108, 140, 160
and narcissism, 174
and the occult, 22, 46, 92, 93
as outsiders, 7, 8, 93, 165
and status, 133–134, 165
and technology, 104
traditional categories, 111–112
as vampires, 7, 94–98
young women, 5, 14, 15, 83, 116–117, 174, 193, 200

yagura-daiko (drum), *see* sumo
yakuza (gangsters), 2, 8, 9, 14, 53, 60, 63, 71, 83, 168, 169, 179, 180
Yamauba no bishō, 93
yokozuna (rank), *see* sumo
Yoshida Tiego, 107, 109, 155, 159, 166
Yoshino Kosaku, 10, 18

Printed in the United States
57405LVS00005B/256-312

9 780521 637299